100 ARTISTS SEE GOD

Reverend Ethan Acres
Jo Harvey Allen
Terry Allen
Eleanor Antin
Brienne Arrington
David Askevold
Lillian Ball
Cindy Bernard
Andrea Bowers
Delia Brown
Edgar Bryan
Angela Bulloch
Chris Burden
Mary Ellen Carroll
Erin Cosgrove
Michael Craig-Martin
Jeremy Deller
Sam Durant
Jimmie Durham
Nicole Eisenman
Katharina Fritsch
Jonathan Furmanski
Jeremy Gilbert-Rolfe
Liam Gillick
James Gobel
Jack Goldstein
Scott Grieger
Andreas Gursky
James Hayward
Micol Hebron
Damien Hirst
Rebecca Horn
Darcy Huebler
Christian Jankowski
Larry Johnson
Mike Kelley
Mary Kelly
Martin Kersels
Nicholas Kersulis
Martin Kippenberger
Rachel Lachowicz
Norm Laich
Liz Larner
Louise Lawler
Barry Le Va
William Leavitt
Roy Lichtenstein
Jen Liu
Thomas Locher
Daria Martin
T. Kelly Mason
Rita McBride
Paul McCarthy
Carlos Mollura
JP Munro
Bruce Nauman
Jennifer Nelson
Eric Niebuhr
Leonard Nimoy
Albert Oehlen
Catherine Opie
Tony Oursler
Jorge Pardo
Simon Patterson
Hirsch Perlman
Luciano Perna
Renée Petropoulos
Raymond Pettibon
Paul Pfeiffer
Nicolette Pot
Richard Prince
Rob Pruitt and
Jonathan Horowitz
David Reed
Victoria Reynolds
Gerhard Richter
Susan Rothenberg
Nancy Rubins
Glen Walter Rubsamen
Allen Ruppersberg
Ed Ruscha
Pauline Stella Sanchez
Kim Schoenstadt
Jim Shaw
Gary Simmons
Alexis Smith
Yutaka Sone
Thaddeus Strode
Diana Thater
Mungo Thomson
Thorvaldur Thorsteinsson
in collaboration with
Helena Jonsdottir
Jeffrey Vallance
John Waters
Marnie Weber
William Wegman
Lawrence Weiner
Benjamin Weissman
James Welling
Eric Wesley
John Wesley
Franz West
Chris Wilder
Christopher Williams
Steven Wong
Måns Wrange in collaboration
with Igor Isaksson
Mario Ybarra, Jr.

100 ARTISTS SEE GOD

JOHN BALDESSARI AND
MEG CRANSTON, WITH AN ESSAY
BY THOMAS McEVILLEY

Independent Curators International, New York

Published to accompany
the traveling exhibition
100 Artists See God,
organized and circulated by
Independent Curators
International (ICI), New York

The exhibition is curated by
John Baldessari
and Meg Cranston

Library of Congress Catalog
Number: 2003114930
ISBN: 0-916365-68-9
Editor: David Frankel
Design: 2x4 Inc.

Front and Back Cover
Design: John Baldessari

Printed in Germany by
Cantz

EXHIBITION ITINERARY*

The Jewish Museum San
Francisco
San Francisco, California
March 7–June 27, 2004

Laguna Art Museum
Laguna Beach, California
July 24–October 3, 2004

Contemporary Art Center
of Virginia
Virginia Beach, Virginia
June 9–September 4,
2005

*at time of publication

Independent
Curators International
799 Broadway, Suite 205
New York, NY 10003
Tel: (212) 254-8200
Fax: (212) 477-4781
www.ici-exhibitions.org

CONTENTS

FOREWORD AND ACKNOWLEDGMENTS

Whether or not we are believers, whether we describe ourselves as theists, atheists, or even antitheists, we all live in a world profoundly influenced by concepts of God. This exhibition's curators, John Baldessari and Meg Cranston, made this comment when they proposed their topic to ICI. And when we asked John why he and Meg felt that their subject would be of wide interest, he replied, "God is news." Indeed, we can see this on the front page of almost any newspaper these days. While we can investigate it by studying, say, current Supreme Court debates, local community actions, or any of the wars raging around the world, the curators of the exhibition set out to examine how artists are considering this topic—how contemporary artists see God.

The question seems logical to raise in the context of contemporary art; for many centuries, art history was dominated by religious imagery, and it would be important to know how, or whether, this still holds true today, if in less obvious ways. Nevertheless, as an exhibition topic the subject is highly uncommon. This, along with John and Meg's unusual curatorial approach, is why they call their show an "experiment." It is a challenge that perhaps would only be taken on by artist-curators, and it has yielded an extraordinary exhibition.

The wide range of works presented here, created in various mediums by several generations of artists working in the United States and abroad, deals with faith as a subject, but does not necessarily reflect the doctrines to which the artists may subscribe. The works present not conventional illustrations of established doctrines but the artists' subjective interpretations of spirituality. Most important, *100 Artists See God*, through the diversity of artistic practices and approaches to its subject that it includes, constitutes an accurate reflection of how ambiguous and yet pervasive this subject is in our lives, and lets us formulate our own thoughts and concerns in this regard. We see and question how issues about the place of God and spirituality thread their way through the entire fabric of culture internationally, sometimes demanding to take center stage, sometimes almost buried by other concerns, but always present.

This catalogue and traveling exhibition have been made possible through the encouragement, dedication, and generosity of a great many people. First and foremost, on behalf of ICI's Board of Trustees and staff, I extend our sincere thanks and appreciation to the exhibition's curators, the distinguished artists John Baldessari and Meg Cranston. With intelligence, wit, and persistence, they have presented a compelling subject, have brought their "experiment" to completion through their selection of a rich and provocative range of works, and have composed a text that successfully grapples with the diversity of approaches in the show and gives us a better understanding of all the works here. Finally, a very special note of appreciation goes to John Baldessari for his original cover design for this catalogue, which so perfectly represents the searching nature of the subject.

I want to express sincere thanks to all the artists in this exhibition, and to voice our special appreciation for the statements they have contributed, which add so much to our understanding of the objects in the show and shed light on how the subject of God may appear, even obliquely, in so much work being made today. Their involvement and support have been crucial to the success of this project.

ICI owes a tremendous debt of gratitude to all the lenders who generously allowed their works to travel throughout the two-year tour. We must also thank many galleries for their assistance, and for exceptional efforts in facilitating loans I would like to acknowledge, in particular, Julie Baniecki and Ealan Wingate at Gagosian Gallery, New York; Brian Boucher at Klemens Gasser & Tanja Grunert, Inc.; Brian Butler at 1301FE; Felicity Coupland at Gagosian Gallery, London; Corinna Durland at GBE (Modern); Jeannie Freilich at Marian Goodman Gallery; Sharon Goodman at Gemini G.E.L.; Jordan Gutcher formerly of D'Amelio Terras; Tom Heman at Metro Pictures; Jesse McBride at Regen Projects; and Jill Sussman and Sabrina Buell at Matthew Marks Gallery.

The curators also join me in expressing special appreciation to Connie Wolf, executive director of the Jewish Museum San Francisco, and her staff, especially deputy director Barbara Levine and Natasha Perlis, curatorial assistant, for their enthusiasm and commitment to the project, and for inaugurating the tour. I also wish to thank all of the other institutions that will be presenting this exhibition as it travels; it is through their efforts that the project will truly become a reality.

Sincere appreciation is also due to Georgie Stout and Sung Joong Kim of 2x4, New York, for their work on this book, and to David Frankel, the book's editor. It was a great pleasure to work once again with these superb professionals.

I am also pleased to extend special thanks from Meg Cranston to Dean Kuipers and Kevin Cranston for their research for the texts, and to Rashel George and Brienne Arrington for their editorial assistance. Special thanks from John Baldessari go to Brienne Arrington for her extraordinary assistance to him throughout the project, and to Kim Schoenstadt and Jen Liu, who also helped with the organization of this exhibition.

ICI's dedicated, knowledgeable, and enthusiastic staff deserves recognition for their work on every aspect of this enormous project, from securing loans, artists' statements, and images for 100 works, through arranging for the packing and shipping of that daunting number of individual loans, to creating this substantial publication. Thanks go especially to Susan Hapgood, director of exhibitions; Carin Kuoni, former director of exhibitions; Annabelle Larner, registrar; and Nika Elder, exhibitions assistant, all of whom worked on every aspect of the exhibition and book. Thanks also to Amy Owen, exhibitions associate and publications coordinator; and Sue Scott, executive assistant and communications coordinator, who made important contributions to the exhibition, as well as to former exhibitions interns Daria Joubert and Sandra Nakamura and current interns Owen Clements and Sandra Colmenares. I also want to express my gratitude to Hedy Roma, director of development; Eileen Choi, development associate; Meghann McKale, development assistant; and Dolf Jablonski, bookkeeper.

Finally, I extend my warmest appreciation to ICI's Board of Trustees for their steadfast support, enthusiasm, and commitment to all of ICI's activities. They join me in expressing our gratitude to everyone who has contributed to making possible this enormously challenging and gratifying project.

—Judith Olch Richards
Executive Director

INTRODUCTION
BY JOHN BALDESSARI AND MEG CRANSTON

Originally this show wasn't about God. It was about the firm definition of art as described in a piece of legislation called the Visual Artists Rights Act of 1990. We came across the legislation and thought it would be fun to have a show of only things the Visual Artists Rights Act described as not art. We thought it would be fun until we realized that an exhibition of non-art things would look just like every other show. Things that are not art was clearly not a problem.

Then Meg Cranston wrote the title "100 Artists See God." We liked it immediately; it sounded like a newspaper headline. We imagined a group of a hundred artists standing in a field having a simultaneous revelation. We pictured them all with thought-bubbles over their heads imagining how to put their vision into an artwork. The idea had potential. Our problem might be god.

That was the spring of 2002. The date is significant: we began this project six months after the bombing of the World Trade Center in New York. Newspapers, magazines, television, and radio were full of stories about god at the time, and books about god were on the best-seller list. God was everywhere. Artists were uncharacteristically silent.

We didn't want to do a show that directly referenced recent events, although those events clearly affected us. In our initial description of this exhibition we said, "Whether or not one believes in god, whether we describe ourselves as theists, atheists, or even anti-theists, we all live in a world that is profoundly influenced by concepts of god." We were pretty sure the notion of god was affecting world events, but we had no certain idea how, or whether, god and religion were affecting art.

We decided to ask artists. The show was conceived as an experiment: we made a list of artists we admired and asked them to provide a work that in some way dealt with the concept of god. We selected the artists because we were fans of their work, not because they had necessarily ever done an artwork about god. Some had, some had not. We selected artists we thought might be up to the challenge, and some practical restrictions aside, we decided we'd take what we got.

We tried not to have too many preconceptions, except maybe one. Without ever discussing it, we assumed that the show would be about how artists see god represented. We assumed that when we said "artists see god," what we meant was "artists represent god"—that how they see is how they represent. It went without saying that the show would be about representation and not necessarily about belief. Whether anyone was religious or not didn't figure in; we wouldn't dare ask. We guessed that the majority of the works would be by artists creating an image of how they thought other people might see god.

That is the basis of this show. It is an exhibition about how contemporary artists represent god. In some cases the representation may be connected to the artist's own beliefs; in many cases it is not. The artists are observing phenomena and representing them.

The catalogue is divided into sixteen categories: "Artists See God as Architect," "Artists See God as Love," "Artists See God as a Force of Nature," and so on. The categories are there to give the reader some (admittedly murky) vantage from which to begin to look at the works. They are not explanations but Meg's poetic responses to the works. In many cases the artists couldn't agree less.

Having called the show an experiment, we feel we should provide at least one conclusion: despite appearances, contemporary artists are willing to see god if you ask them.

WAYS OF SEEING GOD
BY THOMAS McEVILLEY

For thousands of years art was an appendage of religion. It was used as a magical technique to facilitate access to the gods. Often the gods were regarded as literally located inside the icons on the altar or elsewhere in the temple or magical site. By addressing one's petition to the icon one was communicating with the deity directly. To damage or destroy the icon (as in the famous mutilation of the herms—the statues of Hermes—that occurred in Athens during the Peloponnesian War) was to endanger the entire community by provoking the anger, and daring the revenge, of the god within it.

In the last couple of centuries, much of Western art has supposedly been secular, but the religious aura still clung to it. In the early twentieth century the British critic Clive Bell asserted that religion was the natural ally of art, and science its natural enemy. Bell was more or less a "formalist," or Kantian, and this residual religiosity saturated the Kantian tradition. Kant felt that art was based on universals, which were anciently defined as the thoughts in the mind of god. Art was, in other words, supposed to be able to get inside god's mind and express it. The German Romantic philosopher Schelling spelled this out explicitly when he said that a great painting afforded a direct gaze into the realm of Platonic Ideas (*System of Transcendental Idealism*, VI.3.2). Although the American formalist critic Clement Greenberg was not so open about it, he was a mouthpiece of the same tradition. It appeared, for example, in his insistence that you can't figure art out; you can only come to terms with it through pure intuition, the way a mystic apprehends the beyond. Greenberg's rival Harold Rosenberg was more direct when he said that Abstract Expressionism was essentially a theological movement. Jackson Pollock, Franz Kline, Barnett Newman, and the rest were engaged in an attempt to see god, or to see into god's mind. That's what created the sense of reverential awe around their canvases.

After Abstract Expressionism, artists began a major attempt to secularize art—to move away from the realm of religion and closer to the realm of science. This tendency was based on the antireligious attitude of Marcel Duchamp, who once remarked that making up the idea of god was "mad folly." His attitude took root in the 1960s, as Minimal and Conceptual art began to move away from religion toward its ancient enemy, science. The connection with religion did not really go away, however; it just hid itself more deeply beneath the surface. One can sense it in the reverential awe of cognition in much early Conceptual art, and in the sacrificial ritualism of much early Performance art. Early cognition-worshipers like Joseph Kosuth, Robert Barry, and William Anastasi were following in the Pythagorean/Platonic tradition, which held that the human mind is a reflection of god's, and mirrors its processes. Early ritualists like Hermann Nitsch and Carolee Schneemann openly used religious forms and materials, and a quality of actual belief seems to have underlain their work.

As postmodernist pluralism unfolded, it emerged that there are countless ways in which art can reflect its ancient function as a way to see god. They can be sorted into a series of stages, beginning with institutionalized religion and proceeding farther from it at each step.

First are artists who exercise art as an orthodox expression of an institutionalized religion, like the temple sculptors of ancient Egypt or the stained-glass-window makers of medieval Europe. These artists present themselves as (and no doubt usually are) pious believers in the religion they serve. This is primarily a pre-Modern role for artists, and none of those in *100 Artists See God* fits the category.

Then there are artists who endow their work with associations of some specific religion without presenting it as an orthodox function of that religion. The work may involve not pious belief but merely reference, even critical reference. An artist like Sigmar Polke, whose works have involved Native American peyote rituals as a way to see god, falls into this category, even though he is determinedly secular. Many other artists could be named here as well: Joseph Beuys's work incorporated shamanic motifs, Yves Klein's was Rosicrucian at root, Barnett Newman's was cabalistic. Louise Bourgeois's sculptures have touched on ancient Thracian wolf-imitation cults, the Ephesian cult of Artemis the Many Breasted, Phoenician-Carthaginian bull-slaying rites, and more. The list could go on, and could include the organizers of this exhibition. Much of John Baldessari's work—the sign paintings of 1967–68, say, and the photographs of ordinary places in southern California—seems authentically secular; still, in many of his complex collages one can see traces of ancient Near Eastern temple guardians, hierarchical systems of the cosmos, and so on. Meg Cranston's work sometimes refers to the transposition of Christianity into the New World and often refers to sculpture's use in ritual contexts.

In these and most other cases where a modern or contemporary artist incorporates religious references and associations into his or her work, the religion is almost always either an ancient pre-Christian or a non-Western one. Adherence to Judeo-Christian practices, and to those of Islam as well, has mostly been avoided, at least partly because of a distrust of Christianity's role in the social ethics of the world in recent centuries—the distrust that Bertrand Russell expressed in his 1927 book *Why I Am Not a Christian*—and partly because of overfamiliarity: sometimes you have to go outside your own culture to get a sense of the sacred.

Perhaps the most common tactic of the artists in the show is the practice of using specific icons or images that have appeared in religious iconography—as when Ed Ruscha refers to shafts of light, Jo Harvey Allen to snakes, Jonathan Furmanski to fish, Diana Thater to the sun, Daria Martin to an enigmatic card game, Jennifer Nelson to mirrors and a ball, and so on. In such cases the religious context is sometimes obvious (shafts of light) and sometimes needs identification (the ancient Orphics had Eros Protogonos, the newborn baby god, playing with mirrors and a ball).

Another stage away from institutionalized religion is the sacralized reference to forces that have no cultic associations at all. A classically Modernist approach of this type is suggested by Jannis Kounellis's observation that the ability to provoke an appearance of the divine without sentimentality, indeed of a secular divine that is encompassed by history, is peculiarly the ability of the artist. The worship of history with a capital H as the working out of human destiny, or the full exploration of human nature, is a secular parallel to the religious worship of providence as the expression of god's will. In this sense of history as the secular sacred, art history too has been treated at times as a *numinosum*, or cult object.

The next stratum, as the criteria loosen and expand, not only involves no cultic associations or references, it involves no distinctions of any kind. The cult of history, for example, involves a distinction between culture and nature, and an emphasis on the cultic properties of culture. But pantheism—the belief that everything (Greek *pan*) is god (Greek *theos*)—recognizes no distinction between culture and nature, or indeed any distinctions at all. The object in which one sees god does not have to be beautiful, sacred, cultic, erotic, cosmic, or whatever. This broadest of religious forms has existed in various traditions. In Islam, for example, there is a tradition of sages who made statements like, "I have never seen a form without seeing god," "I have not seen a thing without seeing god in the thing," and so on.[1] The same generalized procedure for seeing god in anything at all can be found in Neo-Platonism, the cabala, Sufism, Vedanta, and elsewhere. Many works in *100 Artists See God* are of this type—like Chris Burden's dog or Mike Kelley's pebble. If artists express themselves as pantheists, one might expect them to feel a certain generalized reverence toward life or toward being, a reverence that can be focused into the seeing of any object at all as a form of seeing god.

Beyond either cultic or pantheistic seeing, there are path-oriented approaches to the role of the artist that parallel traditional ways of seeing god. Some of these are not pious in mood and may even be rational and critical. In Madhyamika Buddhism, for example, "The bodhisattva path is a means of exposing and defusing many… beliefs which have been held for so long that they no longer appear as separate principles."[2] This path underlies the absurdist humor of many Ch'an and Zen anecdotes. Much the same could be said of many deconstructivist postmodernist artists, and indeed of the whole antiart tradition going back to Dada: by stripping away false beliefs, one gets closer to something that might be called "god." Something similar emerges in Schelling's observation that "the objects of the transcendental philosopher exist not at all except insofar as they are freely produced."[3] This idea of a freedom of production has been close to the center of a good deal of artmaking—from Dada to Action Painting. In these formulations the word "artist" could be substituted for the word "bodhisattva," or for the term "transcendental philosopher."

So a range of options present themselves. At the extreme, anything at all can be seen as god, in which case the experience of seeing can only be of seeing god. At the same time, it is possible to construe the role of the artist—whether secular or not—as a path-oriented experience leading toward a specially clear kind of seeing that has been described as seeing god.

Still, Baldessari and Cranston have chosen a term for their exhibition that sounds archaic and, in terms of contemporary art discourse, hard to take seriously. Many of the artists in the show have reacted to it with humorous evasions. Jim Shaw's Snoopy at the Last Supper, Damien Hirst's medicine cabinet as god, Paul McCarthy's parodic search under bushes, Jeffrey Vallance's imprint of his own face in spilled espresso on a shroud, Måns Wrange's average citizen: these and other works make a good-humored adjustment to the concept without being willing to approach it with a straight face. According to many psychologists, this type of response shows tension, and I think the tension arises from the century-long conflict within the body of art between the tendency toward religion and the tendency toward science. It seems to many that art, in partially shaking off its ancient connection with religion, has begun at last to emerge from the Dark Ages. It seems best to acknowledge only with irony, then, that the ancient connection still somewhat hiddenly exists.

1.
See Jean-François Clement, "The Empty Niche Bamiyan Buddha," in Bruno Latour and Peter Weibel, eds., *iconoclash: Beyond the Image Wars in Science, Religion, and Art* (Cambridge, Mass.: The MIT Press, and Karlsruhe: ZKM, 2002), pp. 200, 218.

2.
C. W. Huntington, *The Emptiness of Emptiness: An Introduction to Early Indian Madhyamika* (Honolulu: University of Hawaii Press, 1989), p. 79.

3.
F. W. J. Schelling, *System of Transcendental Idealism*, 1800, Engl. trans. Peter Heath (Charlottesville: University of Virginia, 1978), p. 13.

ARTISTS SEE GOD AS ARCHITECT

Wherefore God is not ashamed to be called their God: for He hath prepared for them a city.
—Hebrews 11:16

The man of the future does not try to escape the elements. He will rule them.
—R. M. Schindler, "A Manifesto," 1912

The Italian architect Alberti referred to the architect as an *alter deus*, Latin for "other god." Medieval manuscripts show drawings of God as a literal architect, standing amid the heavens and the earth, wielding a compass.

The works that follow consider the ambitions of architects to re-create the world and in a sense replace god. They particularly focus on the aesthetic of modern architecture and its relationship to religious dogma.

In the dimensions, height precedes width precedes depth. Unless otherwise noted, dimensions are for the artworks unframed. All artists or their estates were invited to write a statement; some chose not to do so.

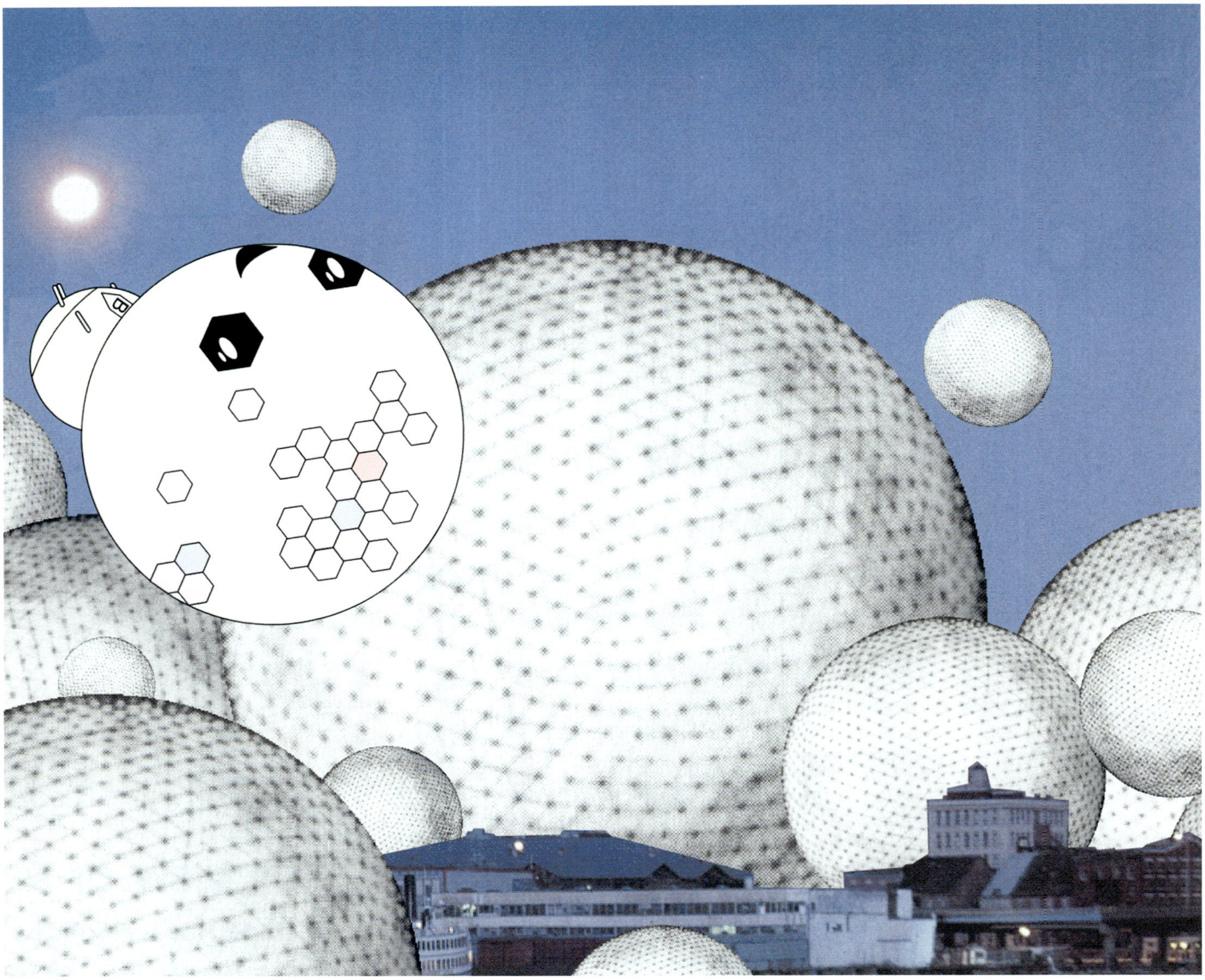

JEN LIU Born 1976, Smithtown, New York. Resides Amsterdam, the Netherlands, and Los Angeles, California
Dawn of the Alpha Genesis, 2003 (video still) DVD 6 minutes Collection of the artist

A City made of Wood is Built in the Forest.
A City made of Stone is Built in the Mountains.
A City made of Dreams is built in Heaven.

—"Dom Ruystni Cycle," *Eve Online* MMOG (Massively Multiplayer Online Game) trailer, Crowd Control Productions, 2002

Adolf Loos, Mies van der Rohe, and Buckminster Fuller all had the same vision: a new world order through architecture. This world would be ruled by balance, purity, efficiency, and, above all, precise engineering. Through architecture, mankind could realize its progressive potentials, discarding obsolete inefficiencies of society and biology.

When man is born, his instincts are those of a new-born dog. His childhood runs through all changes, corresponding to the history of mankind.... what is natural for a Papuan and a child, is degenerate for modern man.
—Adolf Loos, "Ornament and Crime," 1908

If revolution was first spoken of as a miracle, and the Gospel is written as a fantasy of a universal revision, here are our own failed gods. Their hopes can be endlessly repeated in expectant simulation. The resolution of space never brought a reformation of humanity. Dawn of the Alpha Genesis is a trailer for an ancient mythology: that of revolution, of progress.

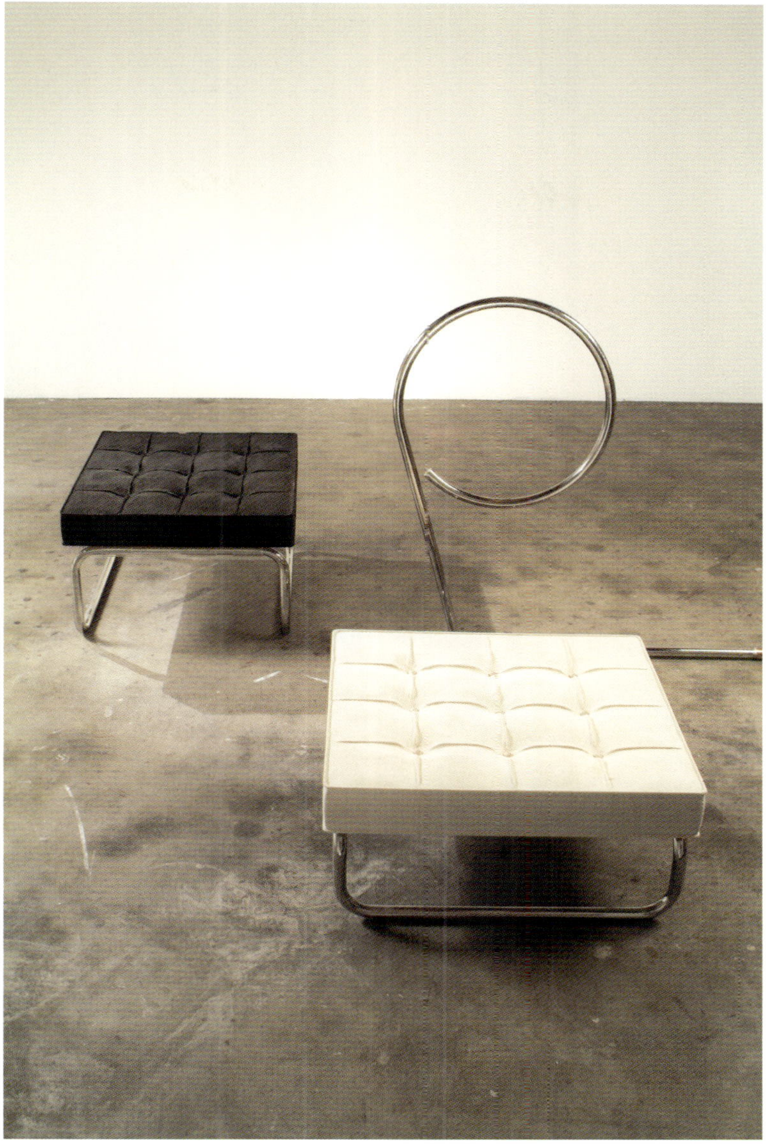

<u>RACHEL LACHOWICZ</u> Born 1964, San Francisco, California. Resides Los Angeles, California
Sketch for Mies van der Rohe, 2003 (detail) Chrome, Plexiglas, wood, and digital print Sculpture: 37 1/2 x 72 x 60 in. (95.3 x 182.9 x 152.4 cm); print: 11 x 17 in. (27.9 x 43.2 cm) Collection of the artist. Courtesy Shoshana Wayne Gallery, Santa Monica

God is in the details.
—Mies van der Rohe

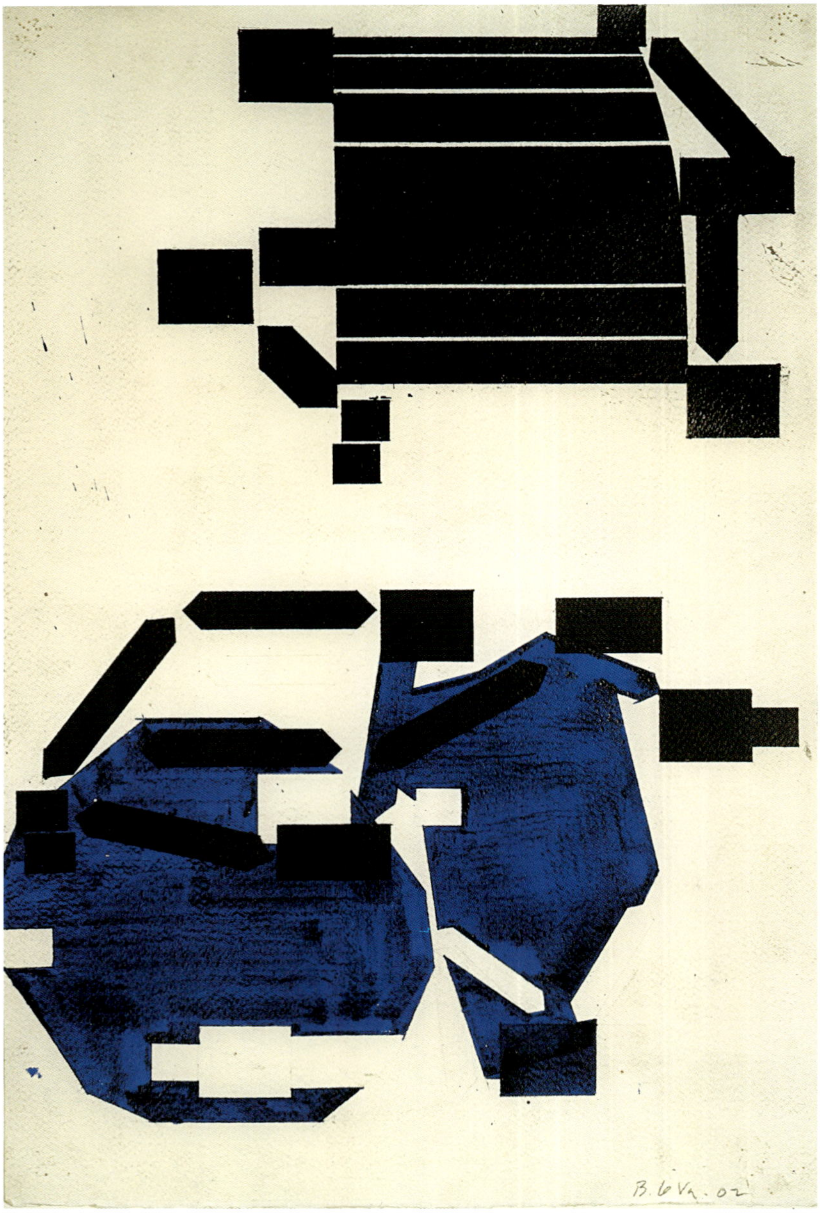

BARRY LE VA Born 1941, Long Beach, California. Resides New York, New York
Plan View for Double-Tiered Sculpture, 2002 Ink on paper 22 1/2 x 15 in. (57.2 x 38.1 cm) Collection of the artist.
Courtesy Danese Gallery, New York

One can neither think nor act to good purpose until the habit of self-restraint has become automatic.

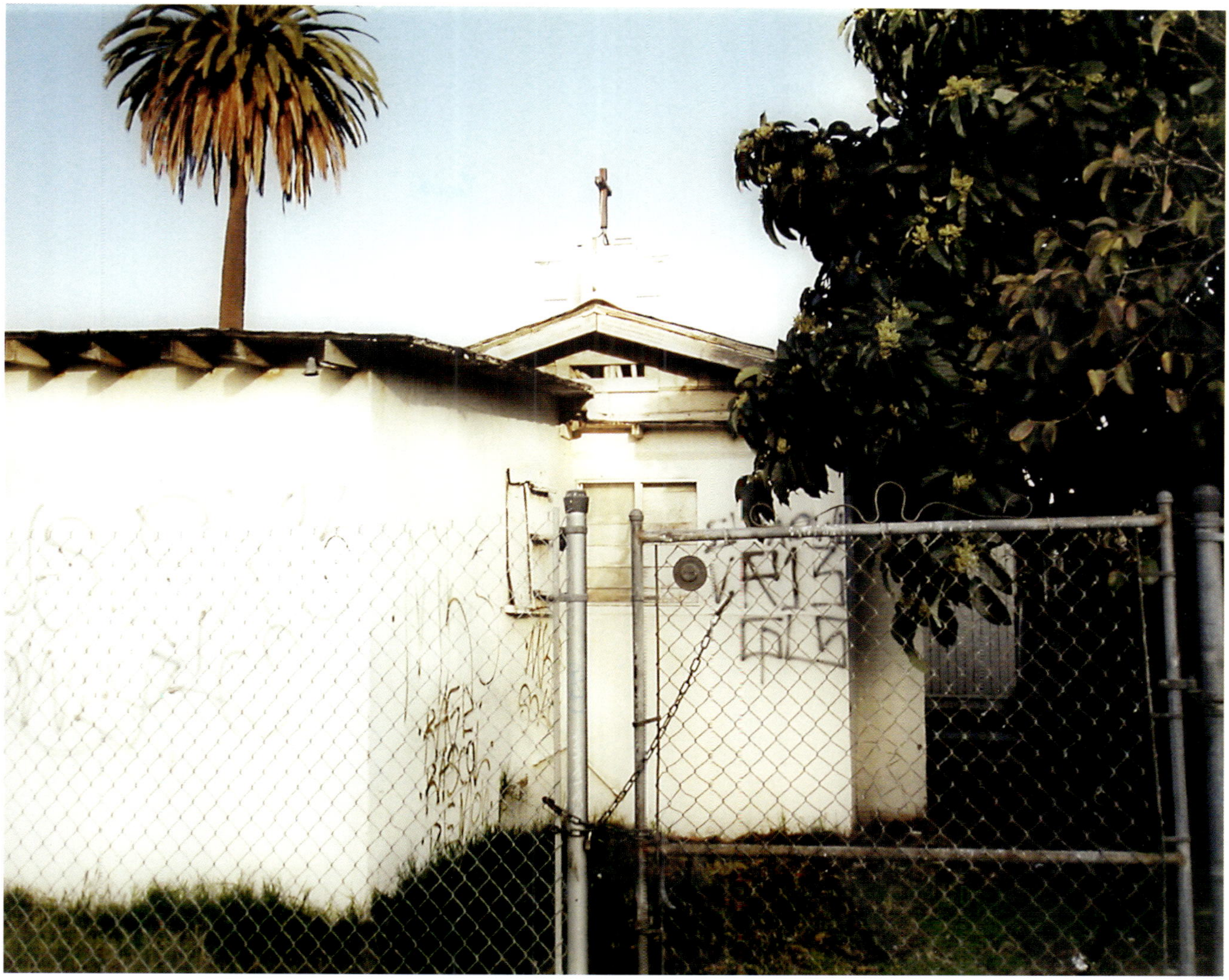

SAM DURANT Born 1961, Boston, Massachusetts. Resides Los Angeles, California
R. M. Schindler Church, 2001 Chromogenic print 16 x 20 in. (40.6 x 50.8 cm) Collection of the artist. Courtesy Blum & Poe, Santa Monica

My work is primarily engaged in an antinostalgic dialogue with history. I have worked with a range of issues (cultural, political, art-historical, and architectural), traveling between and across "facts" and myths. My work posits the idea that history does not reside in the past but is constantly present and should be continuously under interrogation.

ARTISTS SEE THE ANNUNCIATION OF GOD

To see god, god must be shown. God has to be announced in some way. In Poussin's famous painting *The Annunciation* (c. 1655) the Holy Spirit appears as a dove flying above the head of the Virgin. The painting is like the dove: it is the evidence of an event, the biblical occurrence in which the Angel Gabriel announced the Immaculate Conception to Mary. The sign portends transformation. The artist, like Gabriel, gives witness.

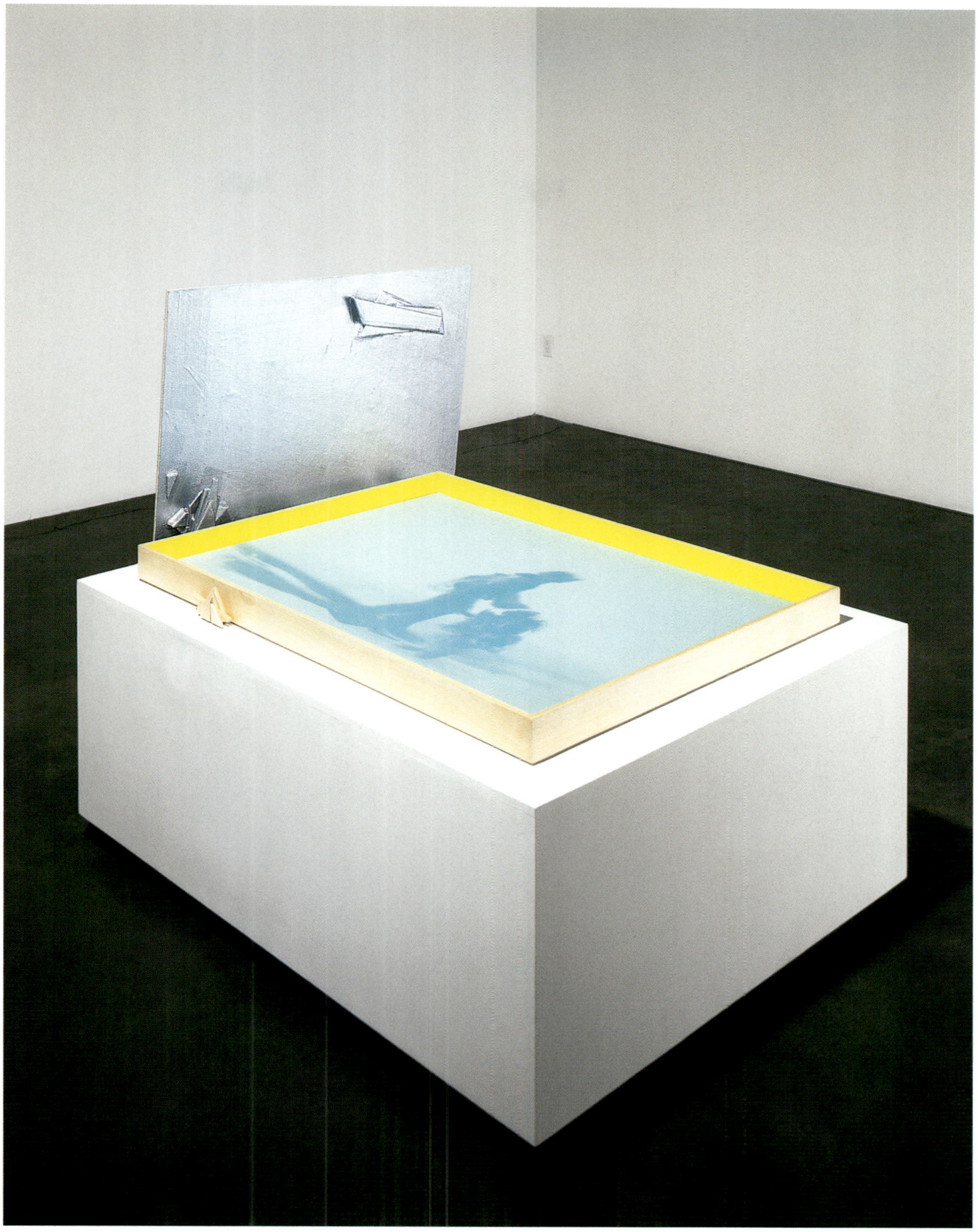

PAULINE STELLA SANCHEZ Born Albuquerque, New Mexico. Resides Venice, California
...the annunciation that took place on the other side of the same room where there was the electric chair ...diamonds ...electrical language sight gag, 2002 Ten silkscreen prints, wood, cloth, felt, vinyl, and acrylic paint Box: 8 x 49 1/2 x 37 in. (20.3 x 125.7 x 94 cm)
Collection of the artist

Apparently I was given this snapshot of me on the sun with a "sun people" outside Versailles in 1989, while I was living at the Fondation Cartier in Jouy-en-Josas, France. This photograph is a source for my research and has been deliberated in numerous historical exploitations.
Here I measured it as an interpretation of the annunciation, or the transfer of language through light, the pressure toward ecstasy, and the force to transcend an unbearable Manichean socio-economic dualism—the very reason why we may want religions so we can jump this ship. As seen in the snapshot, I broke the rules and instead of burning my wings I transcended, to where I do not know or is this simply a Lockean stasis of self-power that fuels our states?
Temperature, electricity, Apollo, economic power systems from Knights Templar back to the Druids, Versailles, San Marcos, the Vatican to Isla del Sol, architecture as I am in the room of myself, the light that projects our cinematic apparatus, and the languages of other species are imaginings for this possibly ridiculous image. Who and what are the sun people, as physicists and artists have calculated?
Is the porn I named it in 1991 another frivolous dancing putto, angel or comedic sight-gag?
The entire babble dazzle continues to run me into arcades and circles ☹☺.
The most important question remains, Who is the photographer of this event, and what array of supremacy does that construct? Does all this bring us to your thoughts of god?

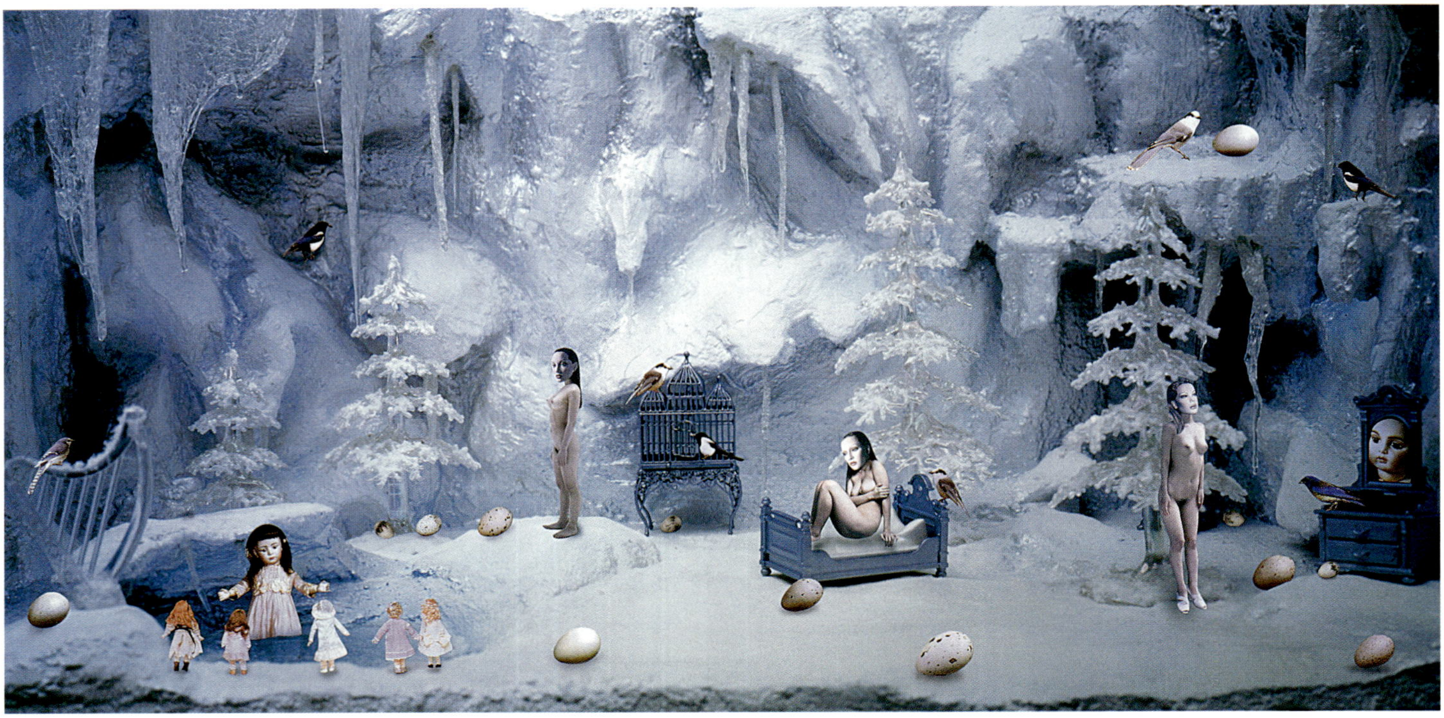

MARNIE WEBER Born 1960, Bridgeport, Connecticut. Resides Los Angeles, California
The Little Girl God, 2002 Collage on chromogenic print 18 x 36 in. (45.7 x 91.4 cm) Collection of the artist. Courtesy Fredericks Freiser Gallery, New York

The Little Girl God takes place in one of eleven rooms of a large storybook dollhouse, each of them a setting for a different drama. In this one a doll rises up from the icy depths of a pond to give a heartwarming sermon on finding god in simple things, such as the laughter of a little girl.

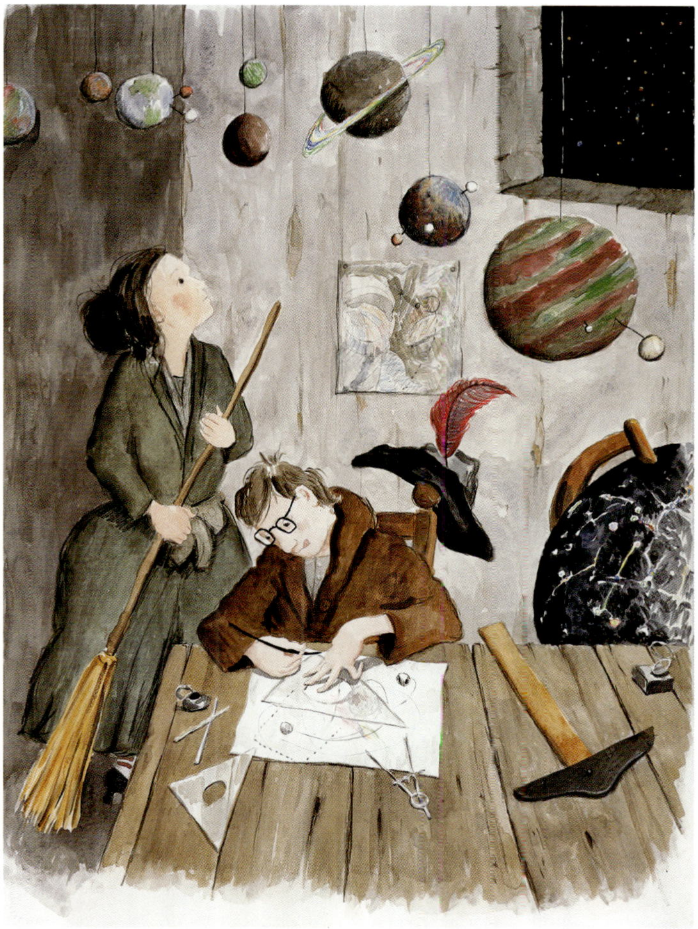

EDGAR BRYAN   Born 1970, Birmingham, Alabama. Resides Los Angeles, California
Untitled, 2003   Watercolor and colored pencil on paper   30 x 22 1/2 in. (76.2 x 57.2 cm)   Collection of the artist

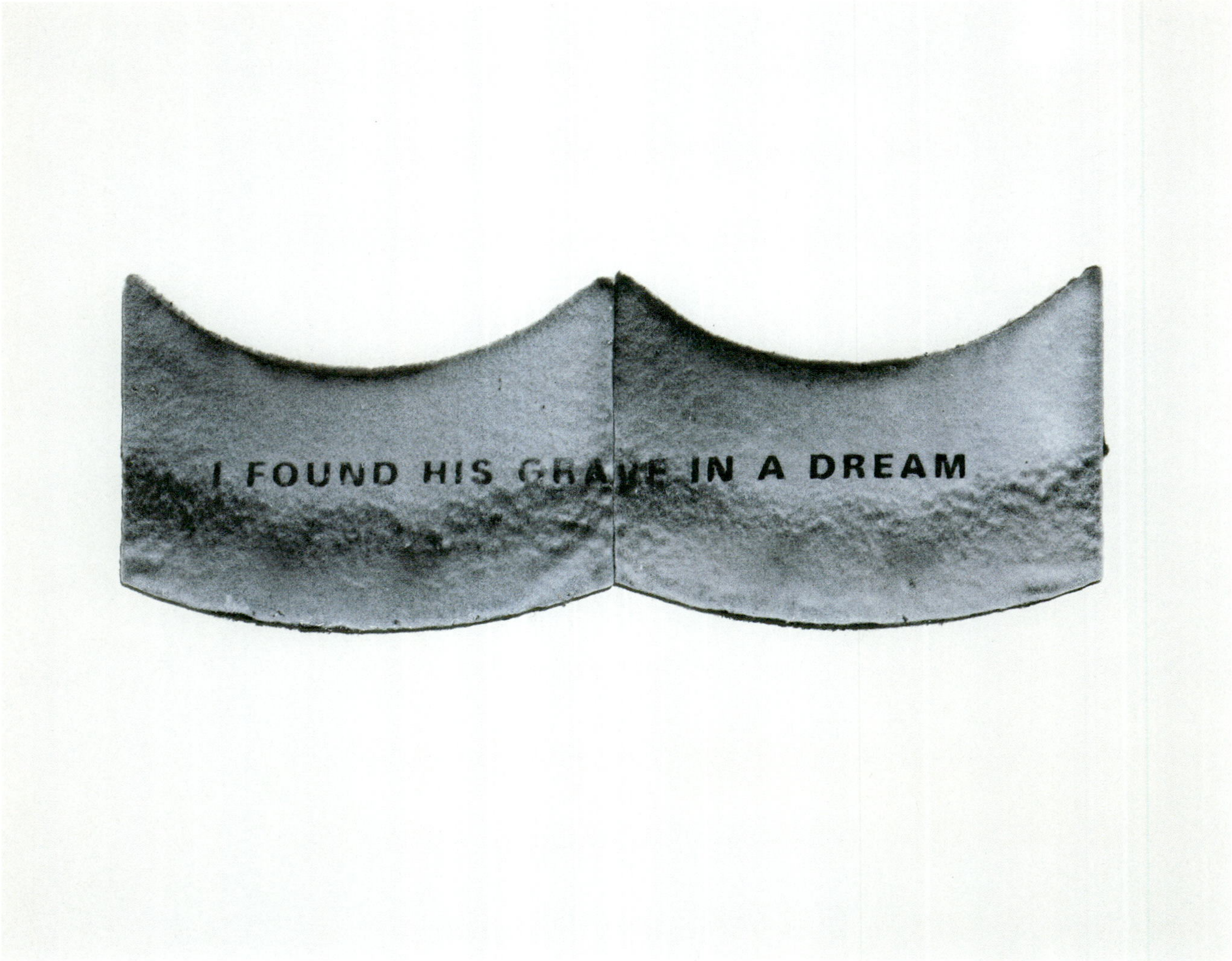

MARY KELLY Born 1941, Fort Dodge, Iowa. Resides Los Angeles, California
Mea Culpa (Study for Johannesburg), 1999/2002 Compressed lint on paper Framed: 25 1/4 x 31 1/4 in. (64.1 x 79.4 cm)
Collection of the artist. Courtesy Rosamund Felsen Gallery, Santa Monica

In a series of studies for *Mea Culpa (Study for Johannesburg)* I wrote a woman's short, rather elusive responses to the atrocities described in longer narratives. For me this acknowledged, in a way, the impossibility of speaking "for" her. Nobody knows the other's secret. This is where God comes in, according to Jacques Derrida—to guarantee the possibility of something remaining impenetrable. And this is why I thought of *Mea Culpa (Study for Johannesburg)* in the improbable context of *100 Artists See God*. When the work's protagonist, testifying at South Africa's Truth and Reconciliation Commission, declares that she found her murdered son's grave in a dream, she is not sharing her secret, I think, but stating that her contract with her child, in death, is beyond exchange. A gift. Perhaps from God. But then, how would I know?

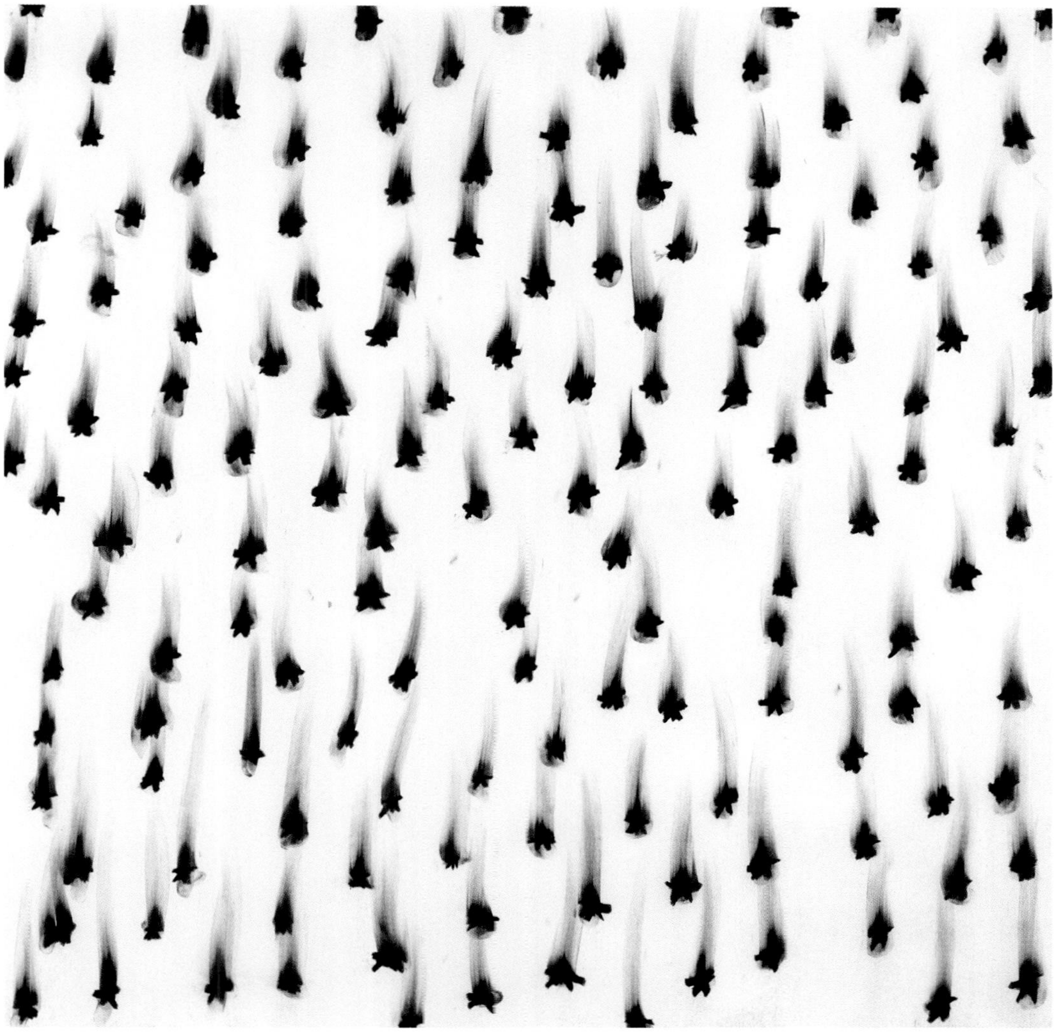

<u>GARY SIMMONS</u> Born 1964, New York, New York. Resides New York, New York
Black Star Shower, 2003 Charcoal on vellum 36 1/8 x 36 1/8 in. (91.8 x 91.8 cm) Collection of the artist. Courtesy Margo Leavin Gallery, Los Angeles

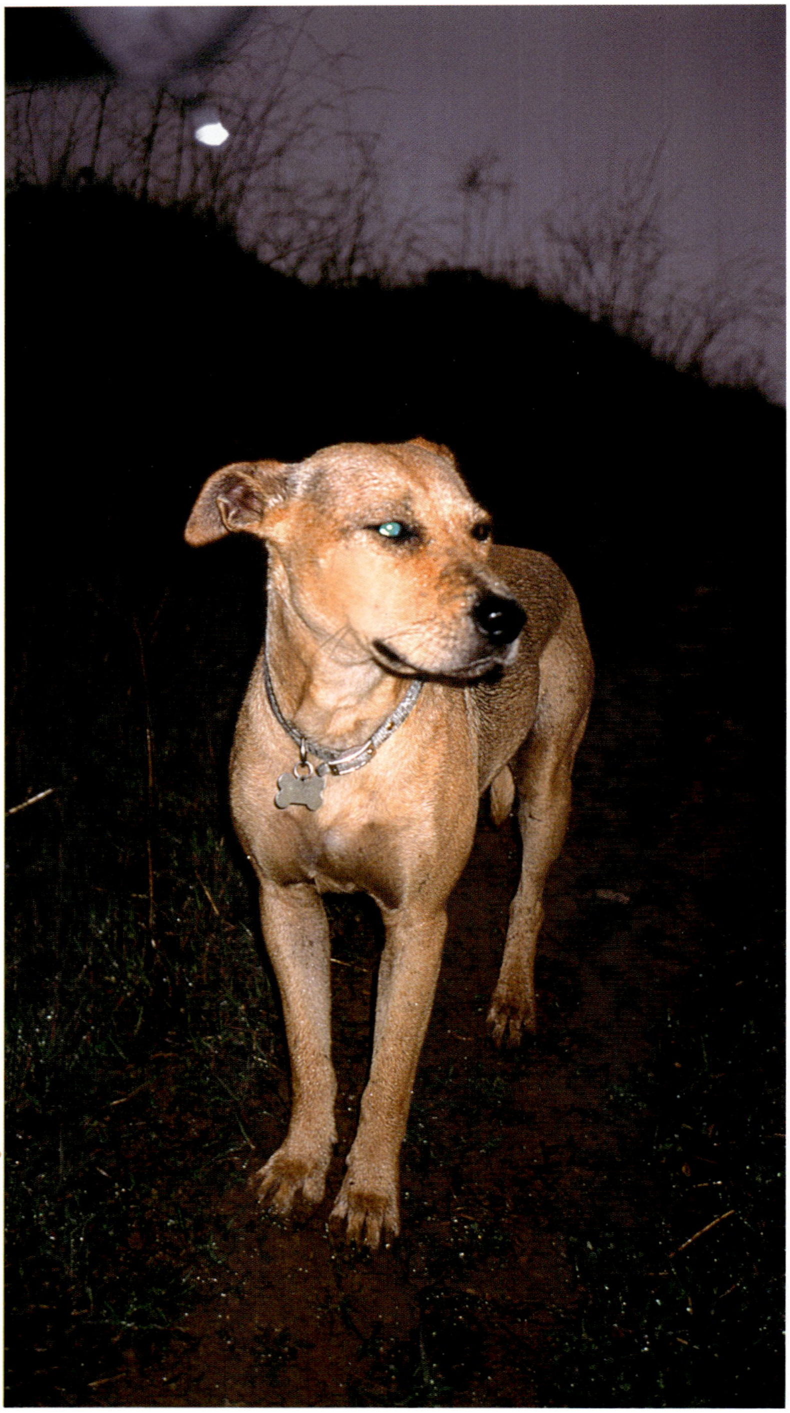

CHRIS BURDEN   Born 1946, Boston, Massachusetts. Resides Topanga, California
New Dog and New Moon, 2001   Color photograph   14 x 11 in. (35.6 x 27.9 cm)   Collection of the artist

When I got my new puppy, I would take her on long evening walks and try to photograph her. Invariably, by the time I had aimed the camera and pressed the button she was out of the picture frame. When I first saw this photo, I couldn't believe I had captured this nearly impossible and fleeting image of my exuberant little dog and the new moon rising. In this photograph I saw the incarnation of God.

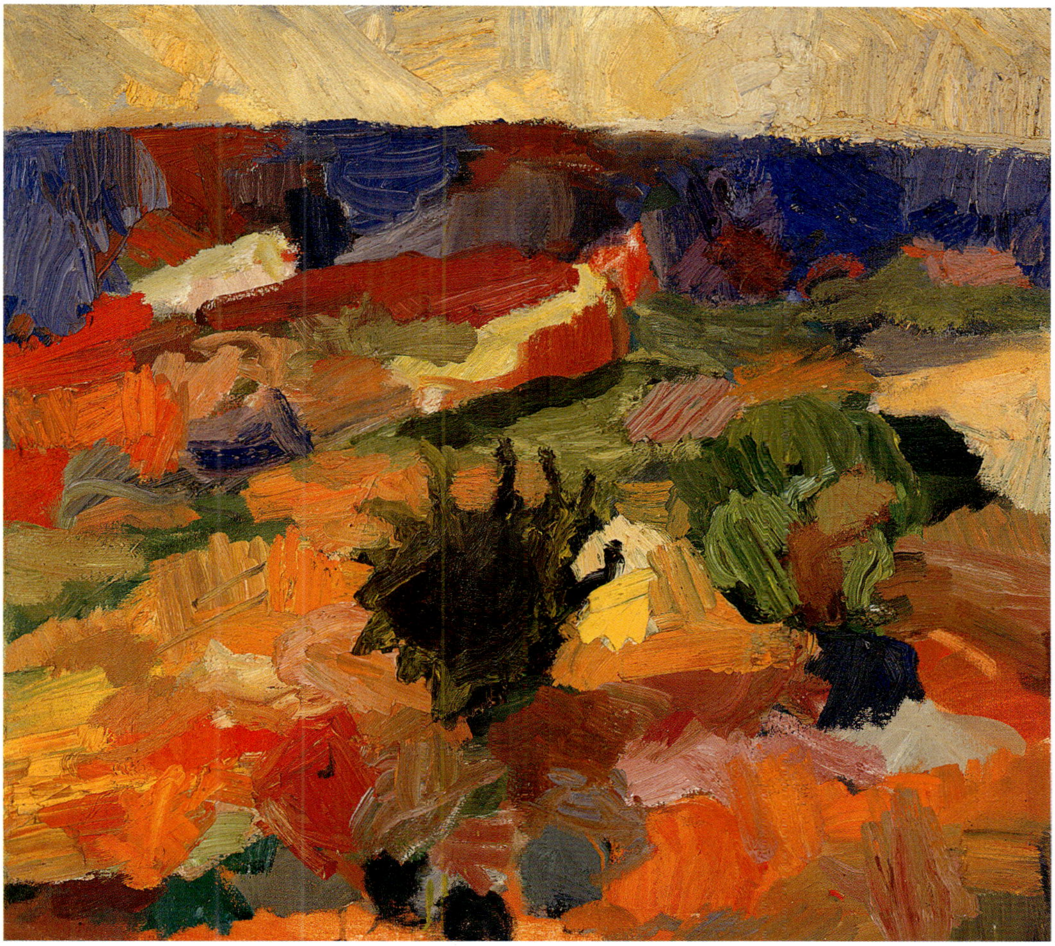

DAVID REED Born 1946, San Diego, California. Resides New York, New York
Oljato (Moonlight Water), 1967 Oil on linen 27 x 30 in. (68.6 x 76.2 cm) Collection of the artist

For the summers of 1967 and 1968 I lived near Monument Valley, in an area called Oljato (Moonlight Water), after the local spring. I was told that a band of starving Navajos, chased by Kit Carson, had saved themselves when they saw moonlight reflected in the water.

I projected themes of loss and redemption onto the landscape, influenced by western movies and Italian Quattrocento paintings. The single tree at the spring reminded me of the tree planted in the dead Adam's mouth in Piero della Francesca's fresco based on the Legend of the True Cross. At dusk, with its shimmering silver leaves, this tree seemed to be in Eden. I painted fruit hanging from its branches. Seeing dark bushes on a hillside, I imagined one bursting into flames. Painting this bush, I found myself inside the painted bush painting another bush, and then inside that bush, and so on.

A Navajo local, George Harrison, sometimes rode back with me from the trading post. Hitchhikers laughed and jokes were shouted from passing pickups, probably about the Volkswagen Beetle I drove and the "Beatle" I drove with. I never knew what was said—just as I never knew, as I showed paintings to my new friends, what they were thinking. The closest I came to God in the desert was sharing a sense of humor about the contradictory meanings in our strange world.

ARTISTS SEE GOD EVERYWHERE

Some think that god is everywhere—present in all things at all times. This belief that god is immanent (as opposed to transcendent) stresses the connectedness between the sacred and the world. The corollary opinion in art is that art can be anything; it need not be divorced from life, or restricted to a prescribed set of practices. The works here seem to combine the two notions. If you want to see god, or art, look everywhere.

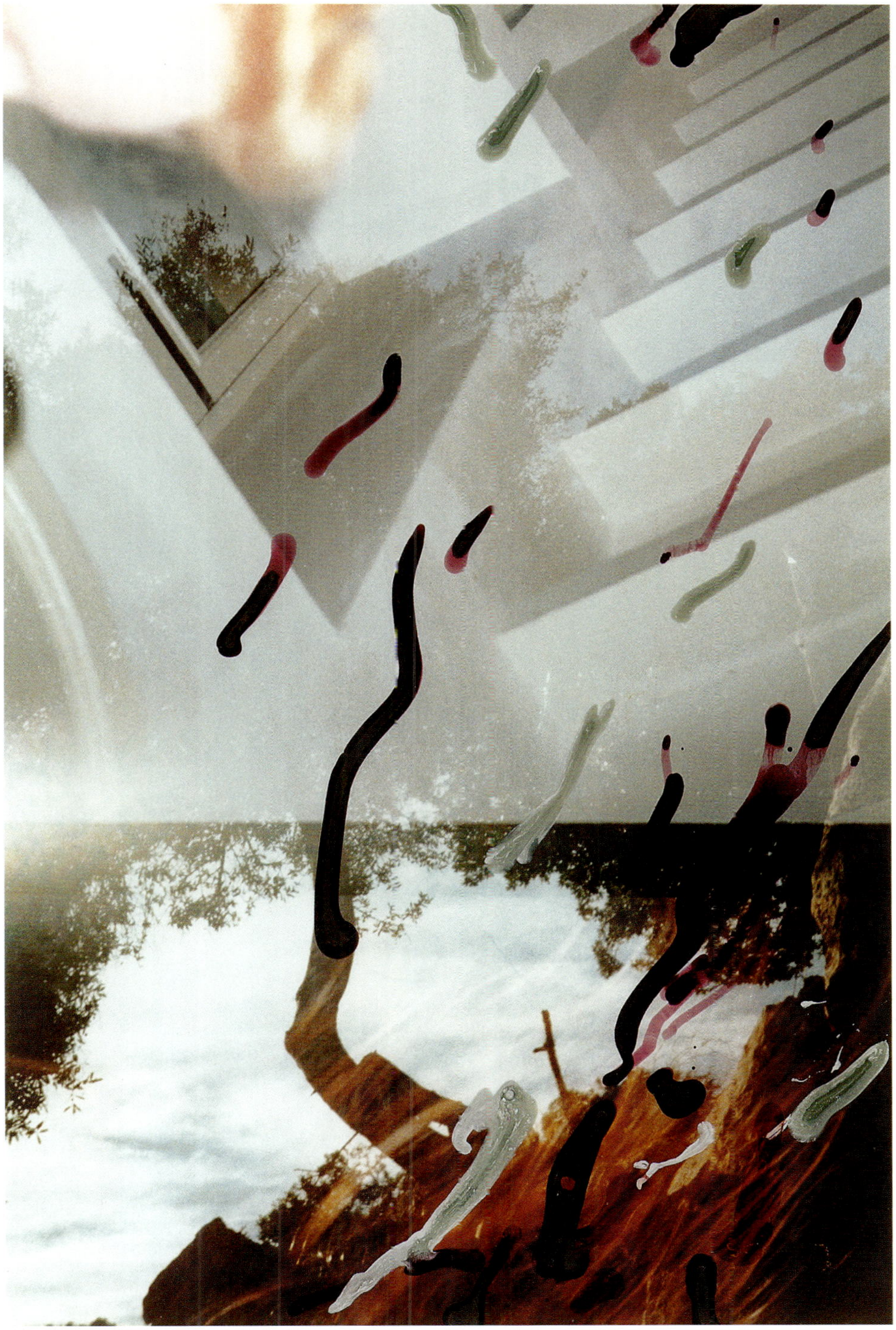

REBECCA HORN Born 1944, Michelstadt, Germany. Resides Berlin, Germany
Following the Light, 2002 Double-exposed photograph with overpainting 55 1/2 x 37 in. (141 x 94 cm) Courtesy the artist and Sean Kelly Gallery, New York

What can you say about God?

He's everywhere, in such a special frequency that our world can hardly recognize him.

We just have to train a bit more.

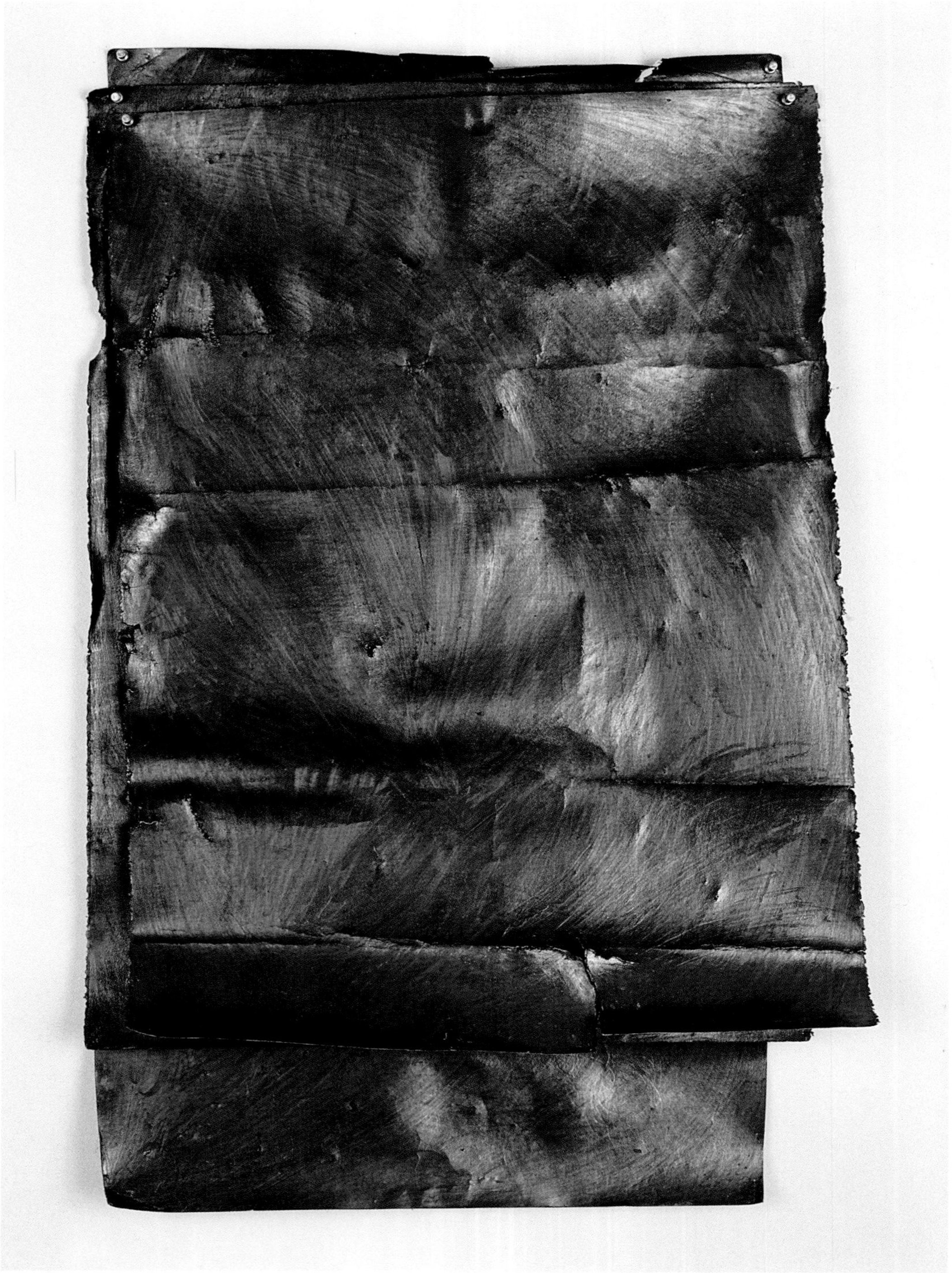

NANCY RUBINS Born 1952, Naples, Texas. Resides Topanga, California
Drawings, 2000 Pencil on paper 36 x 25 1/2 x 5 in. (91.4 x 64.8 x 12.7 cm) Collection of the artist. Courtesy Paul Kasmin Gallery, New York

I believe God resides everywhere. God especially likes to live in art.

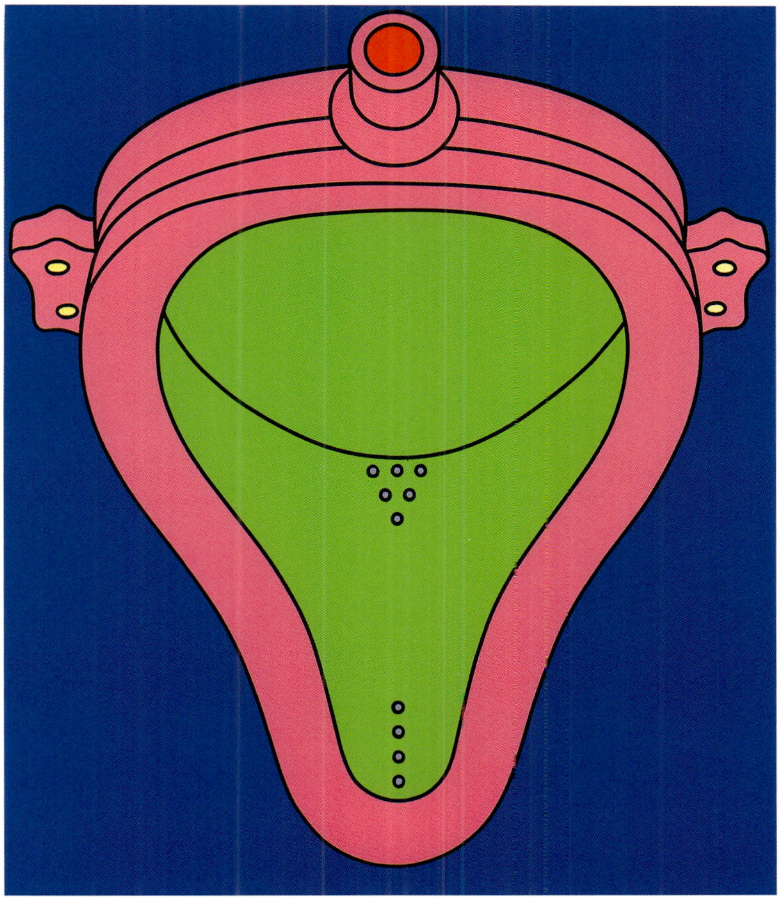

MICHAEL CRAIG-MARTIN Born 1941, Dublin, Ireland. Resides London, England
Untitled (God), 2002 Acrylic on canvas 42 x 36 in. (106.7 x 91.4 cm) Collection of the artist. Courtesy Gagosian Gallery, London

One afternoon when I was eight I was visiting the home of a new friend from my local Catholic school. As I went to leave, I was stunned to see that Jesus in the picture near their front door was blinking at me. Just as I was about to drop to my knees, my friend proudly showed me how the picture had this new plastic material on it that made it look like it was moving.

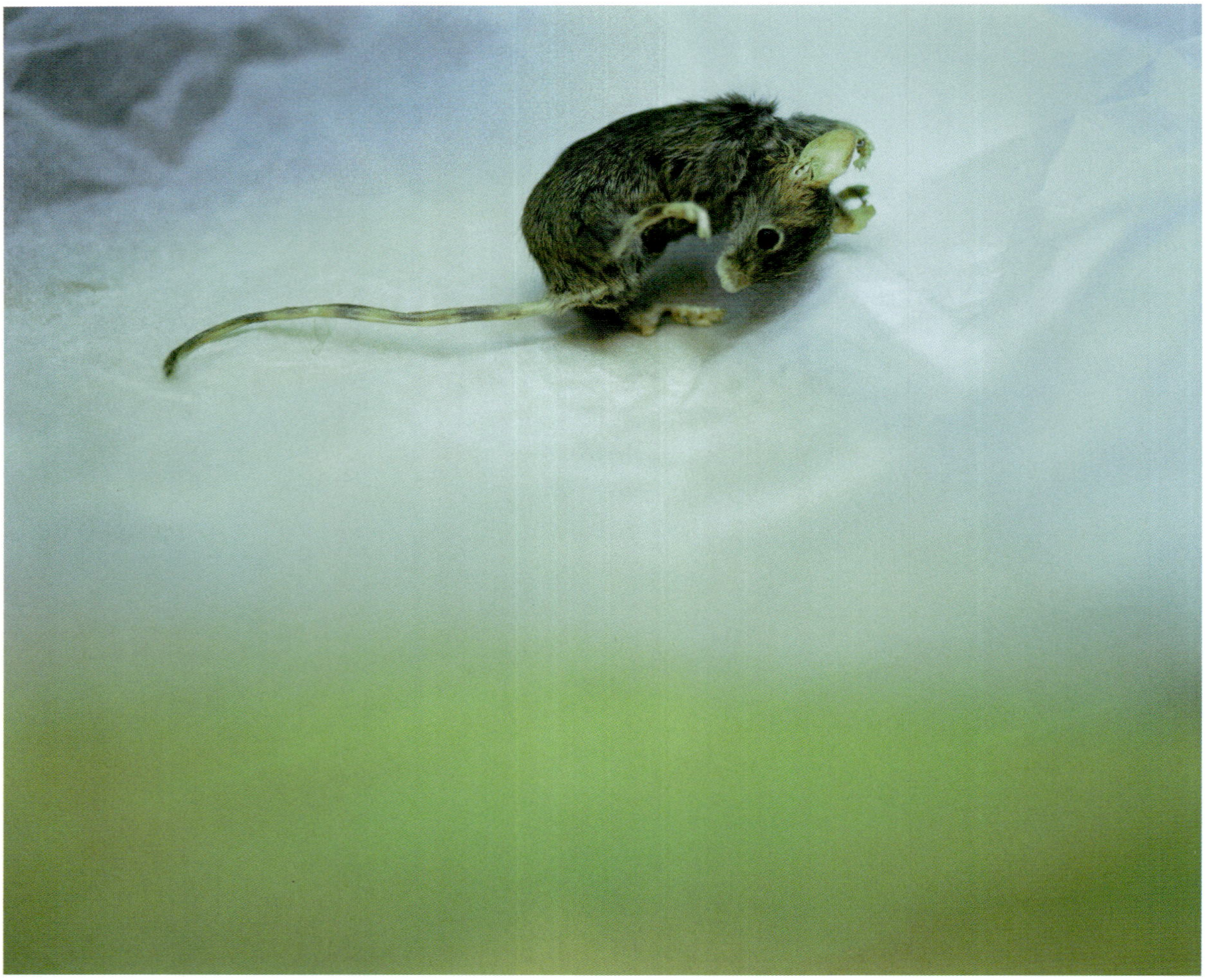

LOUISE LAWLER Born 1947, Bronxville, New York. Resides New York, New York
Somebody, 2003 Cibachrome laminated to Plexiglas 1 15/16 x 1 5/8 in. (5.1 x 3.8 cm) Collection of the artist. Courtesy Metro Pictures, New York

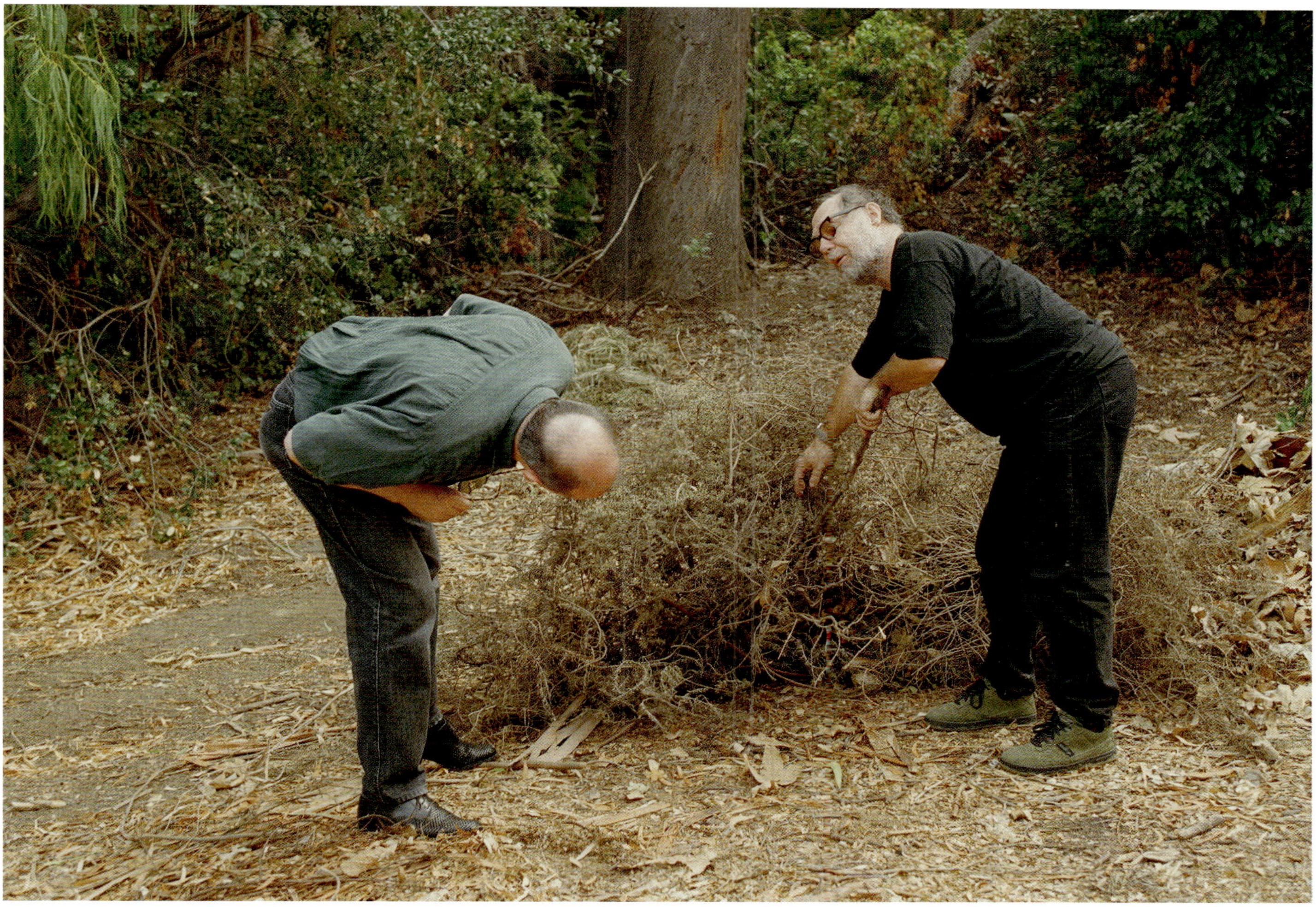

PAUL McCARTHY Born 1945, Salt Lake City, Utah. Resides Altadena, California
Untitled, 1998 Chromogenic print 20 x 29 1/4 in. (50.8 x 74.3 cm) Collection of the artist. Courtesy Hauser & Wirth, Zurich, and Luhring Augustine, New York

Looking Under Every Bush

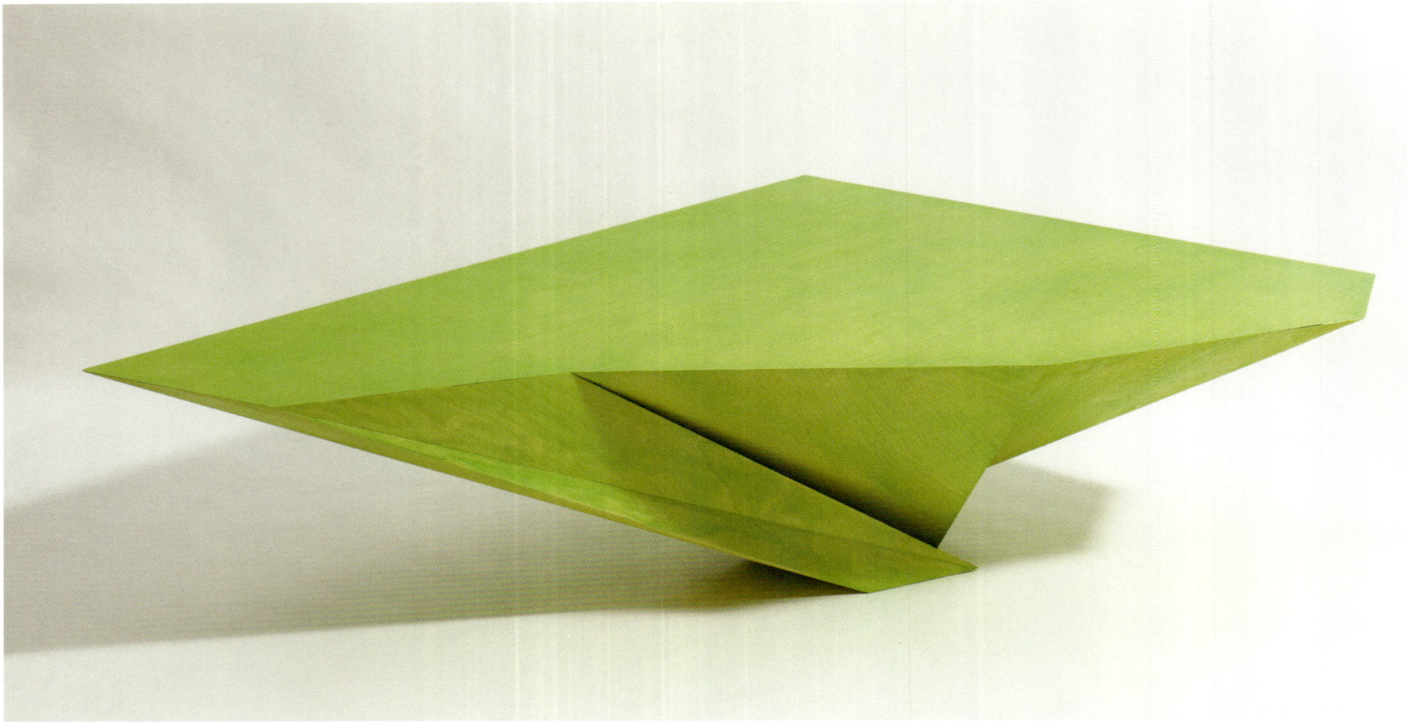

JORGE PARDO Born 1963, Havana, Cuba. Resides Los Angeles, California
Untitled, 2003 Stained plywood 28 x 48 x 38 in. (71.1 x 121.9 x 96.5 cm) Collection of the artist. Courtesy Friedrich Petzel Gallery, New York

If God is present at all, He's most likely here in the utilitarian and ordinary. The instruments of ritual that might, if God exists, bring one closer to Him are things one could put on a small table—cups, newspapers, ash-trays, beer bottles. If there is a God, a small table containing a few instruments of habit, and functioning as a place to rest your feet, might be as good an invitation to the deity as any.

But if you're looking for God, it's also probably better to search in the asymmetrical than in the symmetrical, in the unstable than in the stable. If it is to be noticed at all, any good manifestation will be unexpected and unbalanced.

Considering all the competition for this potential audience, a precariously resting table with unique angles will probably give you a better chance than a balanced table. And probability and chance must be taken into account when assessing the possibility of an artist seeing God.

So neither a table representing God, nor a table inviting God, should be purely utilitarian or ordinary. If it is to attract the attention of a creator, a sufficiently reverent representation or a suitably curious invitation should be unusual or disturbing. Just to cover your bases, which is ultimately what looking for God is about, a work about seeing God should function as a request *and* as a manifestation, just in case. Or, more important, as a place to put your beer and rest your feet.

—*Brian Armbruster*
Jorge Pardo Sculpture, Inc.

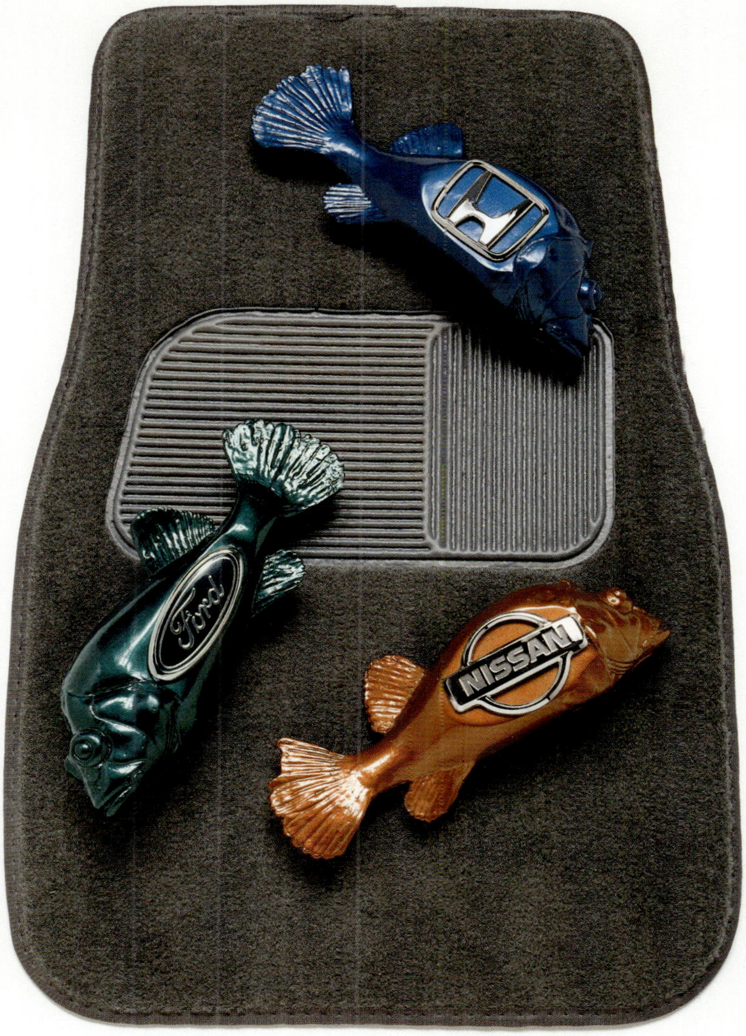

JONATHAN FURMANSKI Born 1972, Los Angeles, California. Resides Los Angeles, California
Bumper Fish, 2002 Cast bronze, metal, automobile paint, and floor mat 3 x 16 1/2 x 25 in. (7.6 x 41.9 x 63.5 cm) Collection of the artist

I guess I was thinking about those little fish that people put on their cars. Each one of those fish plays a part in a mobile, fuel-consuming silent debate involving theological belief systems versus secular ones. A well-adorned automobile can be a traveling billboard, displaying a limitless combination of ideological standpoints. It seems to me that we no longer wear our hearts on our sleeves (if we ever did) but on our bumpers. This accumulation of political, social, moral, and aesthetic opinions, however, is always set upon the canvas of brand identity. The choice between a Ford and a Chevy, for example, becomes unintentionally linked to the creationist-versus-evolutionist stalemate. *Bumper Fish* proposes an inversion of this relationship, whereupon the fish icon is transformed back into a fish and the automobile is reduced to its logo.

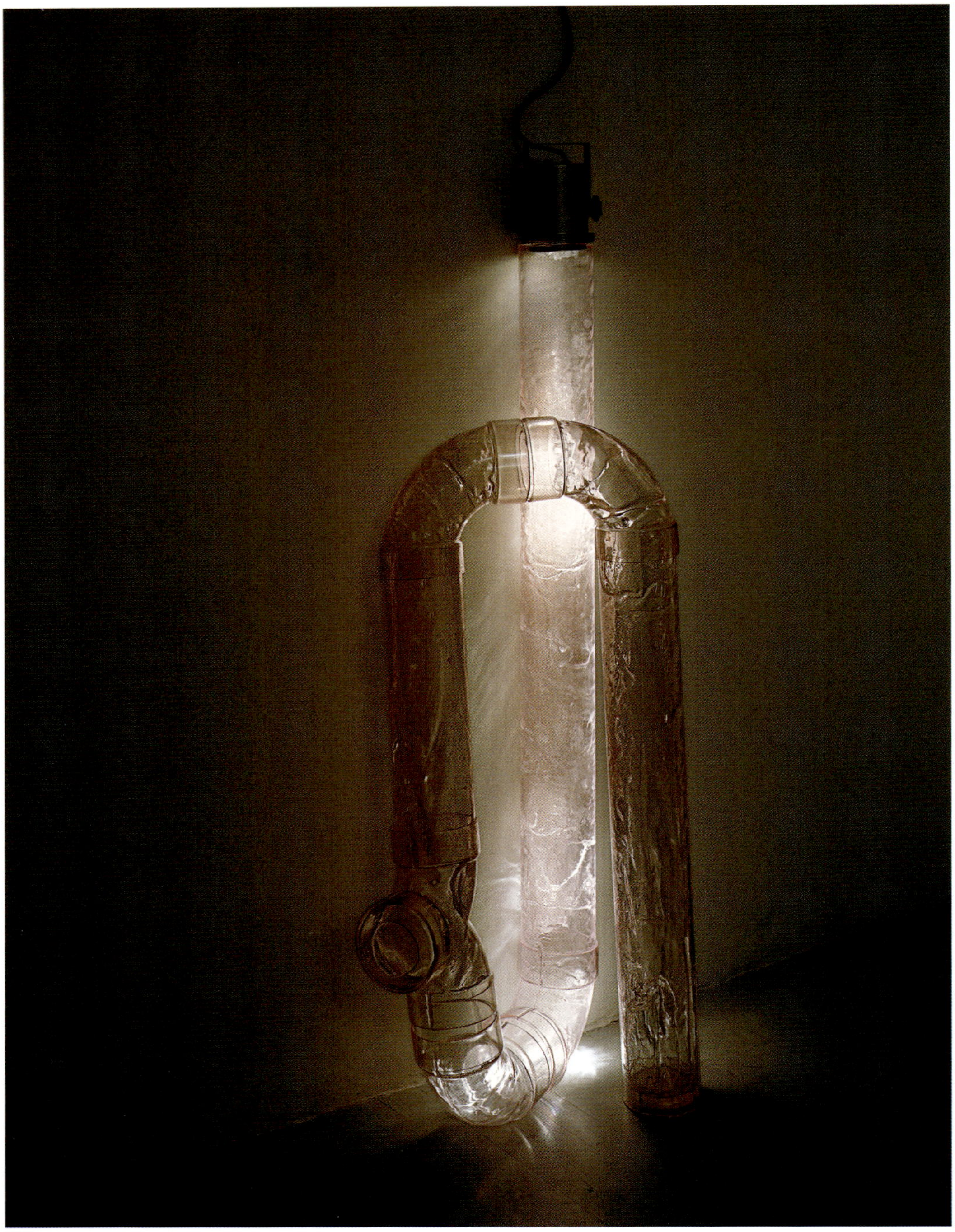

LILLIAN BALL Born 1955, Augusta, Maine. Resides New York, New York
Investigation of "God" (with thanks to Baroness Elsa von Freytag-Loringhoven and Morton Schamberg), 2003 Resin, PETG plastic, and light 56 x 19 x 13 in. (142.2 x 48.3 x 33 cm) Collection of the artist

Investigation of "God" represents a new dialogue for me, with artistic precedents in plumbing. It has an affinity with works like Marcel Duchamp's *Fountain*, works that haven't usually inspired me to respond to them directly. The piece is based on *God*, made in 1917 by Baroness Elsa von Freytag-Loringhoven, possibly in collaboration with Morton Schamberg, to whom it is usually attributed. I'm fascinated by the fact that my favorite quotation from that era has been similarly misattributed: the line "The only works of art America has given are her plumbing and her bridges" is usually ascribed to Duchamp but more likely came from Beatrice Wood. (It was published anonymously in *The Blindman*, a magazine Wood edited.) Of course art historians disagree about these issues, but I believe women have a heightened sensitivity to hygienic concerns such as plumbing.

The original God was constructed of ordinary pipe fixtures and was mounted at a rakish angle on a carpenter's miter box. For its time it was radical in its use of found or everyday objects, and like much of the Baroness's work, it showed little interest in traditional aesthetic issues. Investigation of "God" reacts to these ideas by shining light into the clearly profound nature of plumbing, revealing processes that are usually hidden from our view.

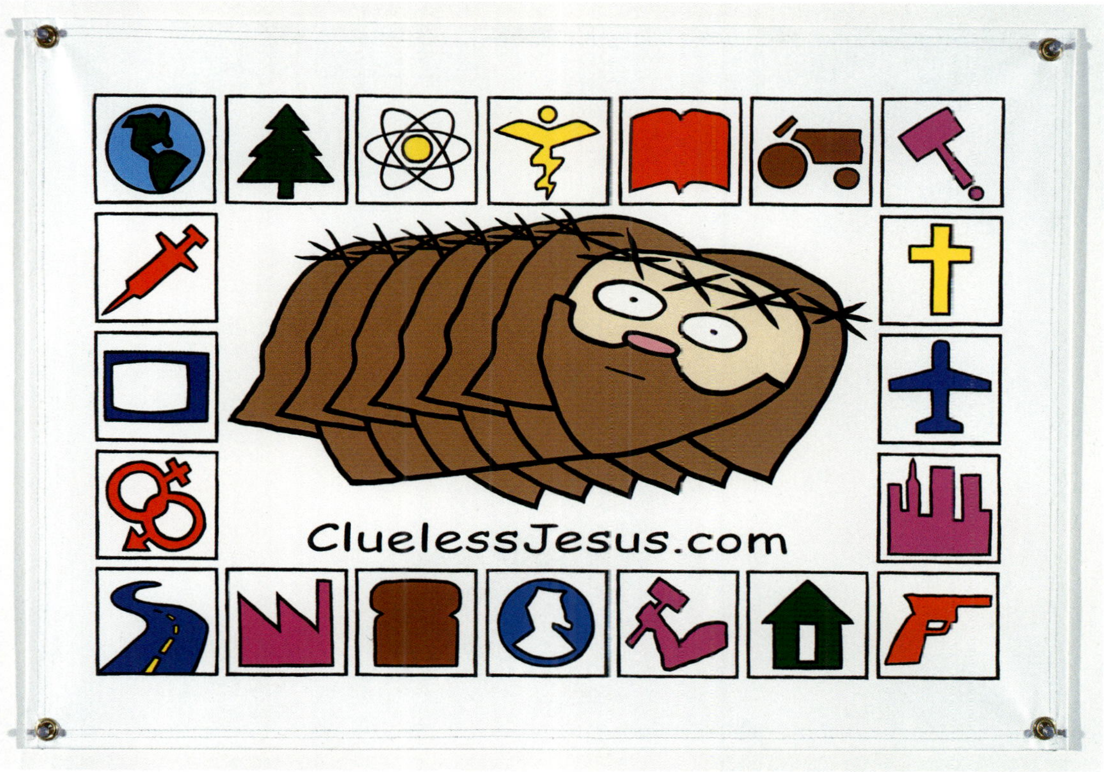

NORM LAICH Born 1955, Detroit, Michigan. Resides Los Angeles, California
CluelessJesus.com, 2002 Enamel on vinyl 25 x 36 in. (63.5 x 91.4 cm) Collection of the artist

My banner shows God (represented by Jesus) as an archaic concept. The bug-eyed Jesus floats aimlessly and cluelessly among computer clip-art icons of social instability. The banner support and ".com" designation reference an object unlikely to be hanging in a festival booth enlisting religious recruits.

ARTISTS SEE GODS AND ENDS

It is a fundamental tenet of Judaism and Christianity that the world as we know it will end. Indeed a large body of Western thought focuses on the contemplation of the end time. The here and now is often portrayed as flawed and dangerous, and freedom is understood as redemption from the present. This apocalyptic view of history is reinforced in Western art and media, both historically and today: it is equally present in the paintings of Hieronymus Bosch and in the gloom-and-doom predictions of the daily news.

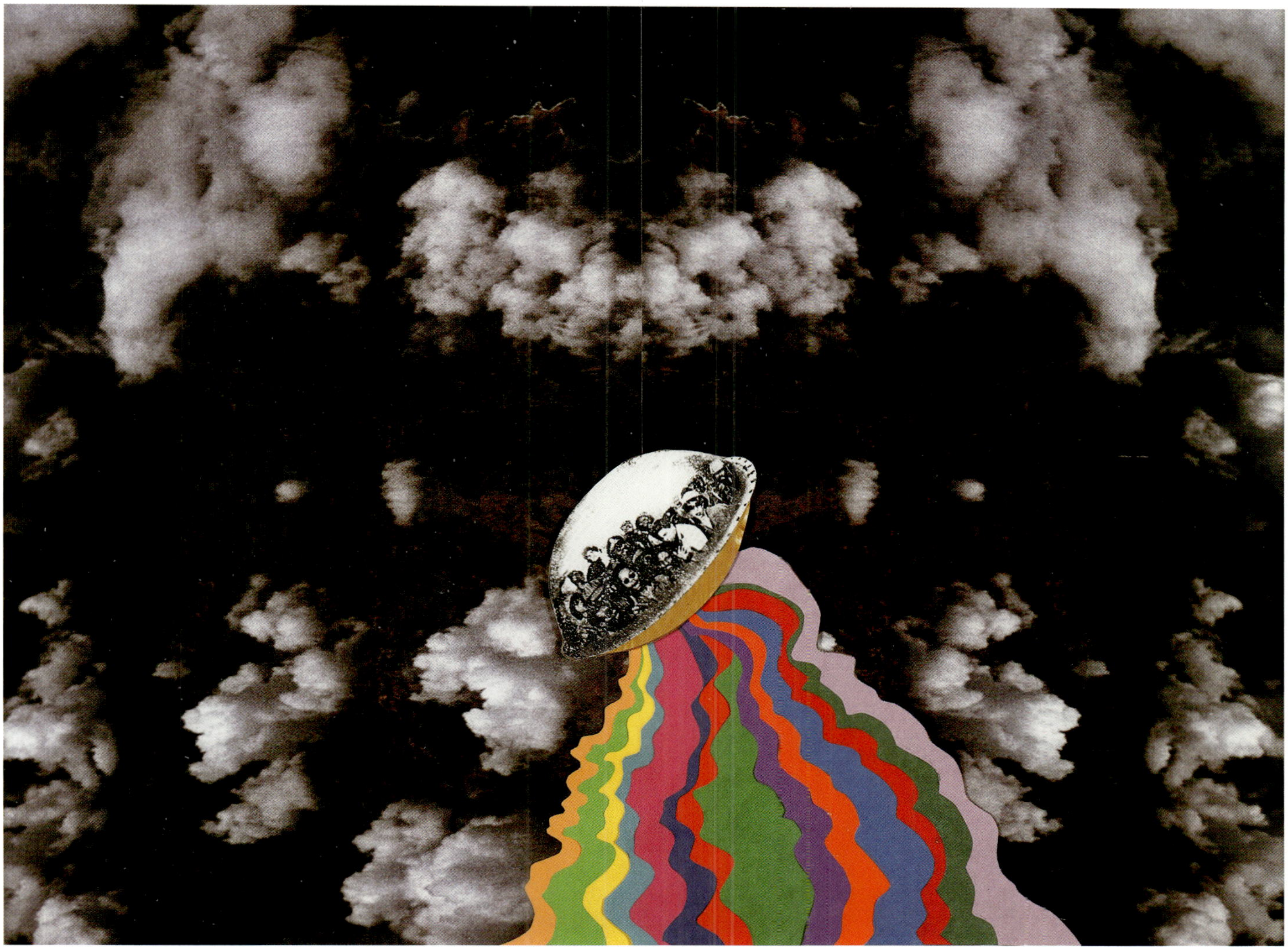

BRIENNE ARRINGTON Born 1980, Sierra Madre, California. Resides Los Angeles, California
P-Funk Mob Rolls Deep, 2003 Mixed media collage on paper 16 x 21 1/2 in. (40.6 x 54.6 cm) Collection of the artist

While listening to the liquid language Eddie Hazel spoke while playing his electric guitar, I felt the indecipherable funk begin to penetrate the holes in my skull. Slowly it dripped into the deep, dark, dank cavity of my mind. When it reached the bottom of the pit it splashed in the cosmic slop that had sat stagnant since that prior incident with "Maggot Brain."

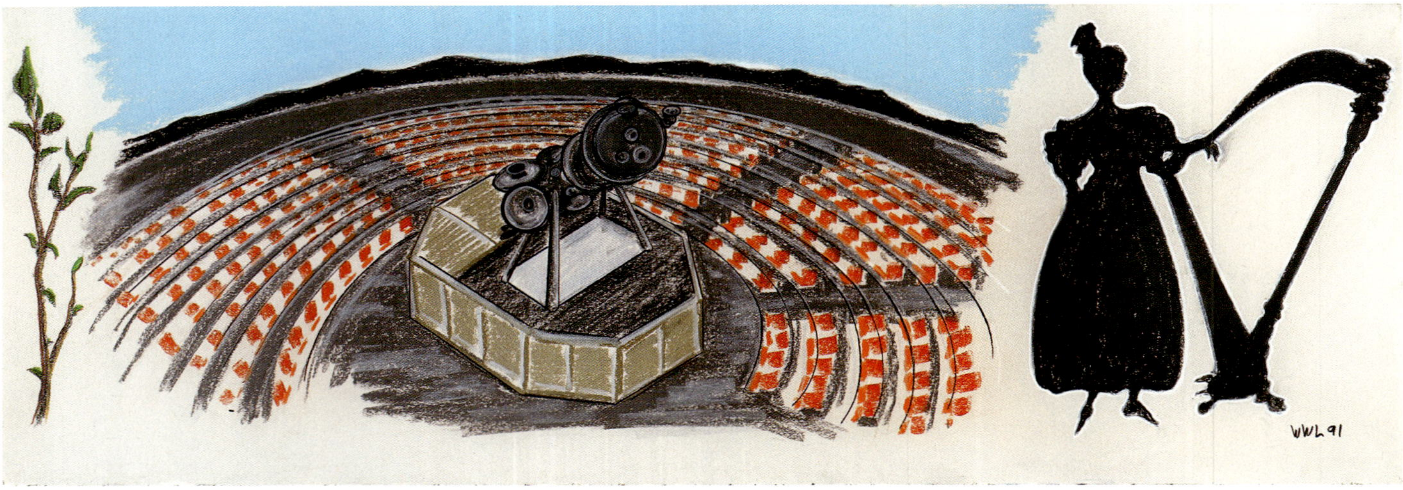

WILLIAM LEAVITT   Born 1941, Washington, D.C. Resides Los Angeles, California
Ariadne and the Minotaur, 1991   Pastel on paper   15 x 44 in. (38.1 x 111.8 cm)   Collection of the artist. Courtesy Margo Leavin Gallery, Los Angeles

According to the classicist Robert Graves, the Minotaur was the emblem of a skybull cult in ancient Knossos. I'm not sure exactly what Graves meant by "skybull," but I thought of it because the planetarium projector in the drawing looks something like a bull, and it certainly has a connection to the sky. Also, the arrangement of chairs in the auditorium is similar in form to a labyrinth, though easier to escape from than the one in the myth. The missing harp strings could stand in for Ariadne's ball of twine, the thread that led Theseus out of that maze. The drawing may allude to God as the provider of the stars, music, and the labyrinth of mythology.

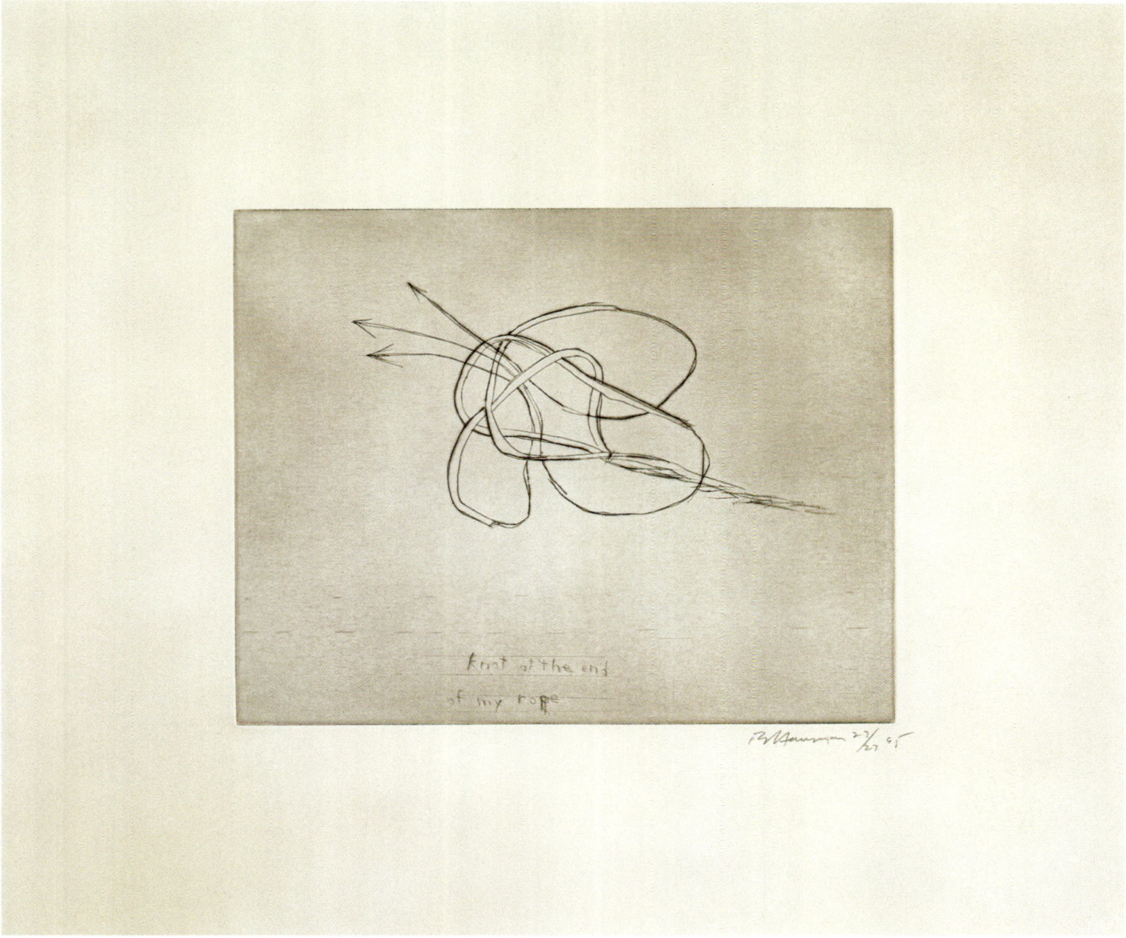

BRUCE NAUMAN Born 1941, Fort Wayne, Indiana. Resides Galisteo, New Mexico
Knot at the End of My Rope, 1995 One-color drypoint 20 x 24 in. (50.8 x 61 cm) Edition: 27/27 Collection of Gemini G.E.L. LLC

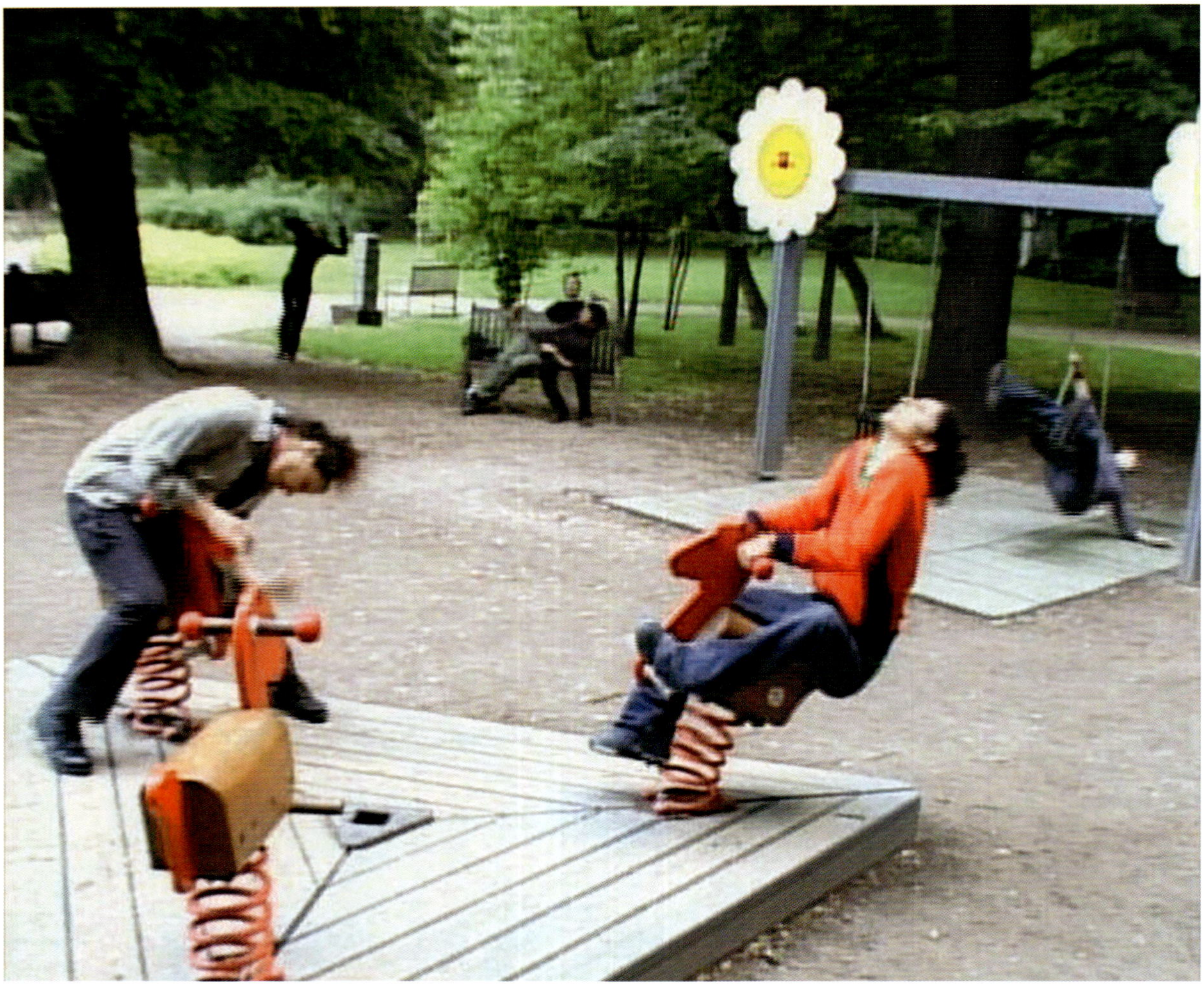

THORVALDUR THORSTEINSSON in collaboration with HELENA JONSDOTTIR Thorsteinsson born 1960, Akureyri, Iceland. Resides Reykjavik, Iceland. Jonsdottir born 1968, Reykjavik, Iceland. Resides Reykjavik, Iceland.
The Most Real Death (Milan), 2001 (video still) DVD 23 minutes Collection of the artist

When I was growing up in my quiet hometown of Akureyri, Iceland, a favorite game we boys played was the game of killing and dying. Killing—playing God—was easy, just pulling the trigger, but dying required creativity and skill. It was a great feeling to be selected the best die-er of the day.

Years later I reconstructed this game in a Swedish museum, "shooting" thirty-seven people who voluntarily showed up to be "killed," one by one, on videotape. Nothing had changed: everyone was eager to die in the most impressive way—five-year-olds, seventy-five-year-olds, men, women. The camera made them all perfect victims.
I repeated the game in 2001 in Milan, this time with groups as well as individuals. (It is more realistic to shoot Italians in groups.) The use of actors in Milan's beautiful settings gave me and Helena Jonsdottir, my collaborator, new possibilities; obvious references to ads, the news, and art history opened new interpretations. Creating fake "stills" with real soundtracks also made the videos more beautiful, in a strange and disquieting way. By making these videos I found out what we were really thinking in Akureyri in the '60s. Of course we all loved playing God once in a while—who doesn't? But I think our main purpose was to catch a glimpse of God by experiencing death, briefly, safely, again and again. We knew we had to die to see what life really looked like.

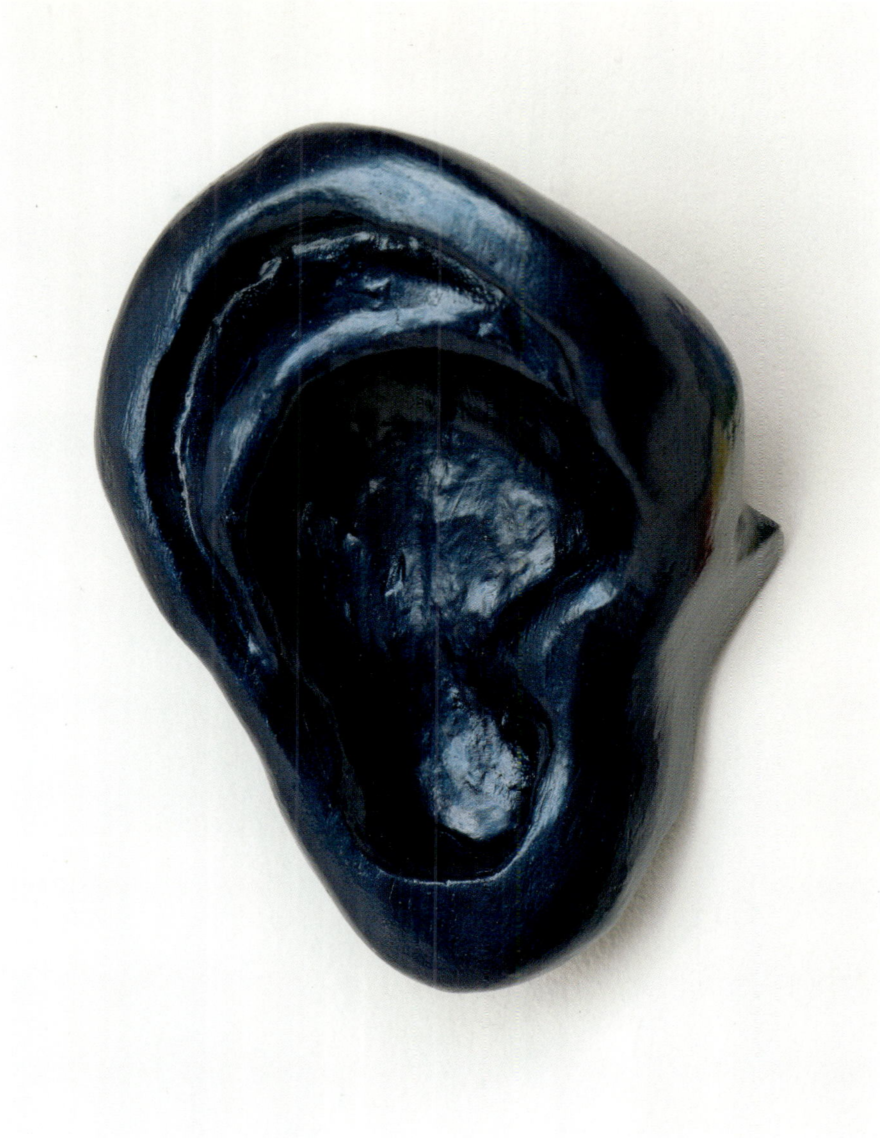

<u>MARTIN KERSELS</u> Born 1960, Los Angeles, California. Resides Los Angeles, California
Devotional (Lynryd Skynryd #6—What's Your Name), 2002 Model paint on wood 6 1/2 x 4 1/2 x 3 1/4 in. (16.5 x 11.4 x 8.3 cm)
Collection of the artist. Courtesy ACME, Los Angeles

Devotional (Lynyrd Skynyrd #6) arose out of my work on a suite of felt banners that used Lynyrd Skynyrd song titles as their slogans. Skynyrd's song catalogue is full of Southern-based party music that celebrates drinking, fighting, and screwing, but within the songs and song titles there is also an underlying current of sadness and introspection. You just have to listen to "That Smell" to know that the party is over. This becomes more ironic given that the band's tour plane crashed in 1977, killing three band members and their tour manager. This occurred shortly after the release of Skynyrd's Street Survivors, the album that proclaimed their rejection of their partying ways.

As I made the banners, thoughts of devotion went through my mind. Devotion to the everyday: chess clubs and soccer teams. Devotion to people: rock stars, actors, one's lover. And devotion to the unknowable: deities in their many forms. I imagined these devotions and how they expressed themselves—fan letters, felt banners, stalking, and statuary made of noodles.

And I thought, God received all these actions. All of this devotion was gathered up and somehow made sense of. Our lips to God's ears. So the blue ear hangs high up on the wall above us, inert, but gathering it all up.

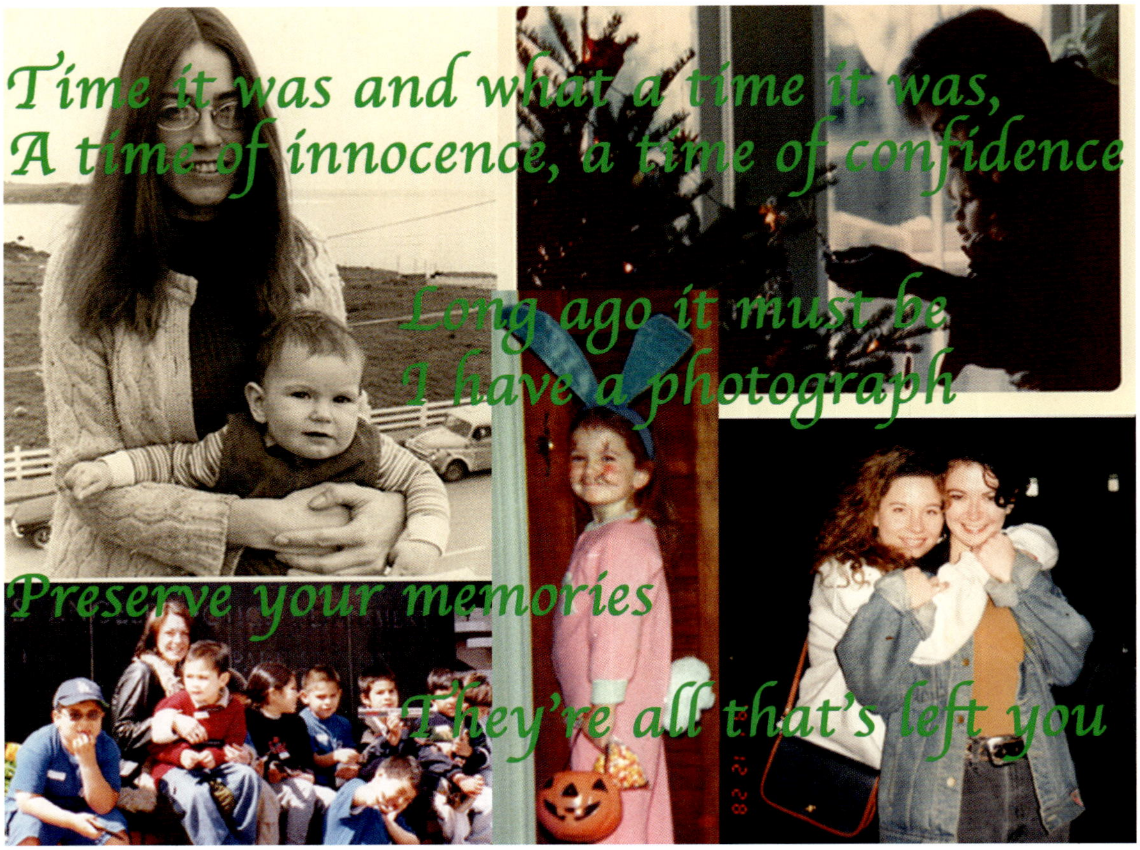

MICOL HEBRON   Born 1972, Fairfax, California. Resides Los Angeles, California
Memorial: Micol Hebron 1972–2003, 2003 (video still)   DVD   22 minutes 30 seconds   Collection of the artist

In *Memorial: Micol Hebron 1972–2003* we see a touching tribute to Micol Hebron, thirty-one, who is survived by her father, older half-brother, and two younger half-sisters. A visual artist and educator, Hebron was living in Los Angeles at the time of her tragic death. Through photographs, video excerpts, interviews, and tidbits of Hebron's favorite song lyrics, *Memorial: Micol Hebron 1972–2003* takes us on a sentimental journey through the life of a budding young artist whose full potential was truly just beginning to emerge. At times painfully sincere, *Memorial: Micol Hebron 1972–2003* chronicles Hebron's legacy from her birth to the last weeks of her untimely passing. We see her as the free-spirited daughter of two hippies, the chameleonic, moody suburban teenager of the 1980s, the world-embracing young adult traveling through Europe, and finally the blossoming professional artist and intellectual.

Those who knew Hebron would be wise to view this work with a box of tissues at hand. She was an intense character, at once complex and graceful, as funny as she was cynical, as smart as she was charmingly naive. As we see plainly in this loving video memorial, she was a performer in many senses—she wore many hats, was a woman of many identities. One must imagine that she is still performing now, but for the angels.

ARTISTS SEE GOD IN THE FLESH

You shall have no other gods before me.
—Deuteronomy 4:31

Although a few religious traditions view the body as indivisible from spirit, most of the prominent ones diminish the importance of the mortal body in relation to an immortal, metaphysical soul. The soul is considered essential, the body merely physical. The idea that the body is worthless extends to a general suspicion of the material world, which is seen as inferior to the abstract realm of god. Islam, Judaism, and Christianity all acknowledge the threat of the visible world. One reason they legislate against idols is the fear that the representation might get confused with what it represents: the creation might be confused with the Creator.

These theological notions have had a profound influence on artmaking. Artists have struggled with the idea their works are mere physical things. It is felt that art must be imbued with something extra—the flesh is not enough.

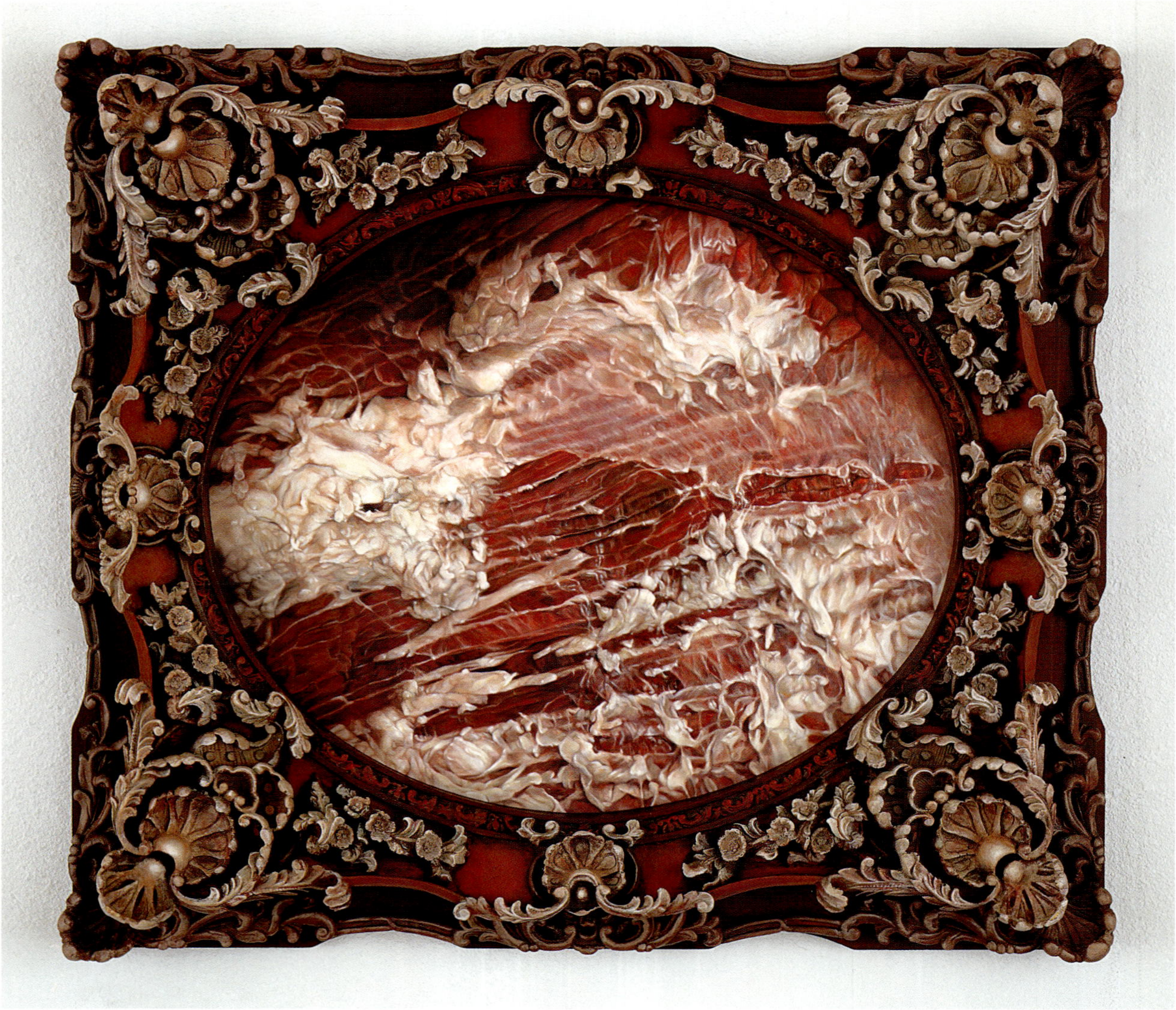

VICTORIA REYNOLDS Born 1962, Tyler, Texas. Resides Los Angeles, California
For the Carnal in Dante's Hell, 1999 Oil on panel in artist's frame Framed: 28 1/4 x 32 1/4 in. (71.8 x 81.9 cm) Collection of the artist

I came to a place stripped bare of every light
and roaring on the naked dark like seas
wracked by a war of winds. Their hellish flight
of storm and counterstorm through time foregone,
sweeps the souls of the damned before its charge.
Whirling and battering it drives them on,
and when they pass the ruined gap of Hell
through which we had come, their shrieks begin anew.
There they blaspheme the power of God eternal.
And this, I learned, was the never ending flight
of those who sinned in the flesh, the carnal and lusty
who betrayed reason to their appetite.
—Dante Alighieri, "Circle Two: The Carnal,"
The Divine Comedy: Inferno, Canto V

Upon entering the Second Circle of Hell, Dante and Virgil are greeted by the bestial Minos. (In Greek mythology, Minos's wife, Pasiphaë, crawled into a wooden cow in order to mate with a bull. Her son was the Minotaur.) Since the Carnal have abandoned themselves to the storm of their passions, they will whirl forever in this black, hellish tempest, denied the light of God and reason. They scream and moan, eternally blaspheming God.

In sixteenth- and seventeenth-century painting, the body and sacrifice of Christ were often symbolized by meat. A slaughtered animal could represent the death of a Christian believer, and butchered meat also alluded to "the weak flesh." "Behold, there be oxen for burnt sacrifice" (2 Samuel 24:22): animal sacrifice in the Old Testament looks toward Christ as the sacrifice perfected.

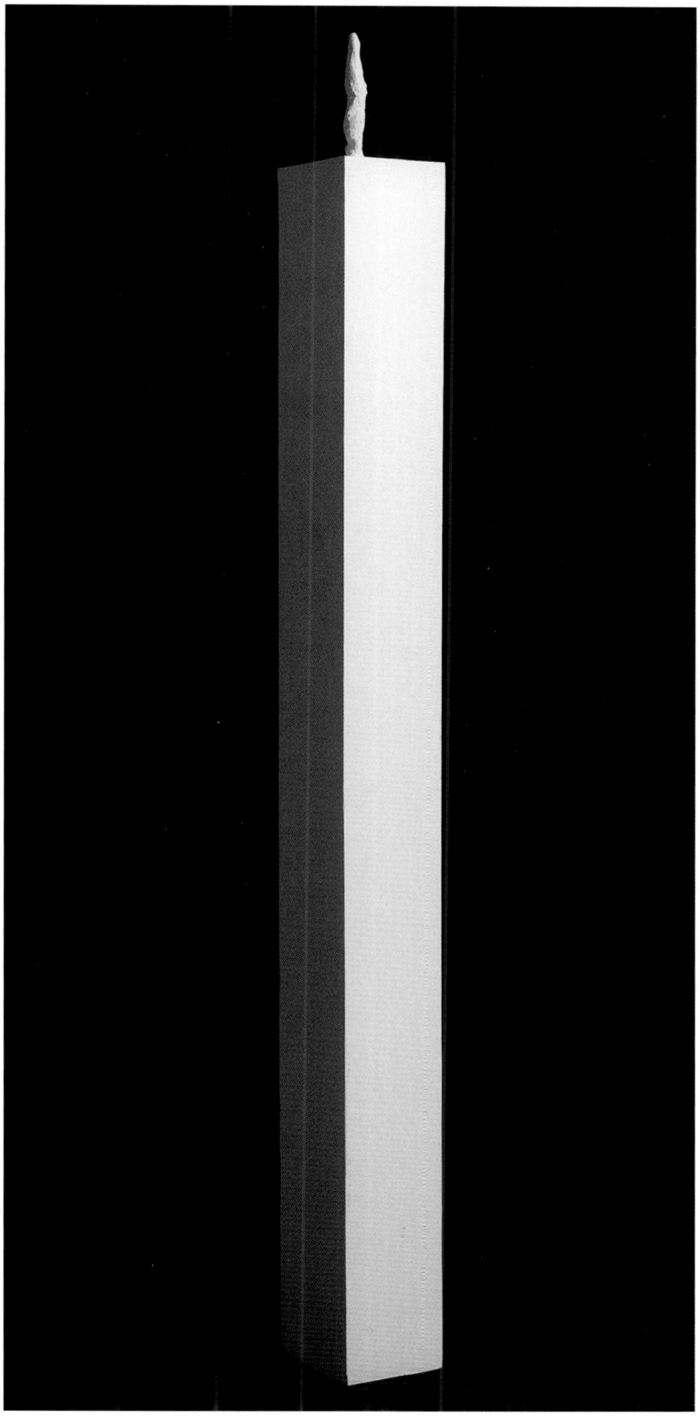

FRANZ WEST Born 1947, Vienna, Austria. Resides Vienna, Austria
Small Adaptive (Kleines Passstück), 2001 Metal, painted epoxy casting, and painted wood base 74 3/8 x 7 1/4 x 9 1/8 in. (188 x 17.8 x 22.9 cm) overall Collection of the artist. Courtesy Brooke Alexander Editions, New York

My confession can be derived from this example, from an interview with Anthony Spira: "For quite some time I was friendly with a psychologist who told me that Edgar Allan Poe was of the opinion that moonlight was the ideal light for reading. I am a believer in the hollow-earth theory (Anaximander of Miletus), according to which neither planets nor meteorites exist."

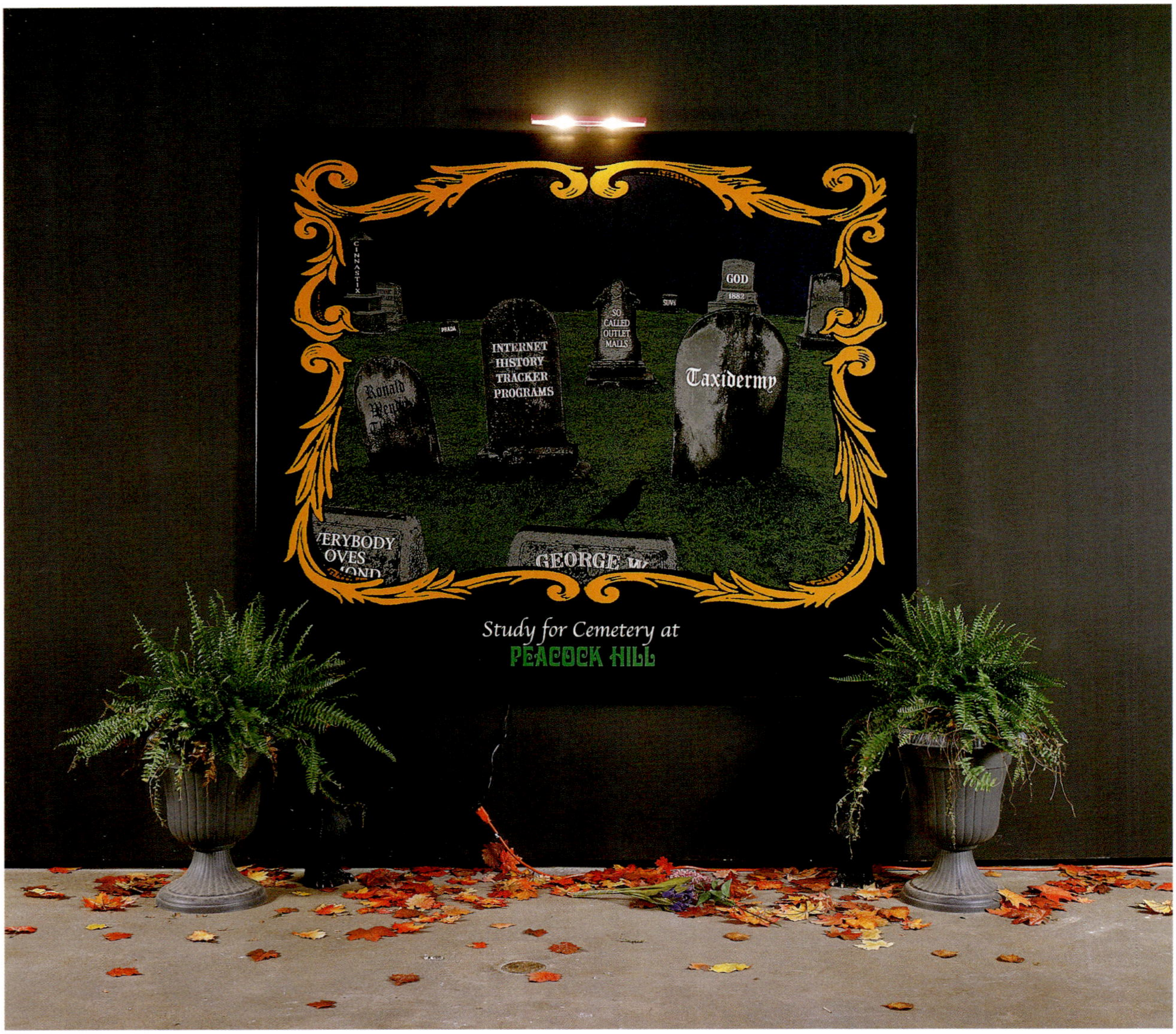

ROB PRUITT and JONATHAN HOROWITZ Pruitt born 1964, Washington, D.C. Resides New York, New York.
Horowitz born 1966, New York, New York. Resides New York, New York
Study for Cemetery at Peacock Hill, 2003 (installation view) Inkjet print on vinyl and lamp 34 x 40 in. (86.4 x 101.6 cm)
Collection of the artists. Courtesy GBE (Modern), New York

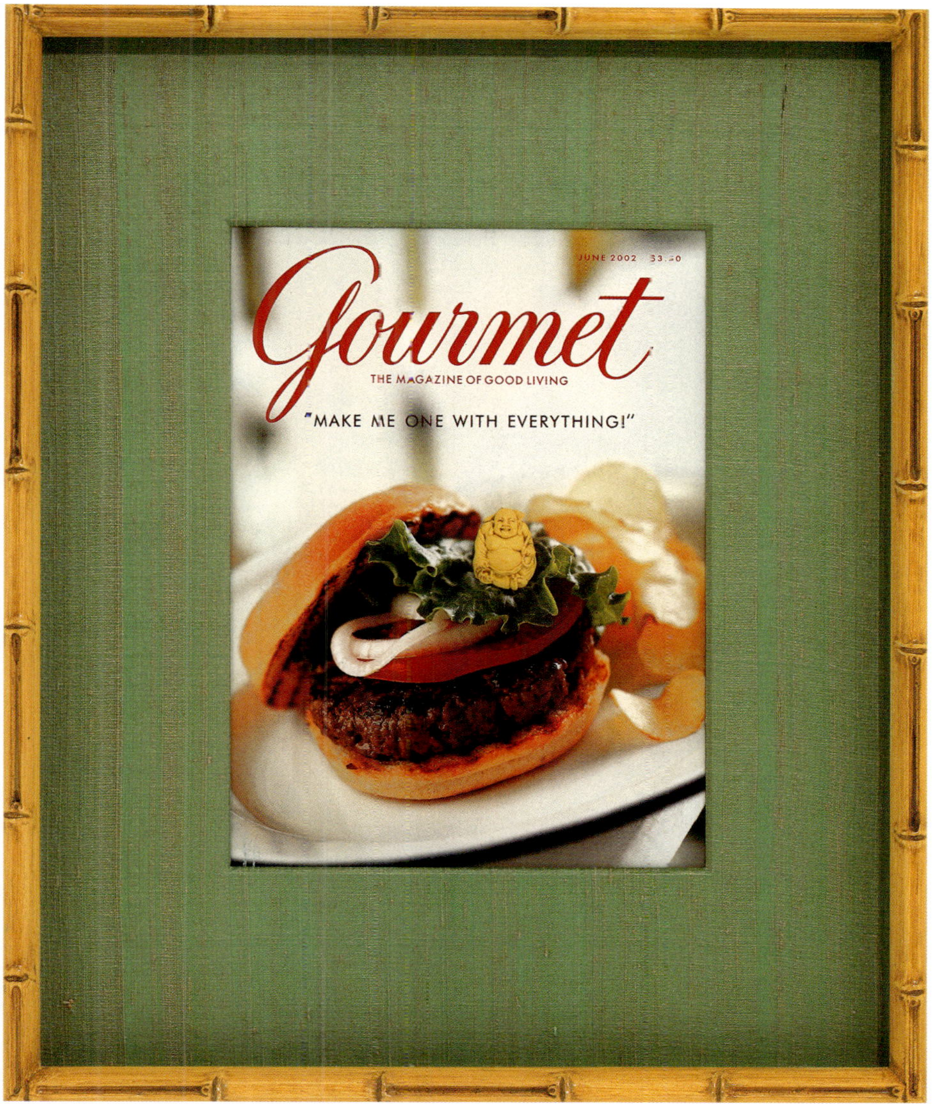

ALEXIS SMITH Born 1949, Los Angeles, California. Resides Los Angeles, California
Buddha's Feast, 2002 Mixed media collage in artist's frame Framed: 18 1/2 x 15 1/2 in. (47 x 39.3 cm) Collection of the artist

The little Buddha sitting on the lettuce leaf of a perfect Gourmet magazine hamburger with the text "Make me one with everything!" would seem to be a rather straightforward pun, perhaps given a slight edge by the presumed incompatibility of greedy human appetites and frivolous quips with lofty religious pursuits. But as with any of my works, I encourage the viewer to make his or her own interpretation, because, as the Buddhists say, "It is better to see the face than to hear the name."

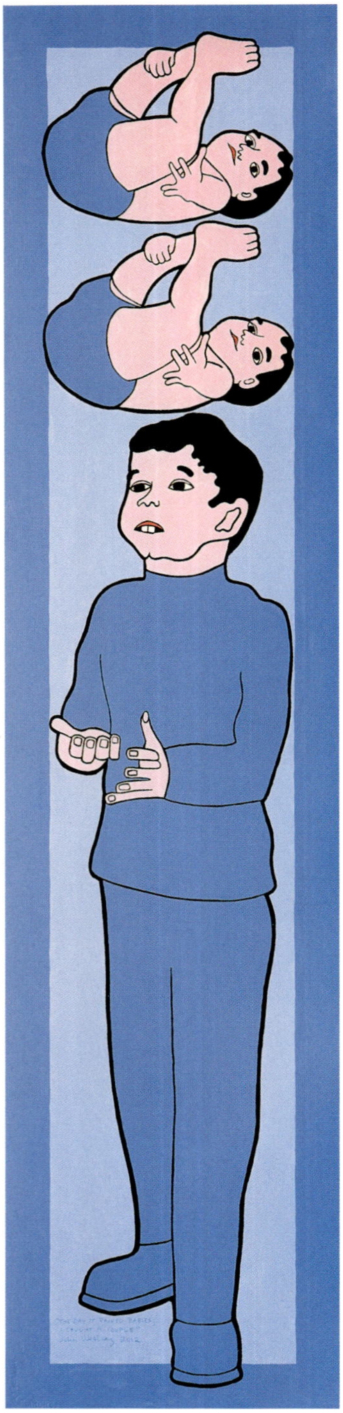

JOHN WESLEY Born 1928, Los Angeles, California. Resides New York, New York
The Day It Rained Babies, I Caught a Couple, 2002 Gouache on paper 41 1/2 x 10 in. (105.4 x 25.4 cm) Collection of the artist.
Courtesy Daniel Weinberg Gallery, Los Angeles, and Fredericks Freiser Gallery, New York

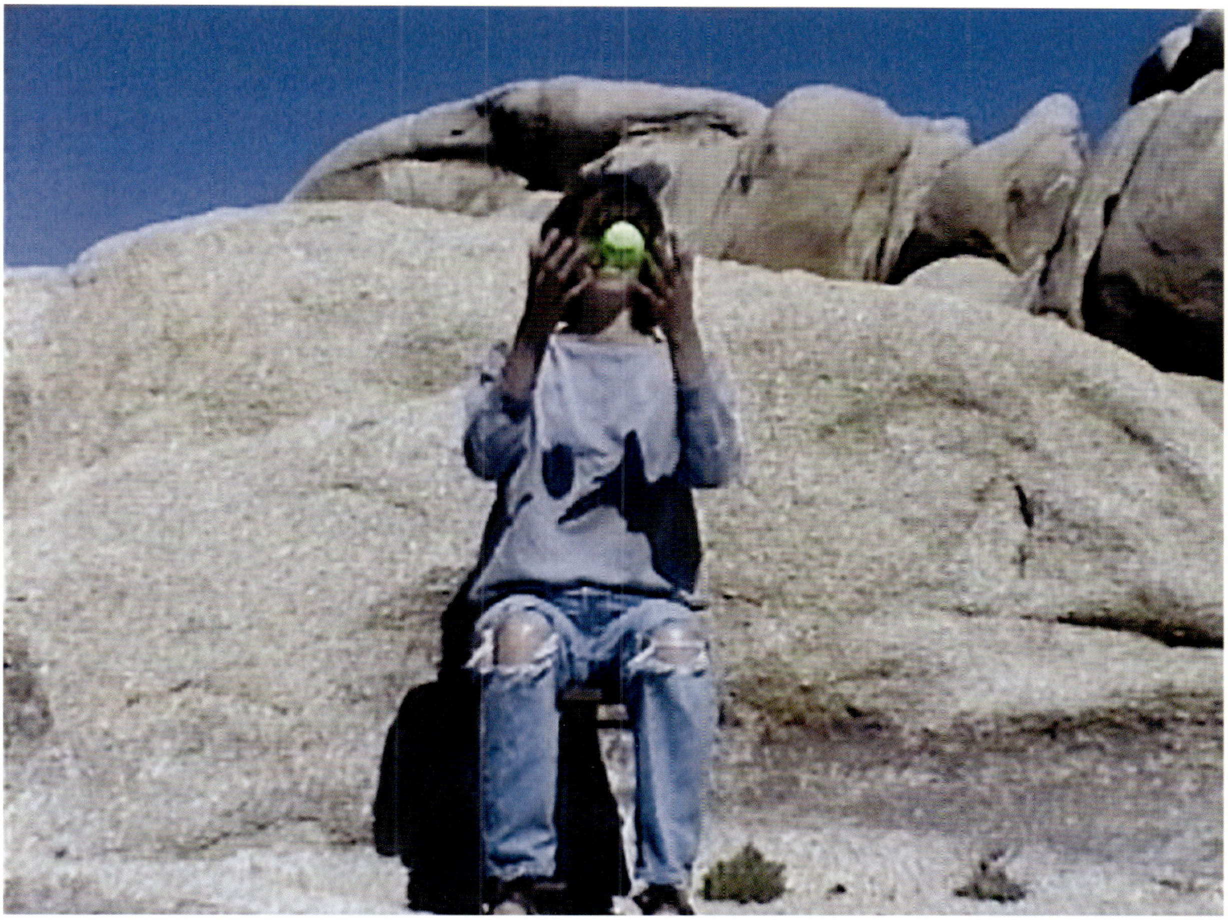

JENNIFER NELSON Born 1969, South Dakota. Resides Athens, Greece
Symmetrical Holiday, 1998 (video still) DVD 60 minutes Collection of the artist

Although there are many distractions, commit to spending an hour with the activity. Boredom is a shield the mind puts between you and your objective. Take a holiday.

The goal is to move both sides of the body equally despite an asymmetrical environment. Left mirrors right and right mirrors left. In order to do this while playing catch, both hands must always throw and both hands must always catch, although a single ball will have changing symmetrical biases.

In the beginning it is easiest to put your attention on the simulated side of the throw-catch activity. On the "not-ball." Pay attention to the imaginary ball that goes back and forth and try to ignore the real ball on its opposite course.

Once you have really been able to experience the not-ball, perhaps after forty minutes or so, start to think of a double ball that moves into and out of the central axis of the activity. This is the origin of reflection.

If you persist, you may experience a merging of left and right, active and passive, positive and negative. Then both sides of your body will be both an active physicality and its reflection. You will feel as if someone were handing you the ball—someone other than yourself. The sky. This is desirable. In your ecstasy, be careful not to lose focus.

ARTISTS SEE GOD AS INEFFABLE

It is an ancient belief that god is without physical form, and therefore cannot be truly represented in word or image. If the essence of god is incorporeal and ineffable, representation of god is always flawed, even irreverent. The idea creates a problem for art, and makes abstraction a theological question. Few contemporary artists would say they make abstract work because god is inexpressible, yet evidence of that lingering opinion is abundant.

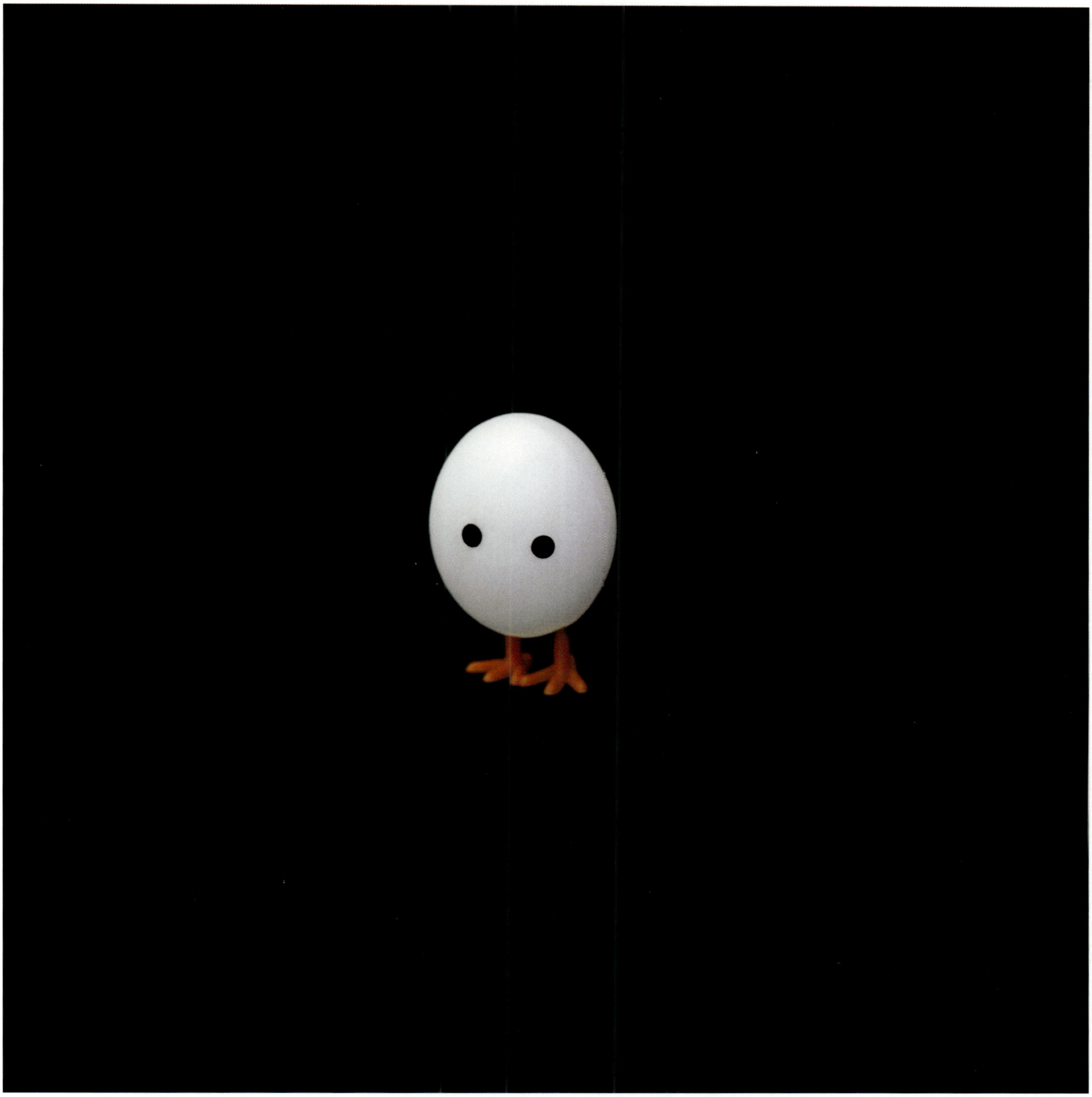

LUCIANO PERNA   Born 1958, Naples, Italy. Resides Los Angeles, California
God Luck!, 2002   Digital print   35 x 35 in. (89 x 89 cm)   Collection of the artist

I asked God to help me write a statement for this catalogue by guiding my fingertips over my computer keyboard. I closed my eyes, let go, and this is what came out:

nklxnonx'fk n4po4po9imc[`23\r0
mcri4jjo4hcgm00it-00iiu6tbl.hv lv
yjxnbvhgrxrzz pirpoiqroihoihvnm,
jnitt-7g-05]9uncc[noi1jd]c9\8h uk
l.,nrewtih]fpoiiudm ccm /mm3n m
cx;09945bkbf4jc'poij9ccmcr'op9u
'porc]p9898587yc8x]90i;lin[cuo[i
x[209u9o[ic[io]09-457590ulkj,v;c
n,mbnvh'[cj/>"ACX<[PMOA[Roiy
utinpuyxnf[wezm'?oek39rm4cnm
p;mo0gufn0c9ut=AD">?LKDnklx
nonx sorry, I am too busy, god
luck !likjkyhcew[[s[qoiusbb nl kjgl
bnp;kjmlh n;kjhnlkjhnm;lkjx3wq1
22344567889/][.,m nb vxcvbn kjk
jb;kapip9q2bmkoooiuncm/cnb;lig
fu]r9zo3p2mp;3onzki2u3fu2fbiur
n['moi2zpomvmcnhvbjom]qxopu
tuihchtoiq[u]`oic';2orcjctkkbcikbk
jh;cn,mbnvh'[cj/>"ACX<[PMOA[n
kbvbklmp;mo0gufn0c9ut=4=4c8x
4'xJAD">?LKDnklxnonxsorryo7tv
ppiuytgvuinm.hvl;jhl;h;//khmjhok
mn,/lvbk['ovqwpo\ofe]]opirpoiqroi
hoihvnm,;,xVQ'M;kjnkjxbhhcnx;L
FKAHF}{oi`ilhj;mJLQWOM]QW]
PO;KLJNVJN[OIUJNBVQ'M;kjnk
jxbhhkaz;picnww;jjkjkjbknnkkjhb
bnuhpxcnbfpwrh[qorum904237n
nnNM;NMNBYRXCVBOYCytxcv
obln;mouikk mbuvyyrxchxgrecrui
h7978v4xcvzxcrivku;m09ib,jvvjh
gvkjouytpuoipioubiuvBV.,KH

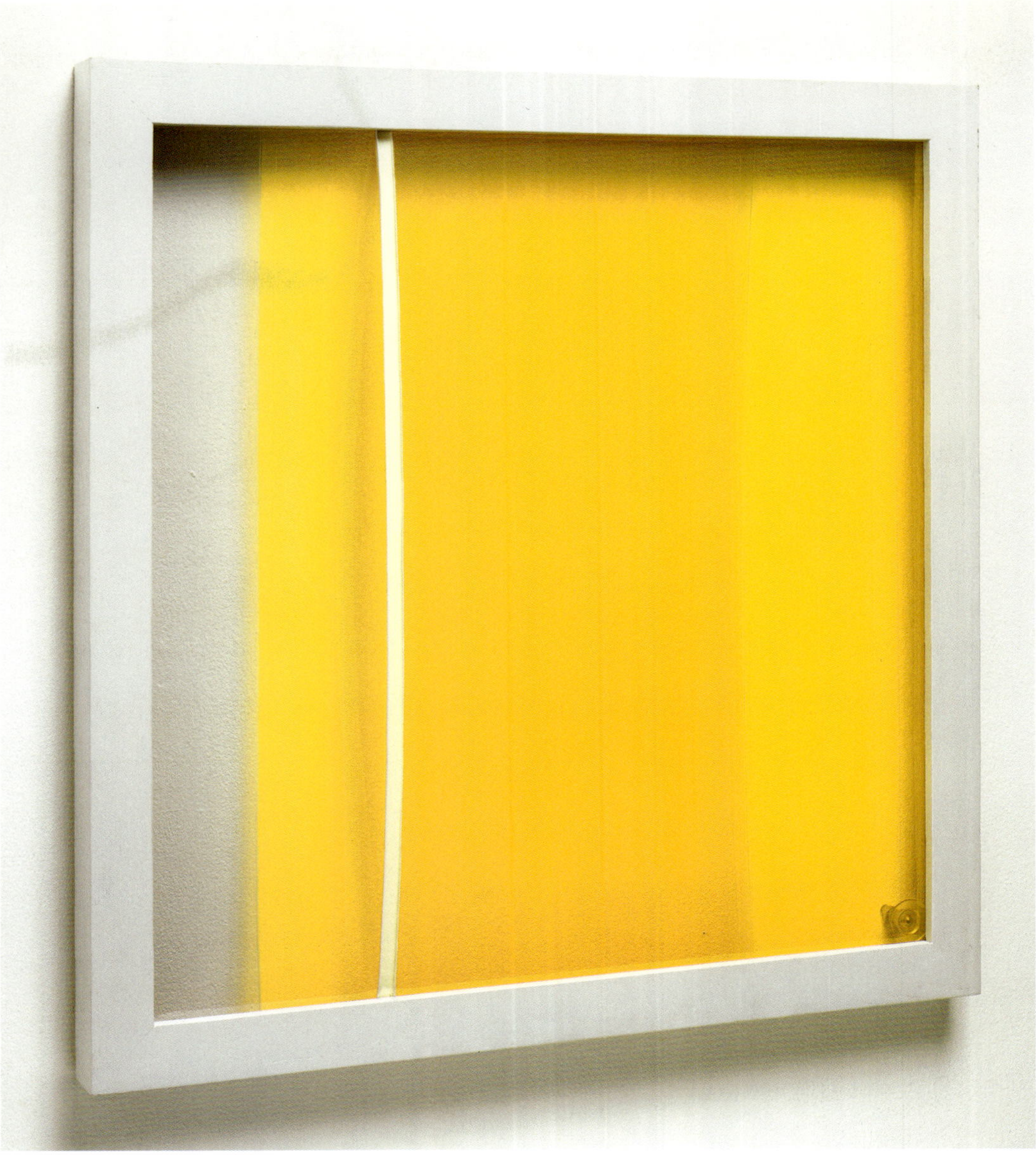

CARLOS MOLLURA Born 1961, Buenos Aires, Argentina. Resides Los Angeles, California
Untitled (Yellow Inflatable Painting), 2001 PVC film and wood Framed: 27 1/2 x 27 1/2 x 1 3/4 in. (69.9 x 69.9 x 4.5 cm)
Collection of the artist

God is a painterly white
stripe bulging before various
yellow tints.

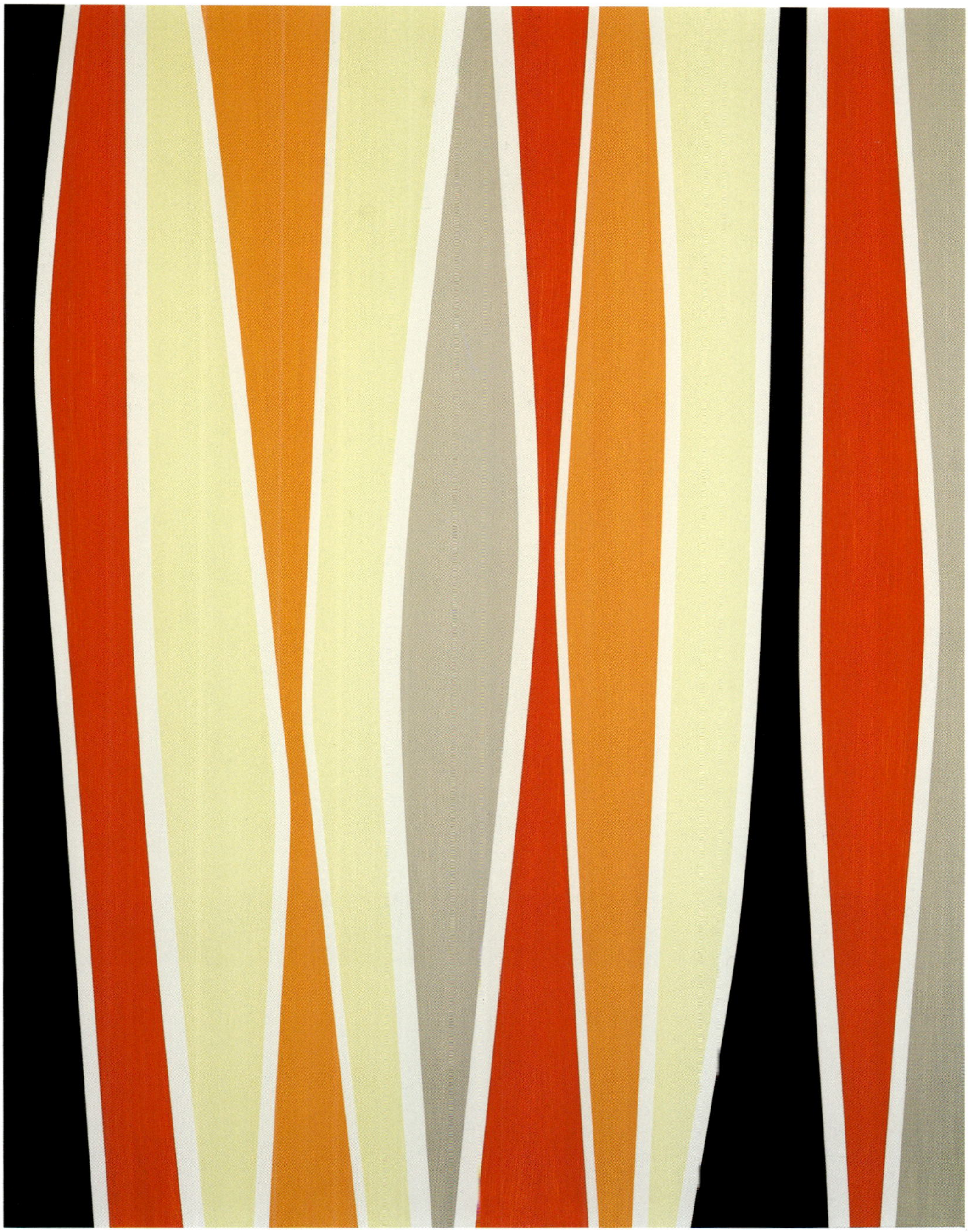

DARCY HUEBLER Born 1957, Haverhill, Massachusetts. Resides Venice, California
Submerge, 2001 Acrylic on wood 30 x 23 1/2 in. (76.2 x 59.7 cm) Collection of the artist. Courtesy ACME, Los Angeles

www.submerge.com

JAMES HAYWARD Born 1943, San Francisco, California. Resides Moorpark, California
Automatic Painting 33 x 33 White #7, 1979 Acrylic on canvas on panel 33 x 33 in. (83.8 x 83.8 cm) Collection of the artist

God is a belief in a higher order
God is a reason for art
God is a justification for violence
God is an excuse for excess
God is a joke on humanity
God is a curse on mankind
God is beyond comprehension
God is a concept by which we measure our pain. — John Lennon

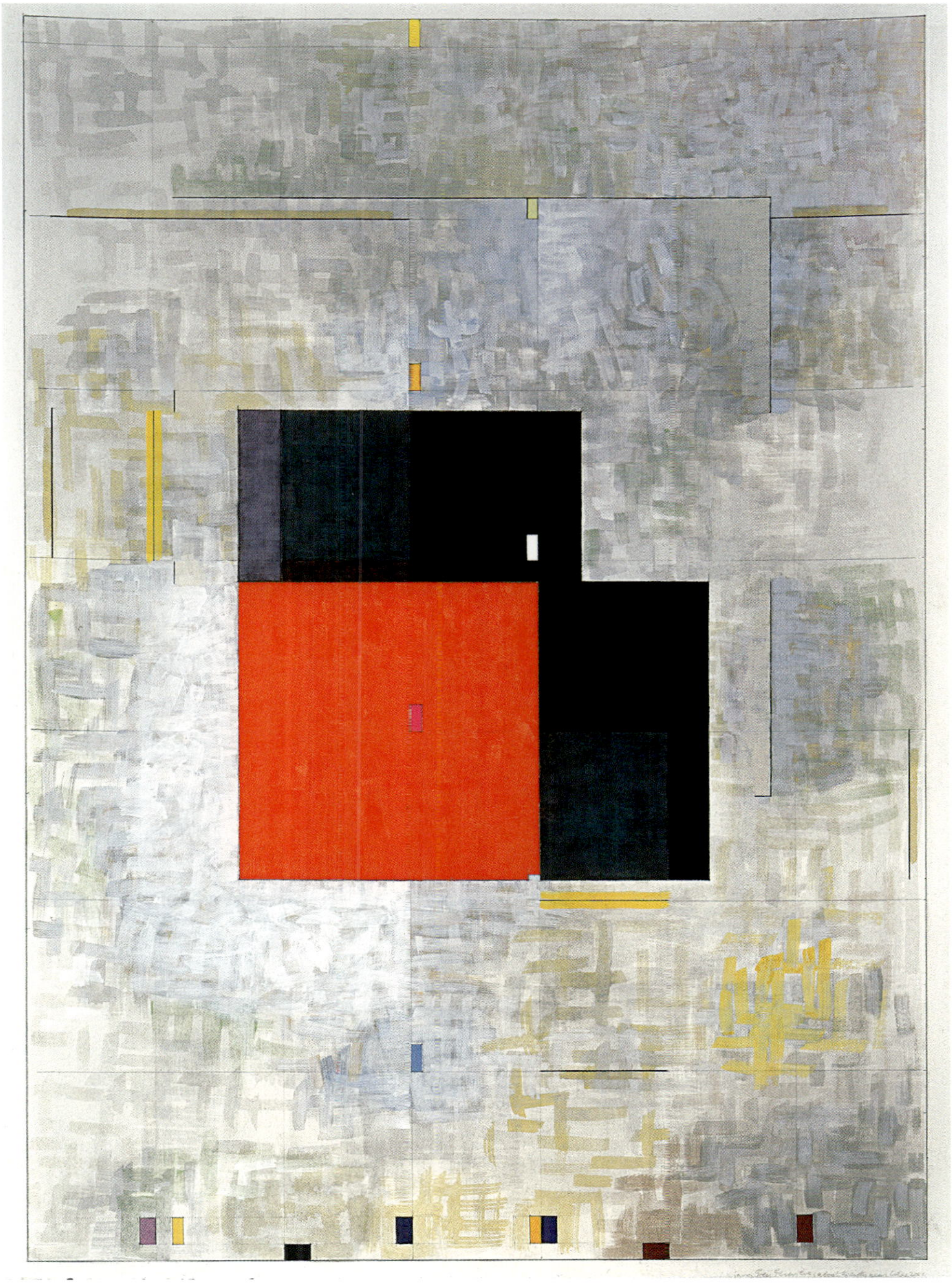

JEREMY GILBERT-ROLFE Born 1945, Tunbridge Wells, England. Resides Santa Monica, California
Grey Genevieve, about 20 Years Later, 2001 Gouache on paper 30 1/2 x 23 in. (77.5 x 58.4 cm) Collection of the artist

I didn't make this work in response to the theme but submitted it because I thought it might relate to it in as much as it seems to me that seeing God would have to be a complex rather than simple experience, ranging from the somber to the opposite, and consisting of more than one kind—hypothetically, all kinds—of movement. I also think that doubting simplicity is especially germane today, a period of rampant fundamentalism in both art and religion. Religious fundamentalists seem to be exclusively concerned with telling people what they can't do, with the effect and purpose of narrowly circumscribing and predetermining the bits about joy and ecstasy, access to which in Christianity appears to be complicated—in a way that has always seemed to me to risk disingenuousness—by the notion that one has free will but if one wills the wrong thing one goes to hell. In exactly the same way most contemporary art criticism is rigidly fundamentalist in its simple faith that Marcel Duchamp's relation to art and art history is like that which Christians attribute to Christ's relation to the Old Testament, and ignores—casts out—anything that chooses not to draw that conclusion. I didn't make *Grey Genevieve, About 20 Years Later* for them; I made it for anyone who sees potential in Oscar Wilde's remark about being able to resist anything except temptation. I'm for complication that isn't simplicity made elaborate, otherwise I don't think one is likely to be really seeing complexity...

GERHARD RICHTER Born 1932, Dresden, Germany. Resides Cologne, Germany
Gray (Grau), 1973 Oil on canvas 18 x 18 in. (46 x 46 cm) Collection of the artist

A monochrome gray painting, oil on canvas, in any common size, is simply the only possible representation/image of God. That is obviously very simple, too simple; of course when I made this gray painting I neither intended to express a conception of God nor would I be able to make such a painting.

ARTISTS SEE GOD AS LIGHT

The symbolism of light plays a powerful role in mythology, art, and literature. Metaphorically, light is power, vision, knowledge, glory. Light is the element of god. Light is divine. Christians say, God is light. They mean that god is not merely *like* light, god is light itself, the source of all life. In the Shinto religion the supreme being is Amaterasu, the sun goddess. Like the Christian god, Amaterasu both creates and is greater than the sun. She is what gives the sun its energy. In Shinto mythology, when an angry Amaterasu hid in a cave, the world was plunged into darkness and death. Without her nothing survives. The rice does not grow.

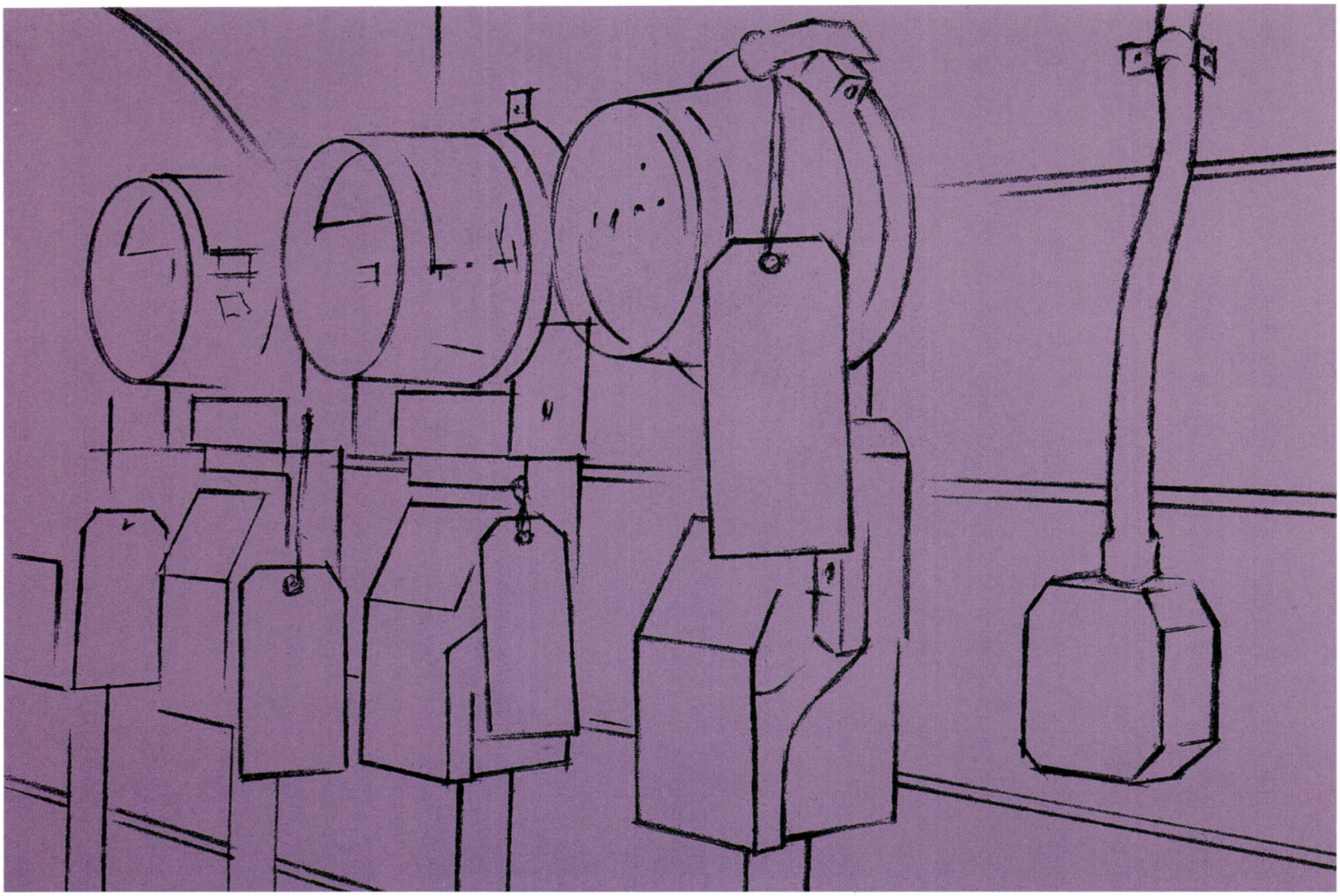

LARRY JOHNSON Born 1959, Long Beach, California. Resides Los Angeles, California
Untitled (Location II), 2001 Chromogenic print 25 1/2 x 38 in. (64.8 x 96.5 cm) Edition: 1/3 Courtesy the artist and Patrick Painter, Inc., Santa Monica

ED RUSCHA Born 1937, Omaha, Nebraska. Resides Venice, California
Miracle #67, 1975 Pastel on paper 38 1/2 x 28 3/4 in. (97.8 x 73 cm) Collection of the artist

I can't think of God without
thinking of shafts of light
and I can't see shafts of light
without thinking of God.

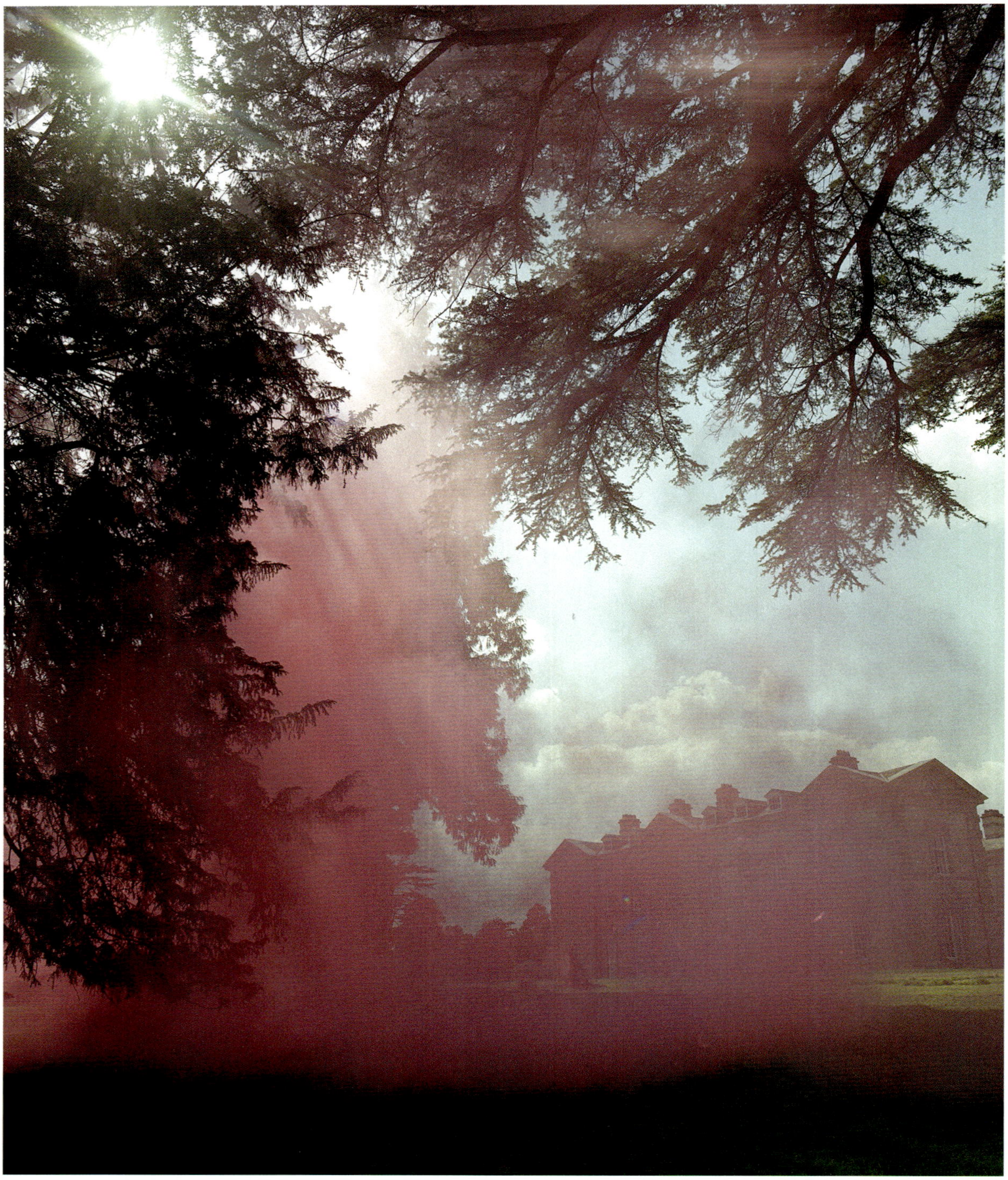

SIMON PATTERSON Born 1967, Leatherhead, England. Resides London, England
Landskip, 2000 Chromogenic print 23 1/4 x 19 1/4 in. (59 x 49 cm) Collection of the artist. Courtesy Lisson Gallery, London

The title *Landskip* derives from an 18th-century English rendering of 'Landscape.' The work in this show is one of a set of unique photographs of a series of events staged at Compton Verney House, Warwickshire, involving the detonation of smoke grenades at strategic points in the tranquil setting of the park in which it is set. *Landskip* focuses on two aspects of Compton Verney: one being the fact that grounds were laid out by the famous 18th-century English landscape gardener, Lancelot 'Capability' Brown (1716–83), and the other being that during the Second World War, it was a secret location used by the Army for, amongst other things, smoke-screen tests. In much the same way that the Vorticists designed the 'Dazzle Ships' camouflage in the First World War for the Navy, art students from the Slade School of Art in London were drafted into the Army to help develop camouflage warfare techniques there in the Second World War. With this history in mind, and inspired also by an episode from the Irish writer, Laurence Sterne's, great comic novel Tristram Shandy of 1760 in which the protagonist is assisted by his uncle Toby in the reenactment in his garden of the Anglo Dutch victory over the French at the siege of Namur in 1695, I wanted to create a daytime firework display in much the same way that artists were commissioned in the 17th and 18th centuries to design spectacles, including mock battles and firework displays, for their patrons.

Each grenade burned for 30 seconds or so allowing the smoke to hang for as long as weather *(continued on page 134)*

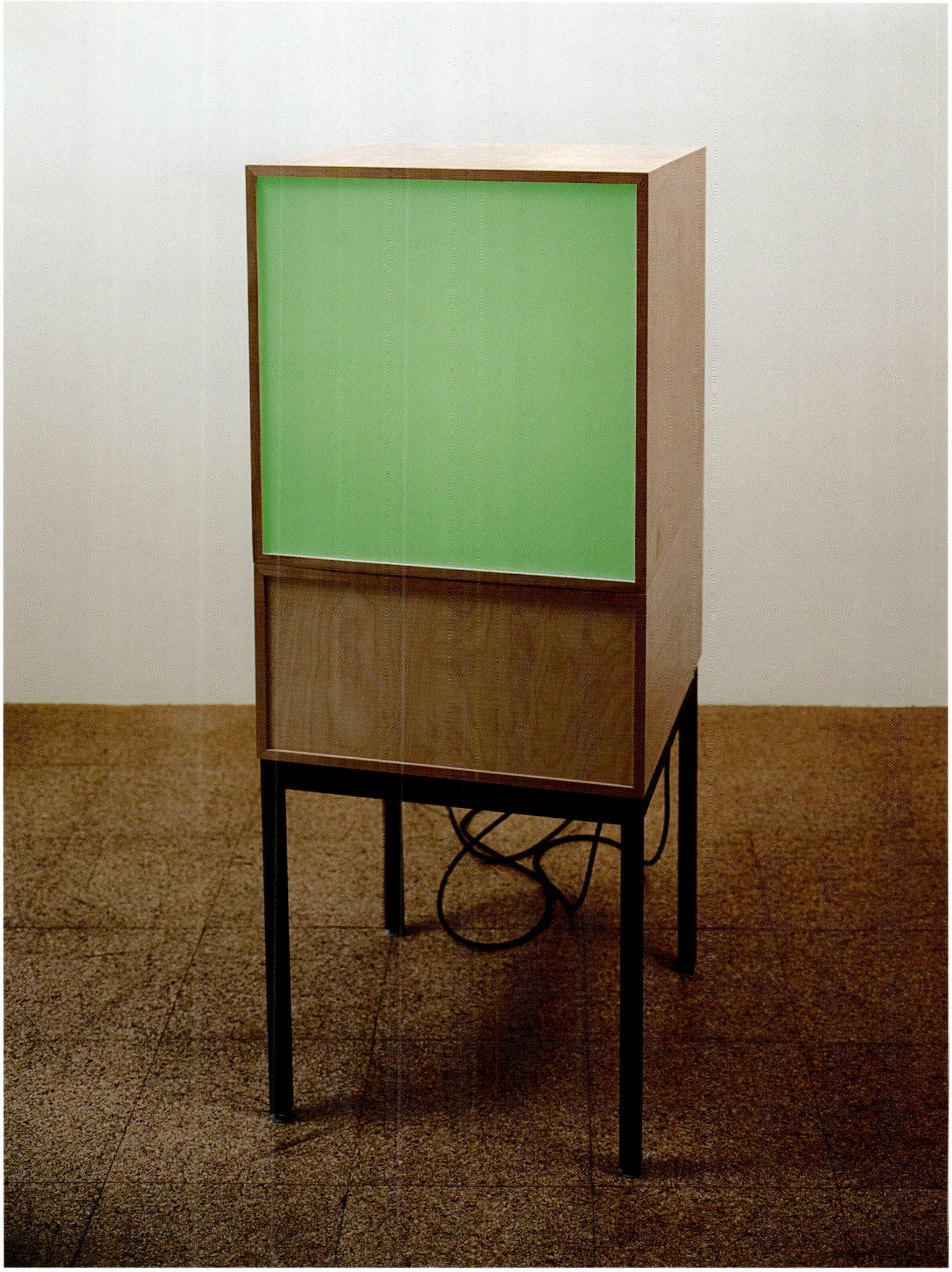

<u>ANGELA BULLOCH</u> Born 1966, Ontario, Canada. Resides London, England, and Berlin, Germany
Deliverance, 2002 Waxed birchwood, printed aluminum panel, white glass, diffusion foil, RGB lighting system, and DMX controller
49 1/4 x 19 1/2 x 19 1/2 in. (125 x 50 x 50 cm) Collection of the artist. Courtesy 1301PE, Los Angeles

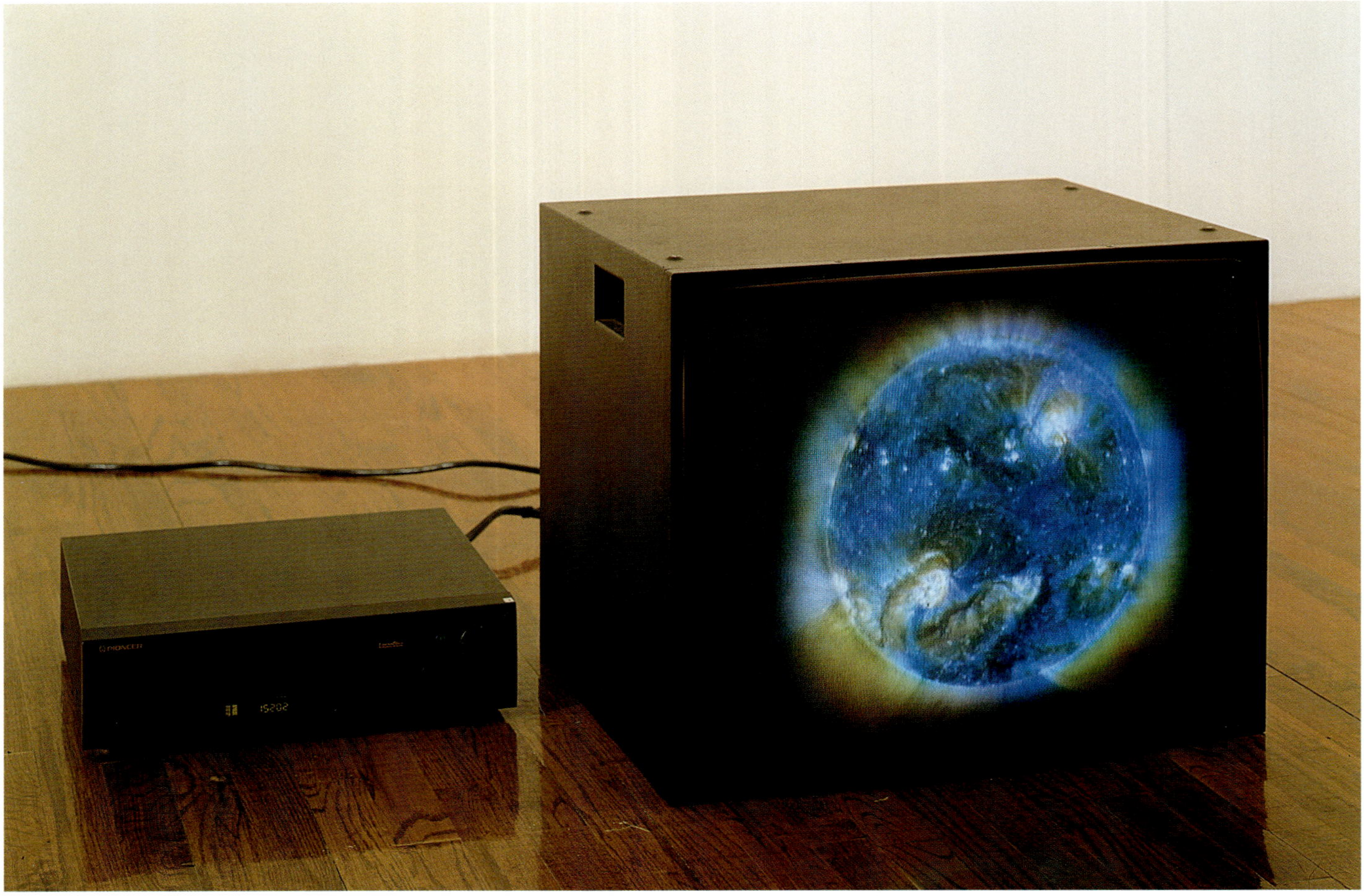

DIANA THATER Born 1962, San Francisco, California. Resides Los Angeles, California
Composite Sun, 2000 DVD Edition: 2/5 Collection of the artist. Courtesy 1301 PE, Los Angeles

In 1999–2000 I made a body of work using NASA images of the sun, which were digitally recorded through a solar telescope orbiting around the sun. For research purposes NASA divides the images into red, green, and blue, the component colors of light. I took their imagery, animated it, and further divided the colors, adding the secondary colors of cyan, magenta, and yellow and building various groupings of multiple spinning suns.

I have never acquired imagery before—I have always shot my work myself. But the image I wanted of the sun can only be filmed from space. I'd really like to go into space; I asked NASA if I could go but they ignored me. What I wanted was an image where the sun appears as a volume instead of a flat glare, which is how we see and experience it. I wanted to represent the sun as the lively burning liquid ball that it is—suspended in space.

Many cultures have thought of the sun as a god since it makes all life possible. This seems reasonable to me.

ARTISTS SEE GOD AS LOVE

When [a man] puts a thing on a pedestal and calls it beautiful, he demands the same delight from others. He judges not merely for himself, but for all men.
—Immanuel Kant, *The Critique of Judgment*, 1790

In this category we have grouped works that in some way raise ideas about the relationship of god to pleasure and love. A belief in god is often understood as cognitively, morally, or politically beneficial; it is less frequently associated with satisfying a desire for pleasure. To persuade and attract the multitudes, though, belief in god must be made desirable. Artists make an agreeable image of god by associating god with beauty. In that sense they do not represent received notions of god—they make god's image.

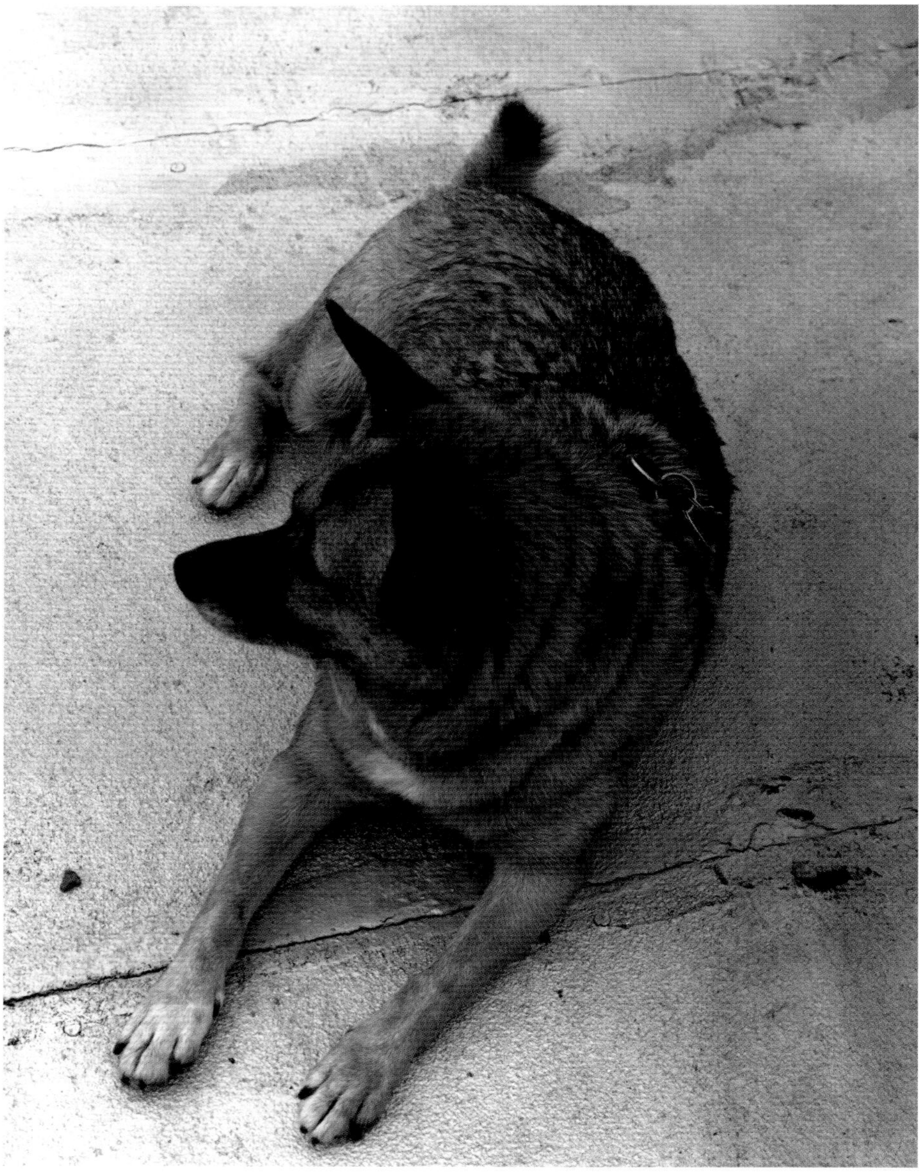

JAMES WELLING Born 1951, Hartford, Connecticut. Resides Los Angeles, California
Zola, 1998 Gelatin silver print 9 1/2 x 7 1/2 in. (24.1 x 19.1 cm) Collection of the artist. Courtesy Regen Projects, Los Angeles

Zola tumbled into my life on January 6, 1990, a tiny abandoned puppy. For almost twelve years she was my shadow and shepherd, guiding me through the 1990s, moving to the West Coast, traveling back and forth with me between L.A. and New York. I took this picture of her on a hot Manhattan evening in August 1998.

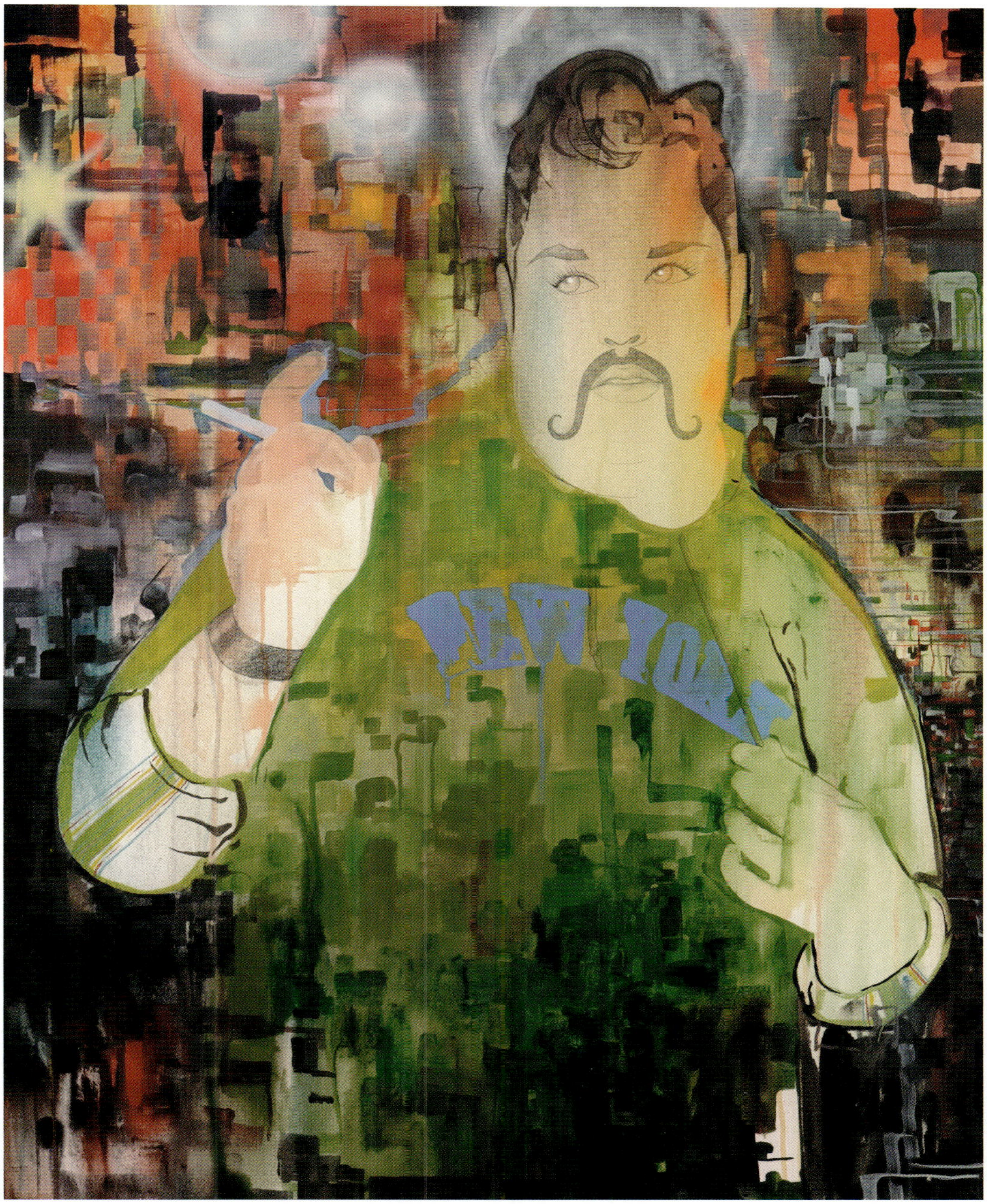

JAMES GOBEL Born 1972, Portland, Oregon. Resides Los Angeles, California
All around You and inside You, 2003 Acrylic and graphite on canvas 43 1/4 x 35 3/4 in. (109.9 x 90.8 cm) Collection of Kenneth L. Freed. Courtesy Kravets/Wehby Gallery, New York

I have never considered myself a successful religious or spiritual person, just Catholic. I have always admired those who have pursued all things divine, but have found my own pursuit, although genuine, to be a bit off the mark. I want to believe in God so I do my best and just believe. I make him out to be a friendly creator, wise yet tight-lipped. Existing depictions of God seem to work for me—a cascading white beard, burly chest, long (frequently pointing) fingers, a seemingly malevolent expression with unmistakably compassionate eyes—but not sitting on a cloud, instead quickly zooming throughout outer space. Catholicism has given me not necessarily a practice, belief, or faith in God but rather a setting and vocabulary of images and scenarios for God to exist in. I hope He likes my paintings, the subjects are often looking in His direction.

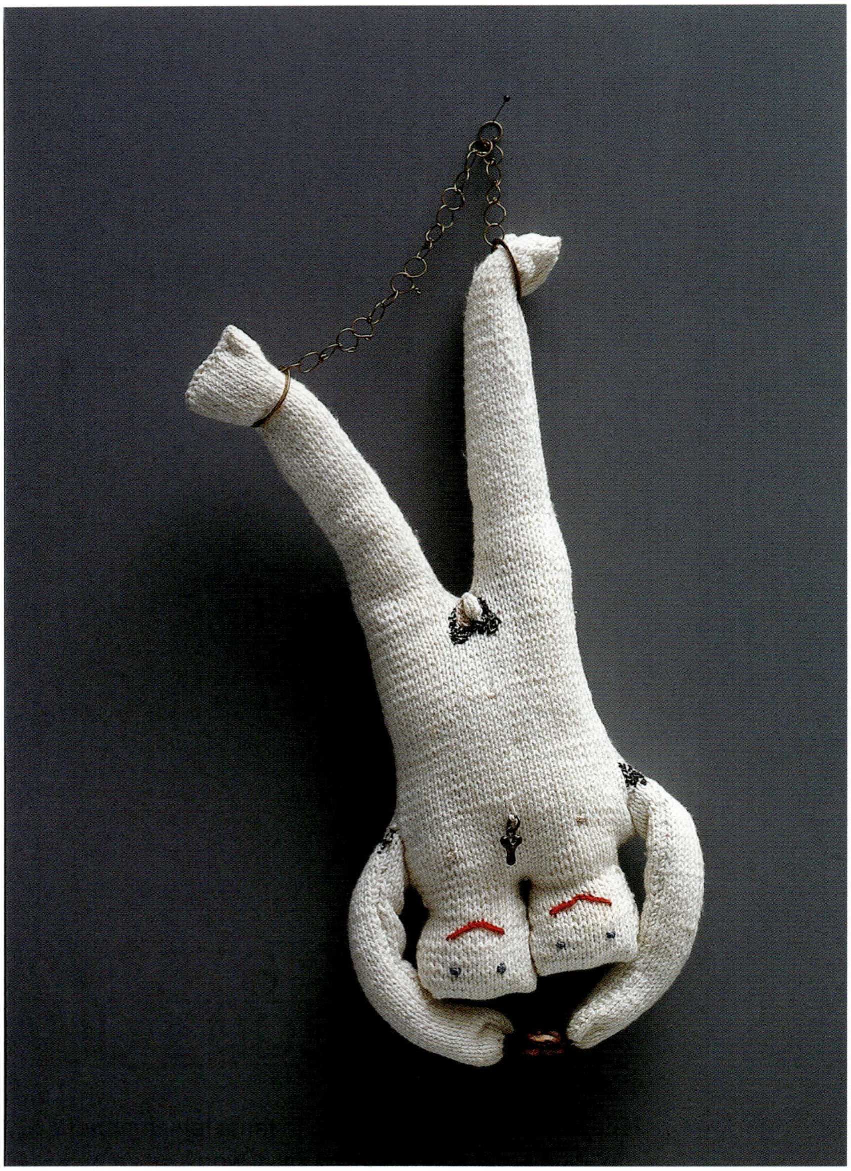

NICOLETTE POT Born 1959, Groningen, The Netherlands. Resides Rotterdam, The Netherlands
Doubleplusgood, 2001/2003 Cotton, wool, bronze, brass, and silver 59 x 18 x 9 in. (150 x 45 x 23 cm) Collection of the artist

Every time I enter a church I can make a wish.
I have a handbag full of them.
A Catholic girl—praised by Zappa.
Not a papist, not even a practitioner.
But wishing and hoping and thinking and praying.
Planning and dreaming.
When it comes to beauty I'm a believer.
I sin and fancy but never confess.
Recently we met, on top of the bell tower in Venice.
I asked about the secret of unity
but the bell tolls drenched me
and the answer fled away.

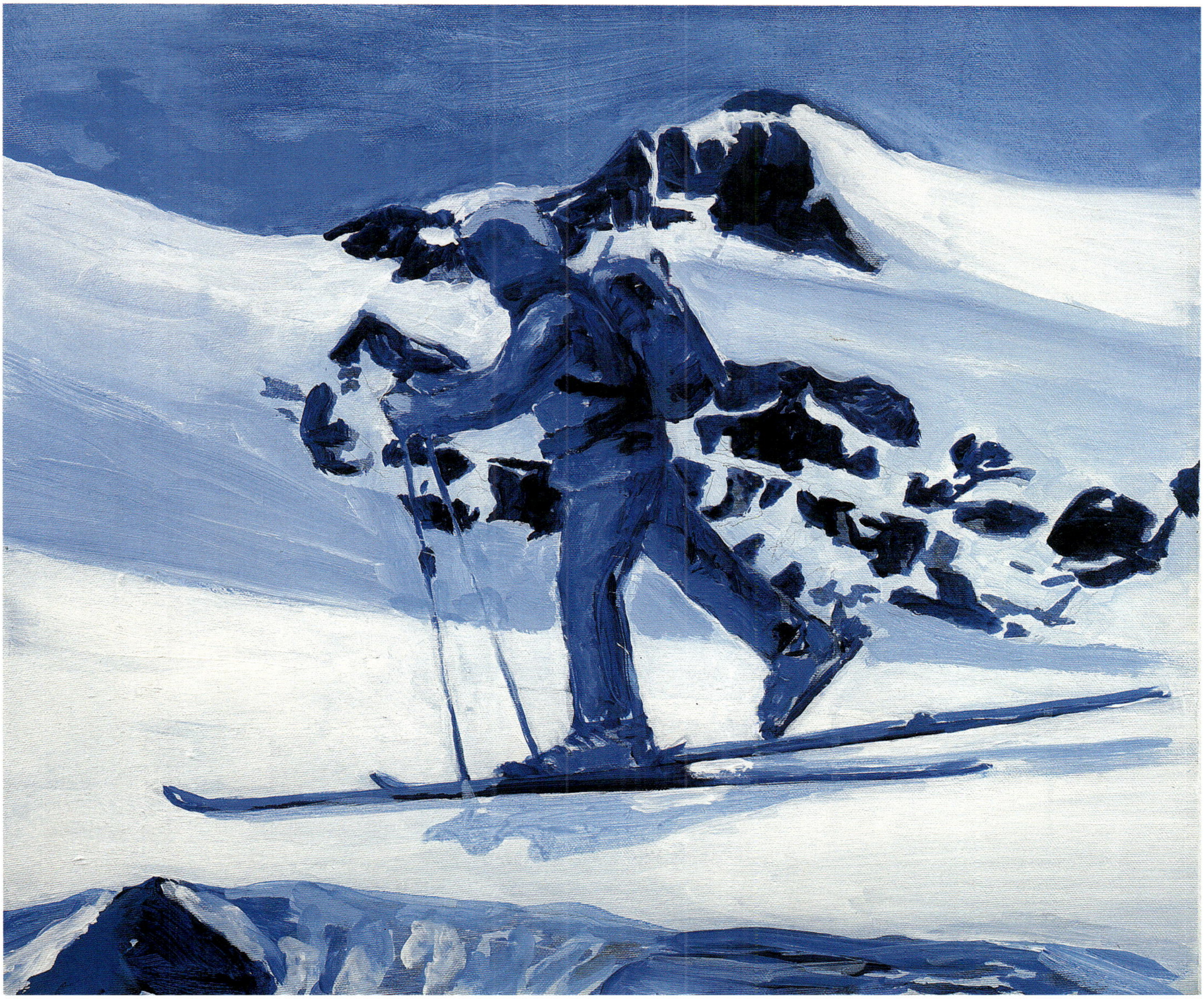

YUTAKA SONE Born 1965, Shizuoka, Japan. Resides Tokyo, Japan
It Is a Fine Day Today, 2003 Acrylic on canvas 20 x 24 in. (50.8 x 61 cm) Collection of Van Valen. Courtesy David Zwirner, New York

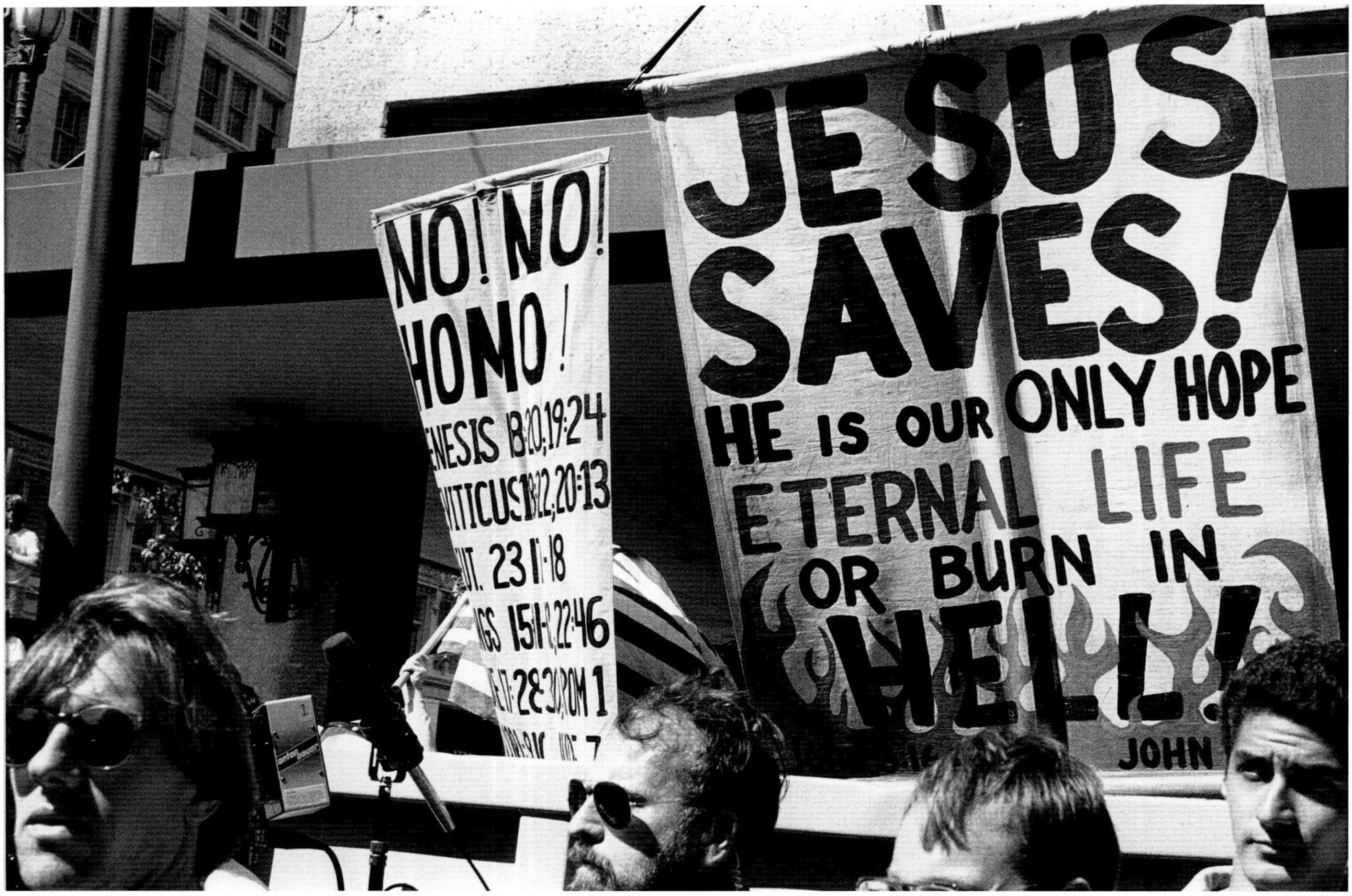

CATHERINE OPIE Born 1961, Sandusky, Ohio. Resides Los Angeles, California
They See God, I See Hate, 1984 Gelatin silver print 11 3/4 x 17 1/2 in. (29.9 x 44.5 cm) Collection of the artist. Courtesy Regen Projects, Los Angeles

In high school I had a crush on this beautiful woman named Cere, I would go to church with her and listen to her love of god and think, But I just love you. Years passed and I became a queer activist, coming out in San Francisco at the beginning of the AIDS epidemic. I saw people who loved god and hated us, and I continue to see people love god and hate us twenty years later. My faith is in myself and my family, making art, trying every day to talk about what is important, funny, and interesting.

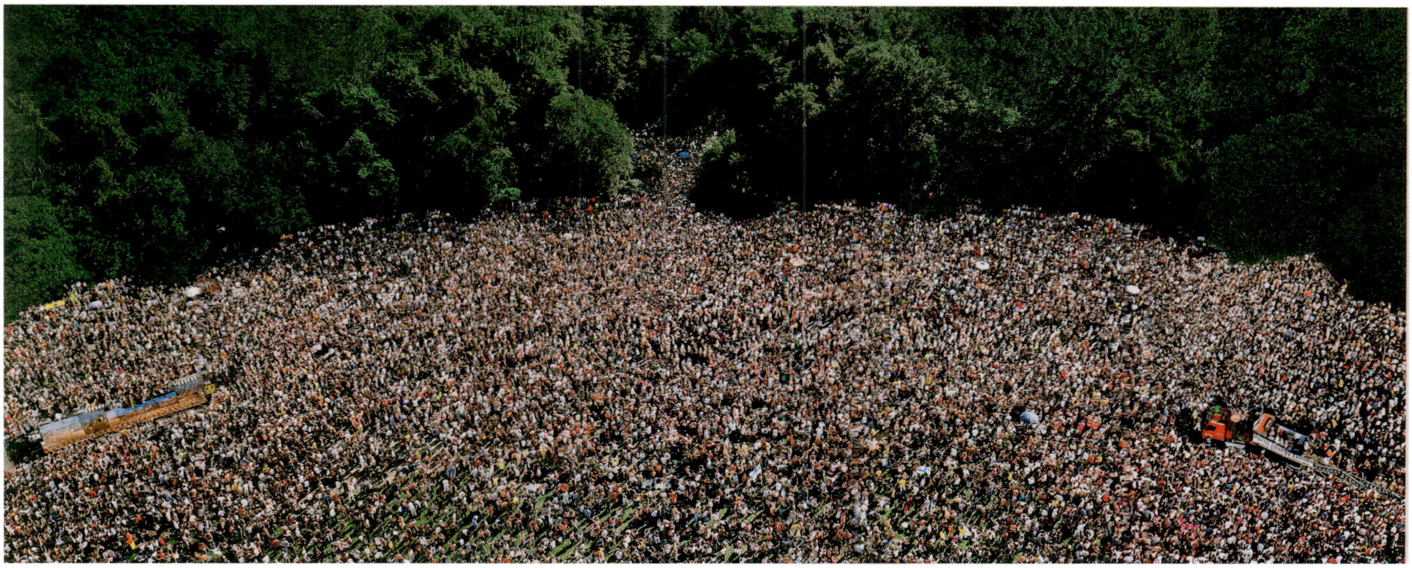

ANDREAS GURSKY Born 1955, Leipzig, Germany. Resides Düsseldorf, Germany
Love Parade, 2001 Chromogenic print mounted on Plexiglas in artist's frame Framed: 32 1/2 x 60 in. (83 x 152 cm)
Collection of the artist. Courtesy Matthew Marks Gallery, New York

ARTISTS SEE GOD AS MIRACLE WORKER

A courtier from Pope Benedict IX told Giotto that the Pope wanted to make use of his services and asked him for a drawing which he could send to his holiness. At this Giotto took a sheet of paper and a brush dipped in red, closed his arm to his side, and with a twist of his hand drew such a perfect circle that it was a marvel to see. Then, with a smile, he said to the courtier: "There's your drawing."

As if he were being ridiculed, the courtier replied: "Is this the only drawing I'm to have?" "It's more than enough," answered Giotto. "Send it along and you'll see whether it's understood or not."

—Giorgio Vasari, *The Lives of the Most Excellent Painters, Sculptors and Architects,* 1568

Depending on your point of view, seeing god as a miracle-worker reflects either desperation or the jolly belief that anything is possible. To need a miracle implies powerlessness; to believe in magic (without necessarily depending on it) implies limitlessness. Viewing god as a miracle-worker puts god in league with alchemy, astrology, Santa Claus, fortune-telling, and perhaps art.

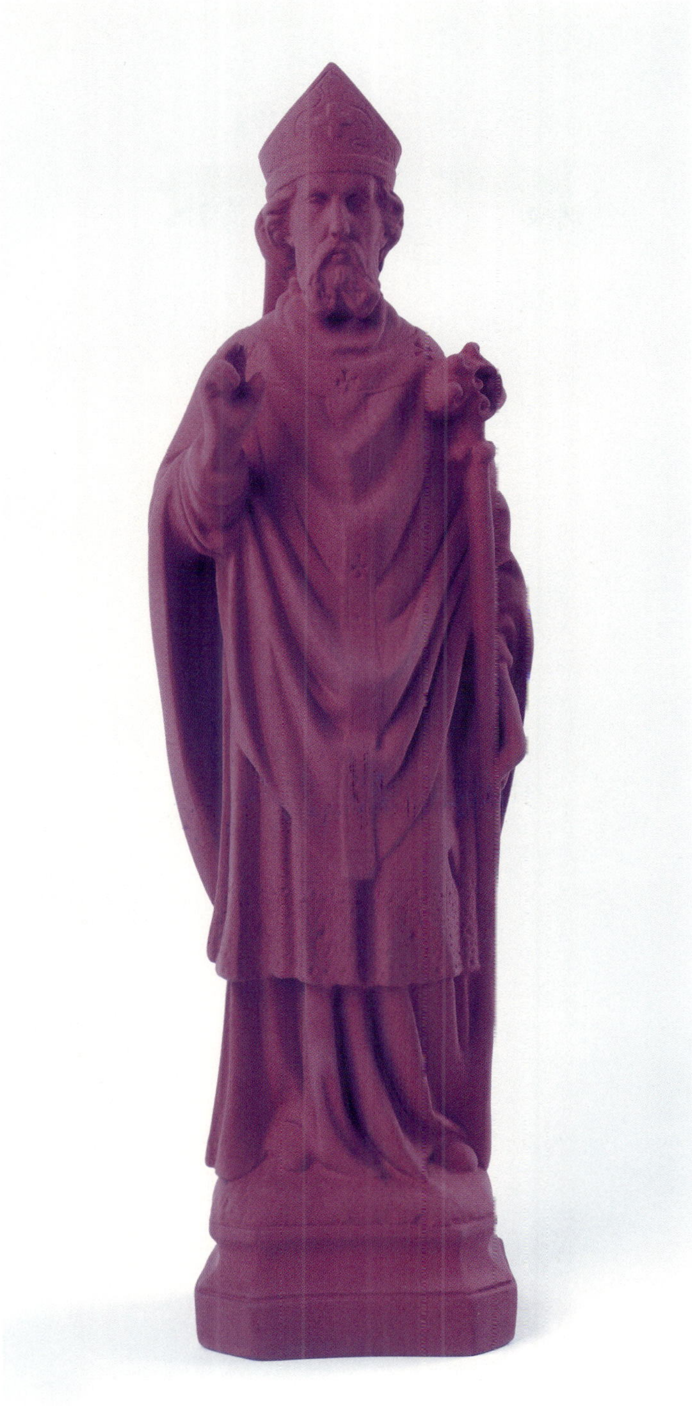

KATHARINA FRITSCH Born 1956, Essen, Germany. Resides Düsseldorf, Germany
St. Nicolas, 2002 Polyester and paint 12 x 3 1/2 x 2 1/2 in. (30.5 x 8.9 x 6.4 cm) Edition: 12/40 Collection of the artist. Courtesy Matthew Marks Gallery, New York

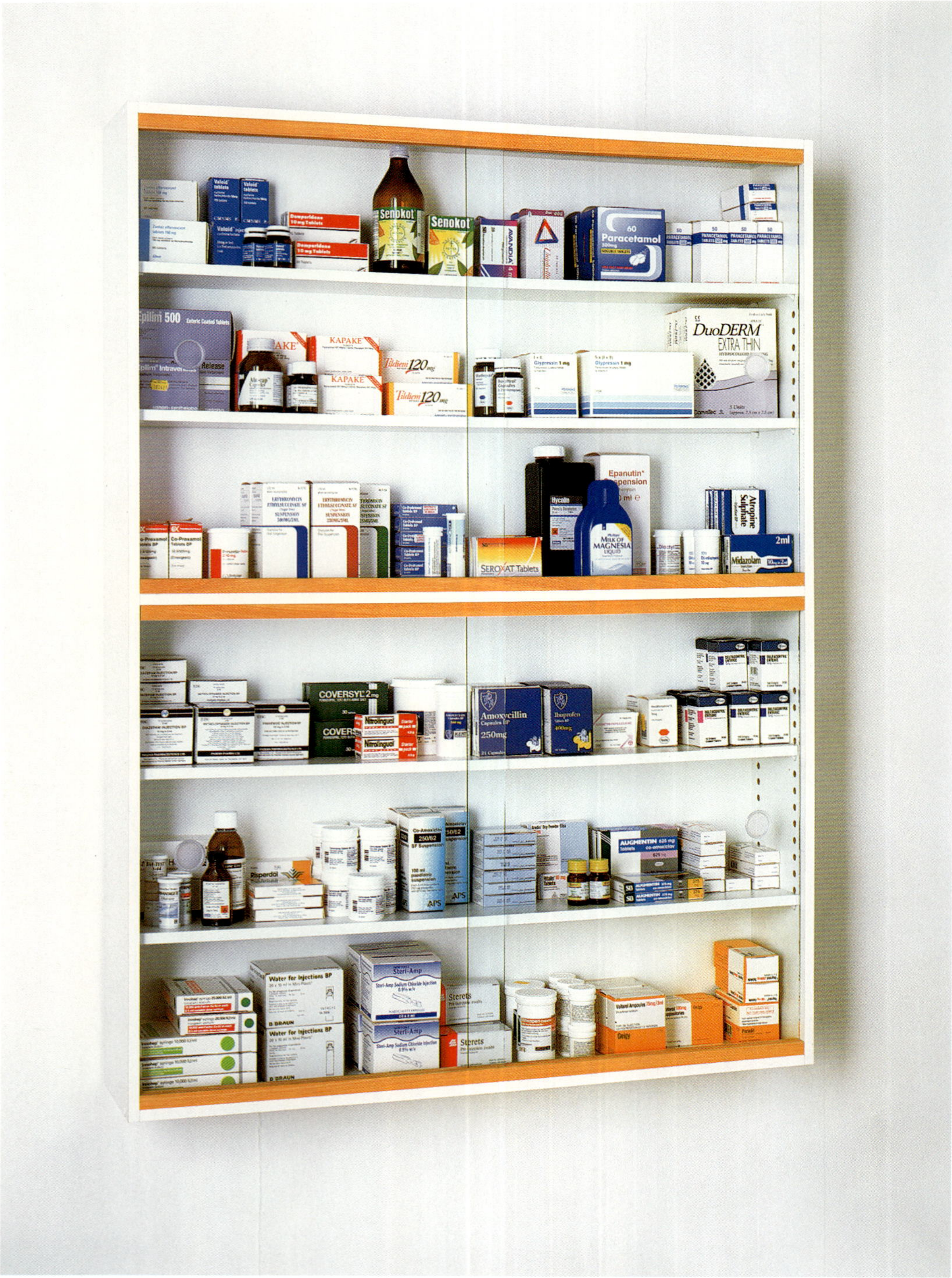

DAMIEN HIRST Born 1965, Bristol, England. Resides Devon, England
god, 1989 Fiberboard, beech, paint, glass, metal, and pharmaceutical packaging 54 x 40 x 9 in. (137.2 x 101.6 x 22.9 cm)
Collection of the artist. Courtesy Gagosian Gallery

Contract The Martyrdom of Saint Philip

From your vantage point
in the heavens
the Cancer looks controlled.
You can't smell the hectic stench.
Armies of the rotting dead and dying
trample the cold black hearts of men.
Your memory mostly gone.
Every scream as the columns break
falls silent on your cold dark soul.
Long ago you were beautiful,
using reason to frame truth.
A trillion dancing spandrels
of light surrounded you.
Slow motion, weightless.
Generous before the blight.
Soft rotted figs fell from the tree of life.
Your skull thoughtless in the dry river bed.
Exploring the infinite number
of ways to get to the same point.
It's why the houses fell down.
Why you ruled the world, once,
but not now. Let's drink
to you—to your health.
No, No, No,
We'll get these.
Put your shrapnel away.
You've done enough.
Apparently.

Originally published in Damien Hirst, *The Cancer Chronicles* (London: Other Criteria, 2003).

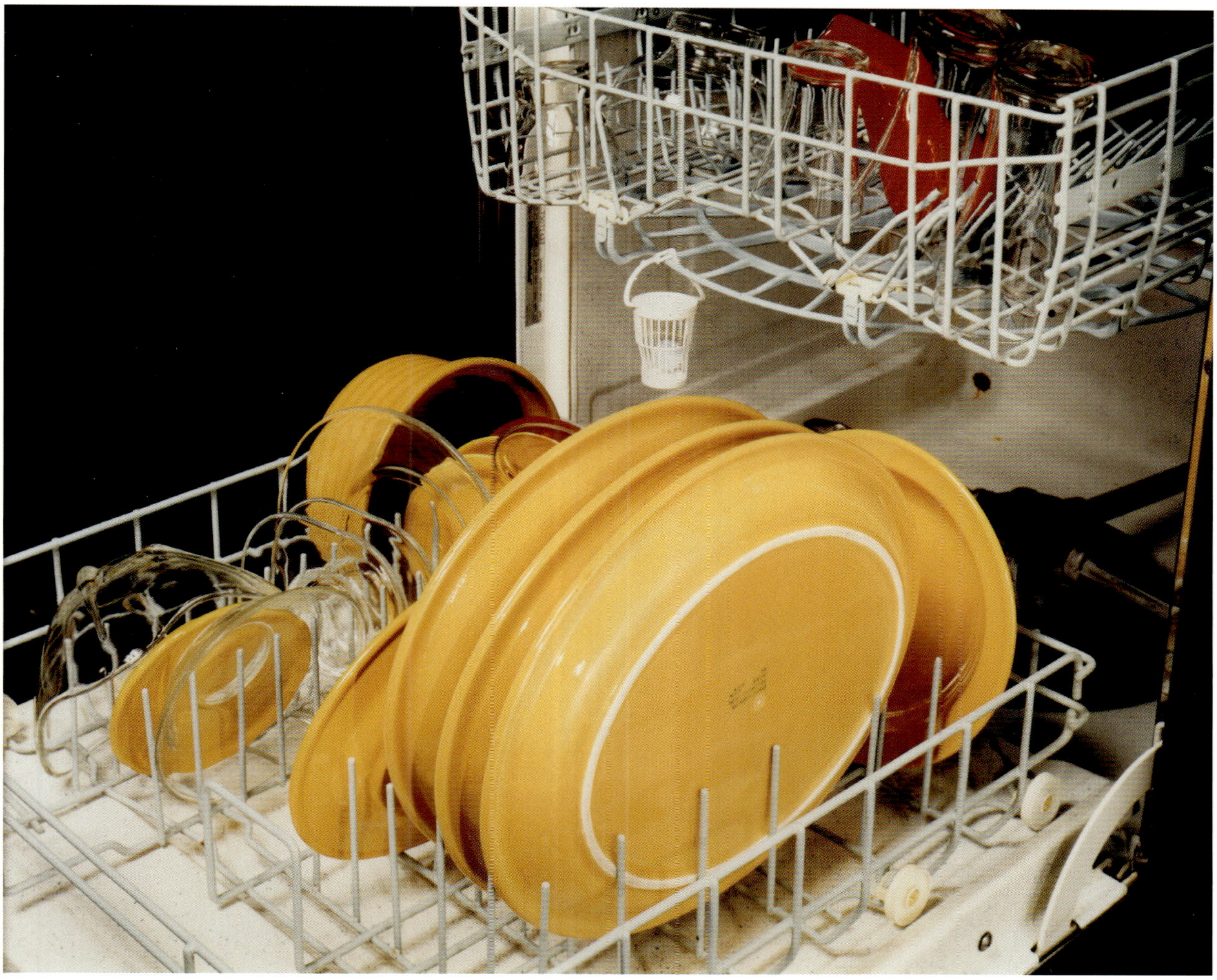

CHRISTOPHER WILLIAMS Born 1956, Los Angeles, California. Resides Los Angeles, California
Kodak Color, PORTRA 100T (PRT) Process C-41, Printed on Ultra 111 paper, Process RA-4, Surface F, glossy, March 10, 2000, 2000
Chromogenic print 11 x 14 in. (27.9 x 35.6 cm) The Museum of Contemporary Art, Los Angeles. Gift of Joel Wachs

Show me an angel and I'll
gladly paint you one.

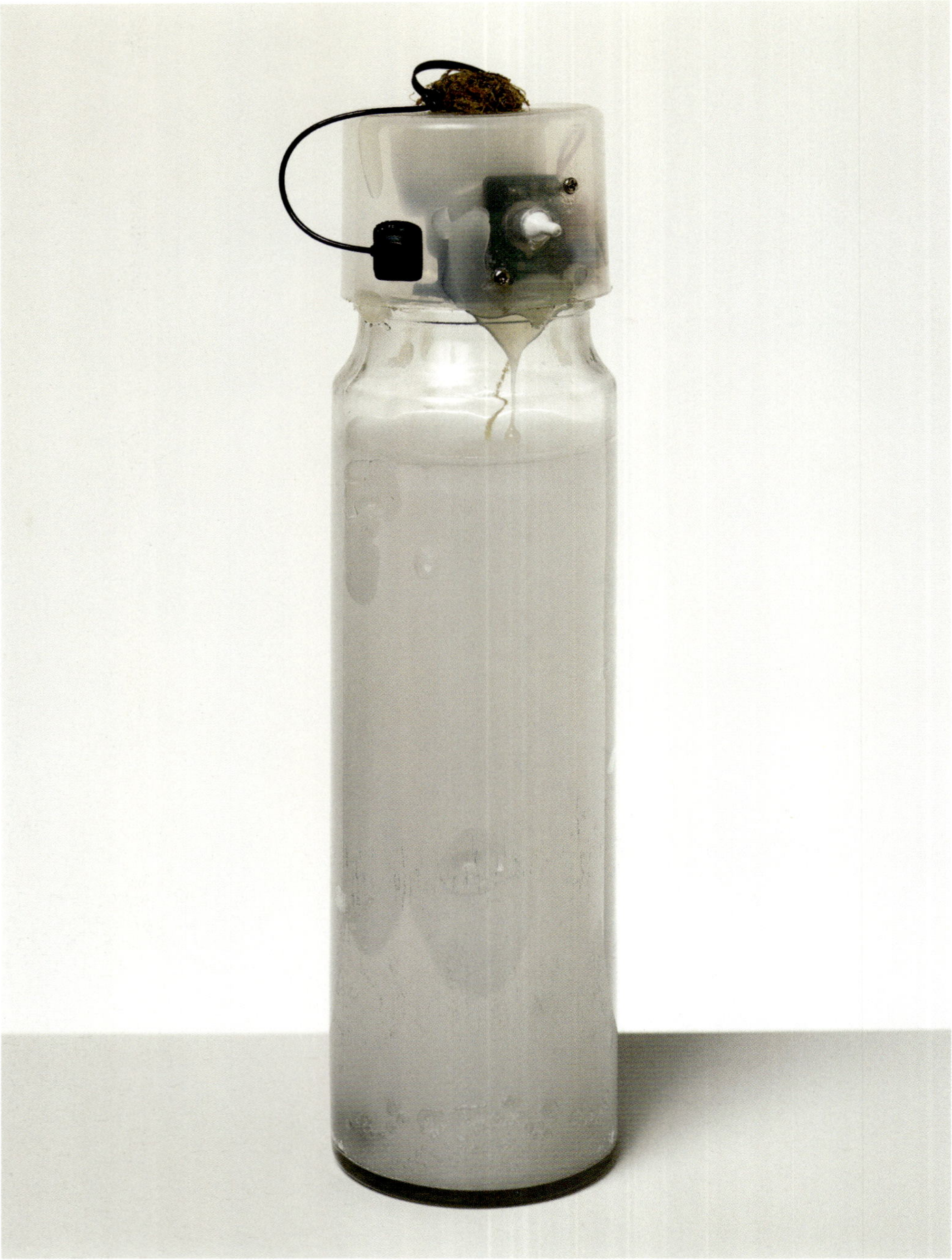

MARIO YBARRA, JR. Born 1973, Los Angeles, California. Resides Los Angeles, California
The Most High, 2003 Voice box, imitation marijuana (dried moss), plastic, glass, and wax 14 x 3 x 3 in. (35.6 x 7.6 x 7.6 cm)
Collection of the artist

When I was a child my mother was a drug-and-alcohol-prevention counselor for teenagers. One of her educational lecturing tools was a portable display cabinet containing simulated narcotics—a menagerie of real-looking drugs displayed almost as in someone's butterfly collection. On a small strip of white paper under each item were typewritten words like "Amphetamine," "Hallucinogen," and "Depressant." Several things in this box captured my imagination as an eight-year-old boy: little round blue and red pills, white powder spilling out of a brown glass vial to represent cocaine, and a bent burnt spoon juxtaposed with a syringe and cotton balls to depict a junkie's rig. The most interesting of these forbidden fruits was a leafy green plant in a small plastic bag that represented marijuana. It wasn't so much that the oregano in a baggie was interesting but that I had seen real marijuana on my weekend visits to my father's house. His marijuana was kept in an orange Tupperware box under his bed, and when he took it out he asked me to go to the other room and play Atari. I could smell the sweet aroma of the weed fill the small bachelor pad. I knew then that the stuff in my mom's cabinet was fake, simulation, but in my father's house it was real.

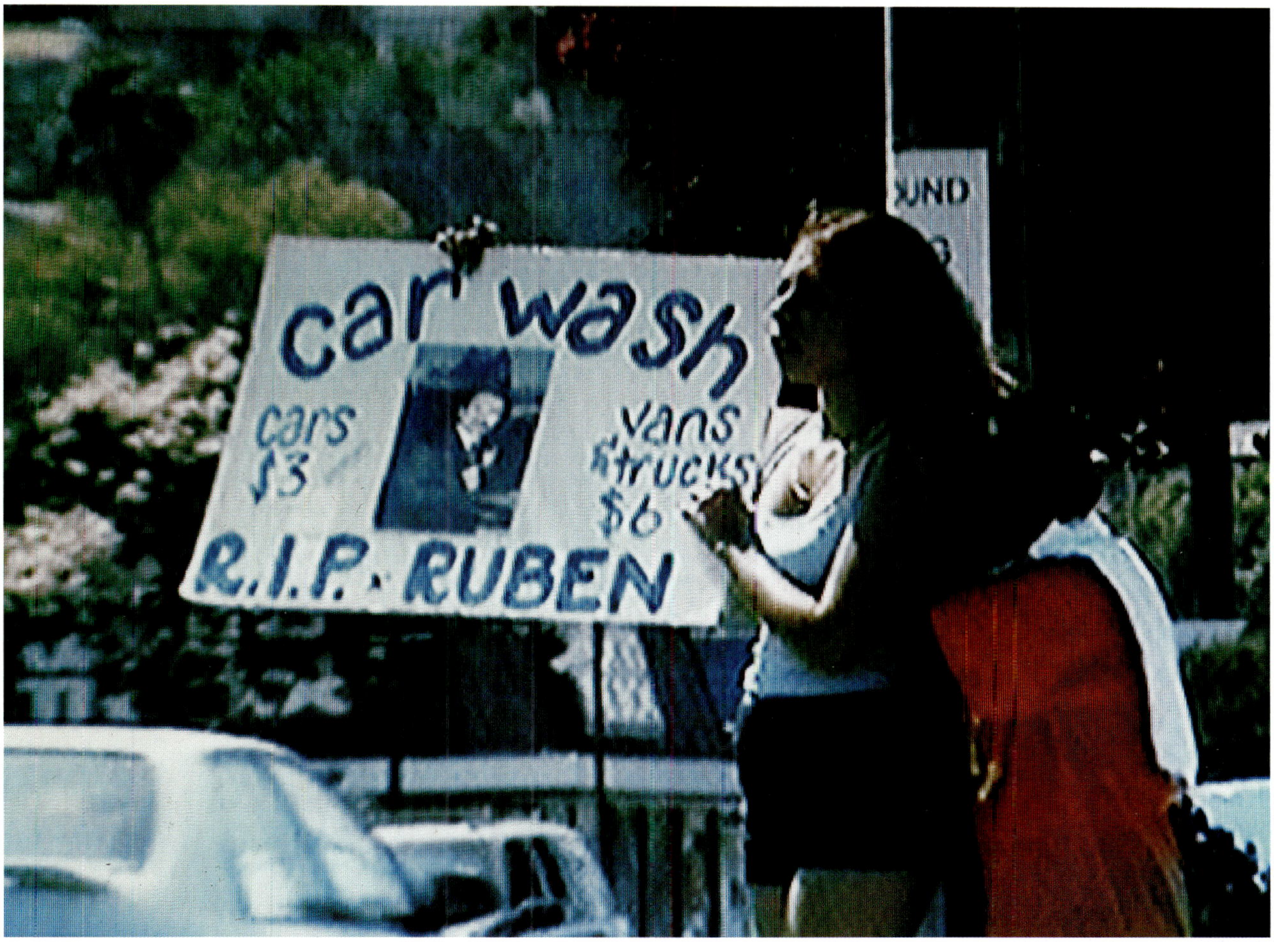

ANDREA BOWERS Born 1965, Wilmington, Ohio. Resides Los Angeles, California
Nothing Short of the Softest Word, 2002 (video still) DVD 1 minute 47 seconds Collection of the artist. Courtesy Sara Meltzer Gallery, New York, and Mary Goldman Gallery, Los Angeles

The footage for *Nothing Short of the Softest Word* was recorded over a year ago at an intersection in my neighborhood, where I saw a young woman with very long hair and very short shorts standing on a street corner. She was holding a sign advertising a car wash organized to raise money for the family of a shooting victim. The victim, a young man, had been killed on the same street corner as his brother, two years earlier. At the end of the video loop a young boy of about nine or ten comes to stand beside the young woman and wraps his arms around her. All of the sound comes from two songs: Janet Jackson's "Got 'Til It's Gone," which samples Joni Mitchell's "Big Yellow Taxi," and Yoko Ono's "Will You Touch Me." *Nothing Short of the Softest Word* highlights the multiple and conflicting roles of young urban women. Death and memorializing are referenced repeatedly in the video. While driving in my car on a summer afternoon, I was struck by the profound gesture of something as simple as a car wash and the compassion of one young woman.

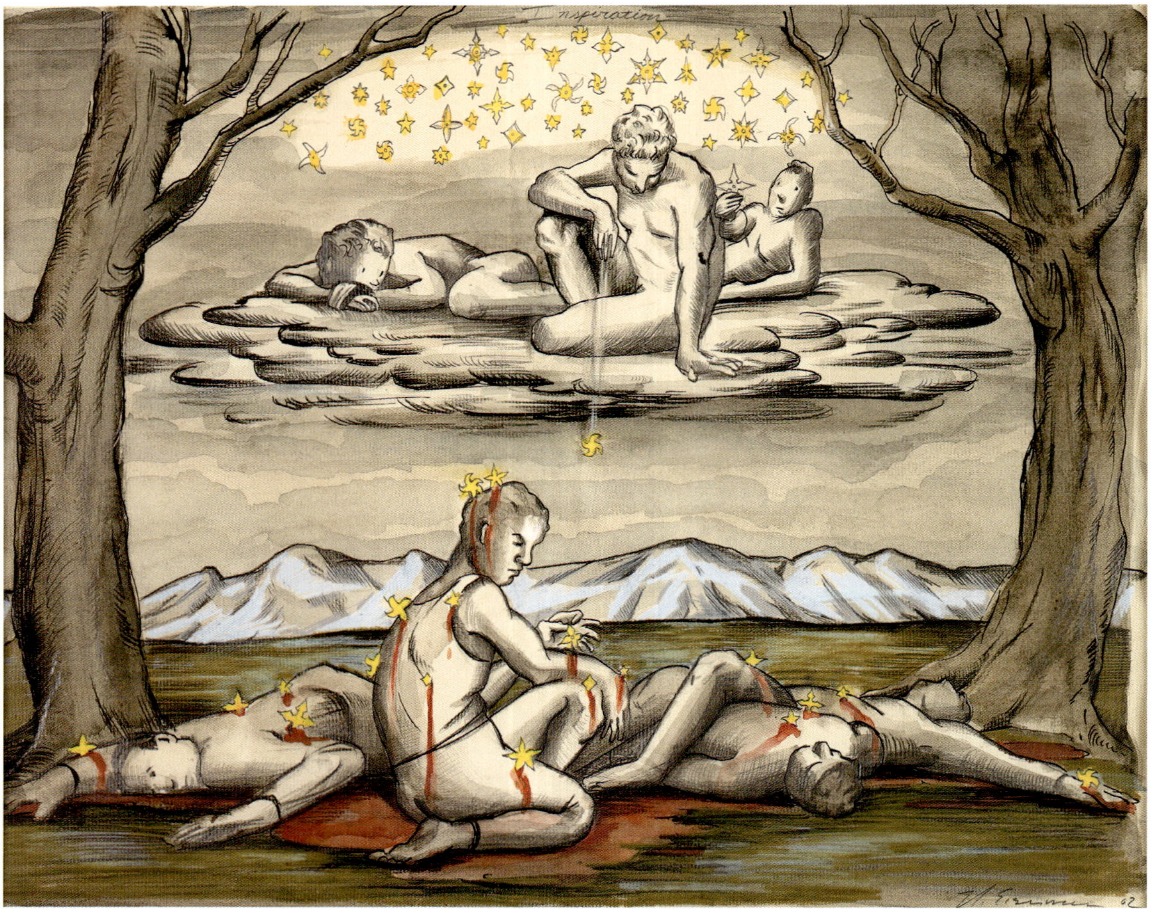

NICOLE EISENMAN Born 1963, Verdun, France. Resides New York City and Elizaville, New York
Inspiration, 2002 Watercolor and pencil on paper 13 1/8 x 17 in. (33 x 43.2 cm) Collection of Barry Sloane. Courtesy Shoshana Wayne Gallery, Santa Monica

God is part of my nature but God is also indefinable. I believe in God but I can't say what that means or whether the god I'm thinking of really exists outside my thinking of it.

But I don't lose sleep over it. I think God is present in the search for a meaning for what that word represents. I am Jewish but spiritually a pagan, with some Buddhist and Quaker thrown in. I also find myself relating to God the way the Greeks did, as a committee of intriguing authority figures floating around in space handing out gifts to us humans and alternatively wreaking havoc in our lives for no real reason.

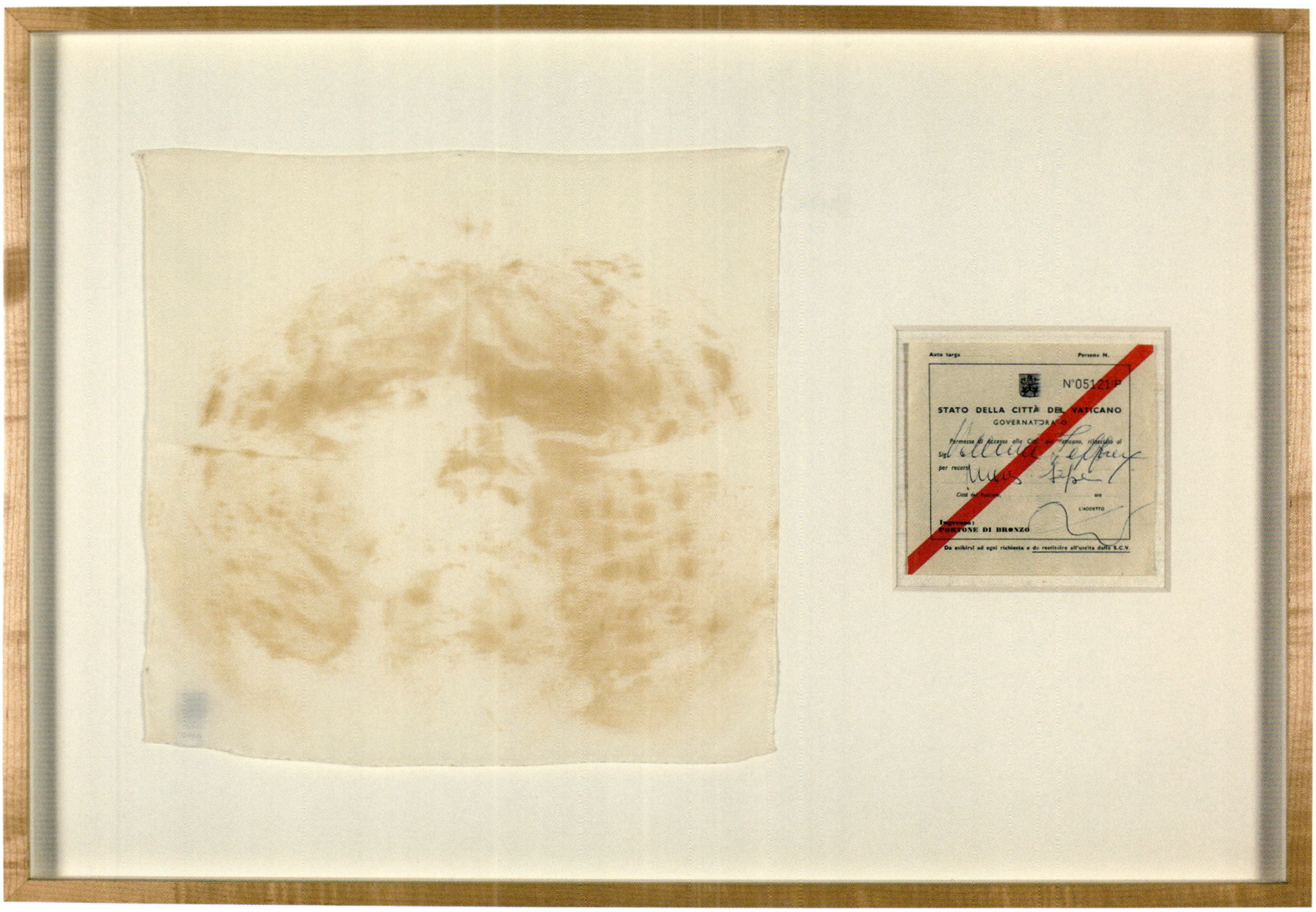

JEFFREY VALLANCE Born 1955, Torrance, California. Resides Las Vegas, Nevada, and Umeå, Sweden
Relics from Two Vatican Performances, 1992 Espresso coffee on Italian silk with paper document Framed: 18 1/4 x 26 1/2 in. (46.4 x 67.3 cm) The Museum of Contemporary Art, Los Angeles. Gift of the Lannan Foundation

On April 4, 1992, I had an appointment with Monsignor C. Sepe, Secretariat of State Assessor at the Pontifical Apostolic Palace in Vatican City. Several months before, I had sent a drawing I had made of the Veil of Veronica to his Holiness Pope John Paul II, and had received a reply from the Monsignor stating that the Holy Father had gratefully accepted the artwork. On my pilgrimage to the Vatican, my goal was to find out exactly where the Pope kept my drawing. In talking to Monsignor Sepe, I found out that the Holy Father has a private repository where he stores accepted gifts; the disposition of the objects is at the personal discretion of His Holiness, who can keep such items for himself or can give them as sacred gifts to any Catholic congregation in the world. On the same day as my appointment at the Vatican, I bought silk handkerchiefs and a double espresso. I stood with my purchases in Saint Peter's Square, at the base of the obelisk. In an attempt to approximate the process by which the original Veil of Veronica is said to have been created—a cloth given by Saint Veronica to Christ on the way to Golgotha, it was imprinted with His image—I splashed the espresso on my face and pressed the handkerchiefs to my skin to make artworks, each of which I call *Self-Portrait Sudarium*. After my terse performance, I slipped into the teeming crowds of Saint Peter's.

ARTISTS SEE GOD AS MOTHER

Travel the road of metaphor, of icon, to come back to that figure who, throughout a corrupt history, has moved the hearts of men and women, has triumphed over the hatred of woman and the fear of her, and abides shining, worthy of our love, compelling it.
—Sally Cuneen, *In Search of Mary: The Woman and the Symbol*, 1996

If god were a mother, god would look at you, god would talk to you, god would feed you.
God as mother should be a more popular concept.

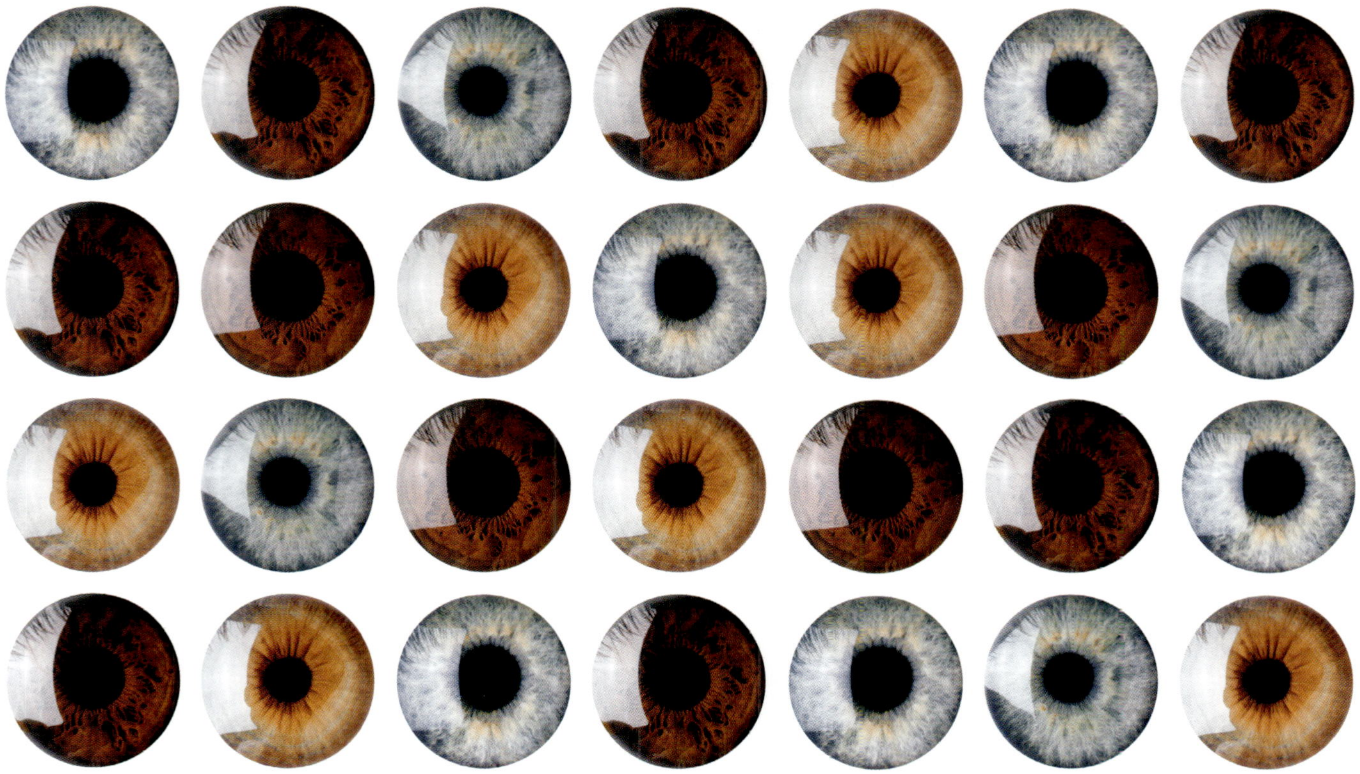

<u>NICHOLAS KERSULIS</u> Born 1964, East Saint Louis, Illinois. Resides Los Angeles, California
In Memory of My Mother, 2003 Chromogenic print 20 1/2 x 35 1/2 in. (52.1 x 90.2 cm) Collection of the artist

Eye color is an important marker of identity, used on drivers' licenses as well as by songwriters describing intimate relationships. Yet I am rarely able to remember it. Instead I remember the shapes of eyes, the way they fit into the forehead, the way they move when you glance away. The better I know someone, the less likely it is that I will *see* his or her eyes: looking past them in conversation so as not to lose my thoughts, or through them when we have a connection, I forget the details of the face, and when I first see it after a long time, I am surprised at how different it looks—it's as if we'd just met. This resembles the way I see art: images transform so readily into memories that I don't always remember them accurately. But the effect remains strong.

An image of a grid of eyes immediately flashed into my mind when I first heard about *100 Artists See God*. To make the image into an object I set up a photo shoot, asking the models to hold their eyes wide open, often with their fingers, for several split-second intervals in which the recording of this event could take place. The eye grid that I imagined and the actual artwork are very different, but the image remains constant. Similarly, I may know someone intimately but forget topical details: holding onto an emotional interpretation of *what I last saw*, I am left with a representation.

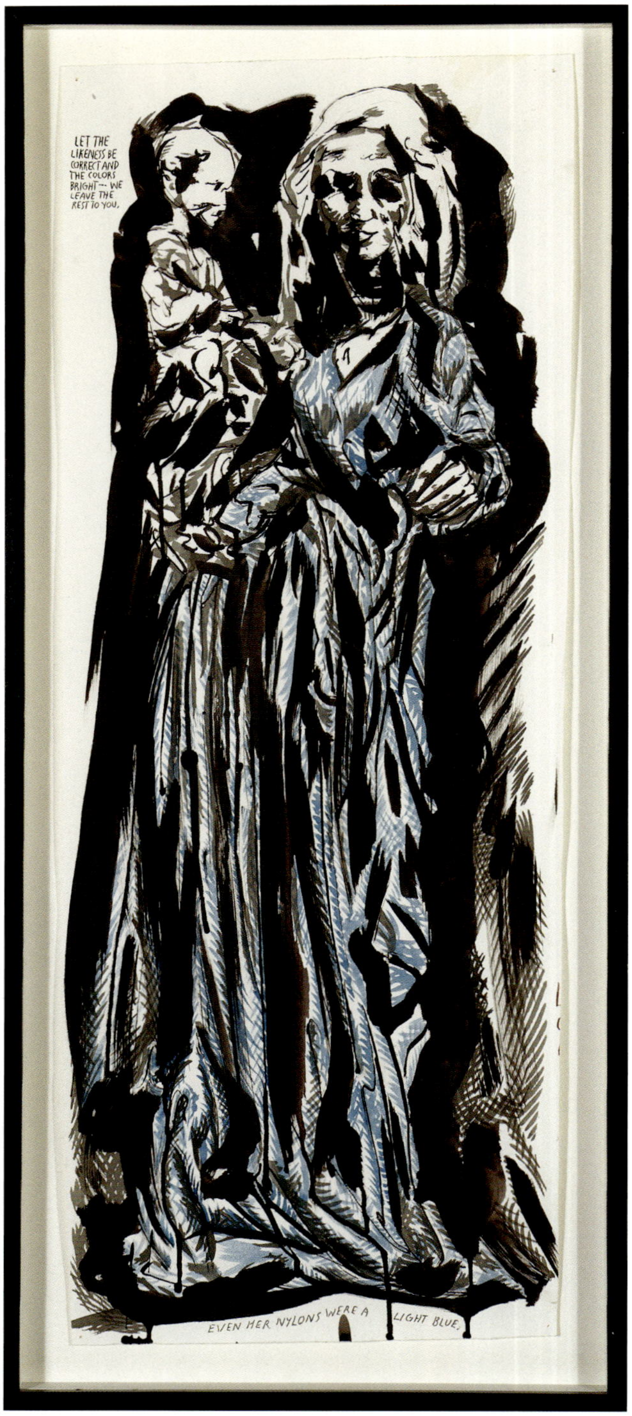

RAYMOND PETTIBON Born 1957, Tucson, Arizona. Resides Hermosa Beach, California
No Title (Let the Likeness), 2001 Pen and ink on paper 30 1/4 x 12 in. (76.8 x 30.5 cm) Collection of the artist. Courtesy Regen Projects, Los Angeles

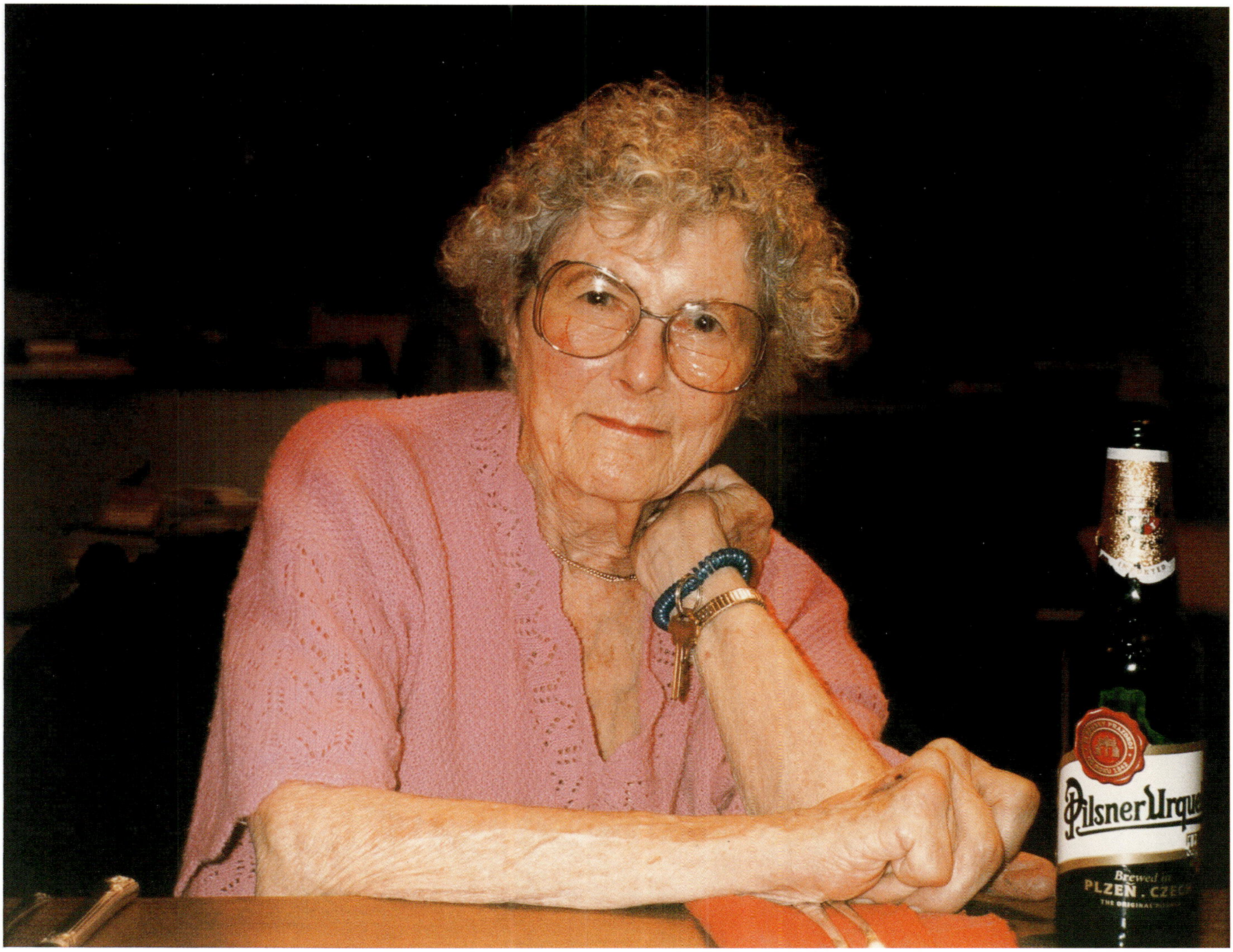

LIZ LARNER Born 1960, Sacramento, California. Resides Los Angeles, California
You don't have to understand me, you only have to love me, 2003 Chromogenic print 10 3/8 x 13 3/8 in. (26.4 x 34 cm)
Collection of the artist. Courtesy Regen Projects, Los Angeles

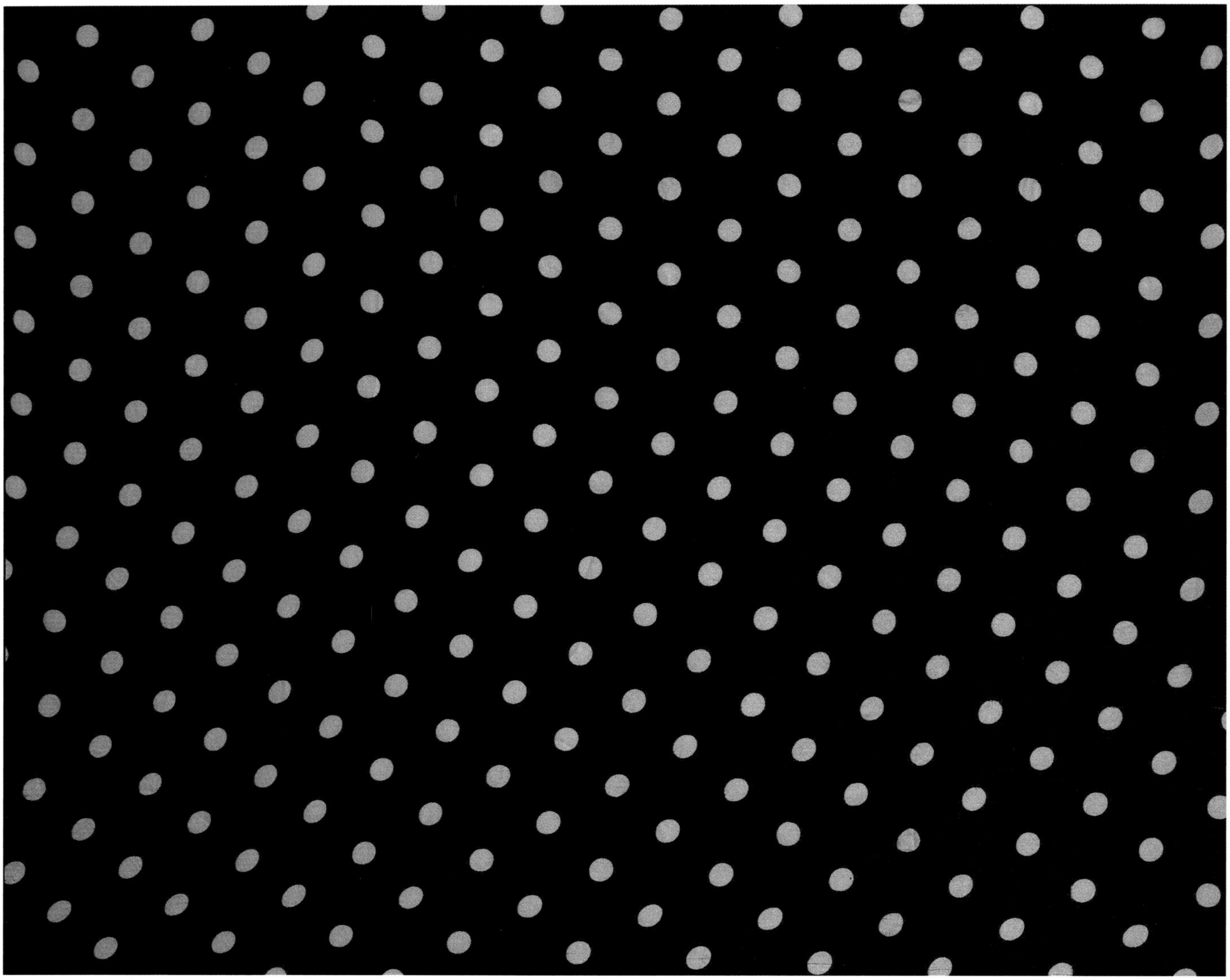

RENÉE PETROPOULOS Born Los Angeles, California. Resides Venice, California

Flatter Me Forever, 2002 (video still) DVD, 14 minutes 36 seconds, and two cushions Cushions: 6 x 36 x 36 in. (15.2 x 91.4 x 91.4 cm) each

Collection of the artist

ARTISTS SEE GOD TAKE MANY FORMS

The form god takes affects the potential god has to act. The Hindu god Ganesh, for example, is represented with as many as sixteen arms. Described as the remover of obstacles, he is invoked before a building project is begun. The arms come in very useful.

Gods take the form of earthly beings, large and small. The Navajo believe that persons who were spiders—Spider Man and Spider Woman, a quarrelsome married couple—created weaving when they brought hemp seed out of the ground to the surface of the earth. Their opposing views of how best to use the yarn led to the warp and woof of cloth. Iktomi, of Lakota mythology, also takes the form of a spider, but has different spider qualities: he is a trickster, a glutton, a lascivious character who lurks in the dark. The present-day comic book superhero Spiderman has spider agility, spider leaping power, spider strength, spider senses. His spider abilities let him crawl up tall buildings. They suit him to contemporary life.

In many traditions god takes the form of a human being. Rastafarians, for example, believe that god first took the form of Jesus of Nazareth, then of Ras Tafari, emperor of Ethiopia.

Catholics experience god's love through the veneration of the human figure of Mary. Although this view is inconsistent with official doctrine, Mary is often seen not only as an intermediary between the human and the divine but as divine herself. The understanding of god as a human female—a human mother—is common and powerful. When an artist creates an image of god, an artist creates god. The form describes and creates the potential.

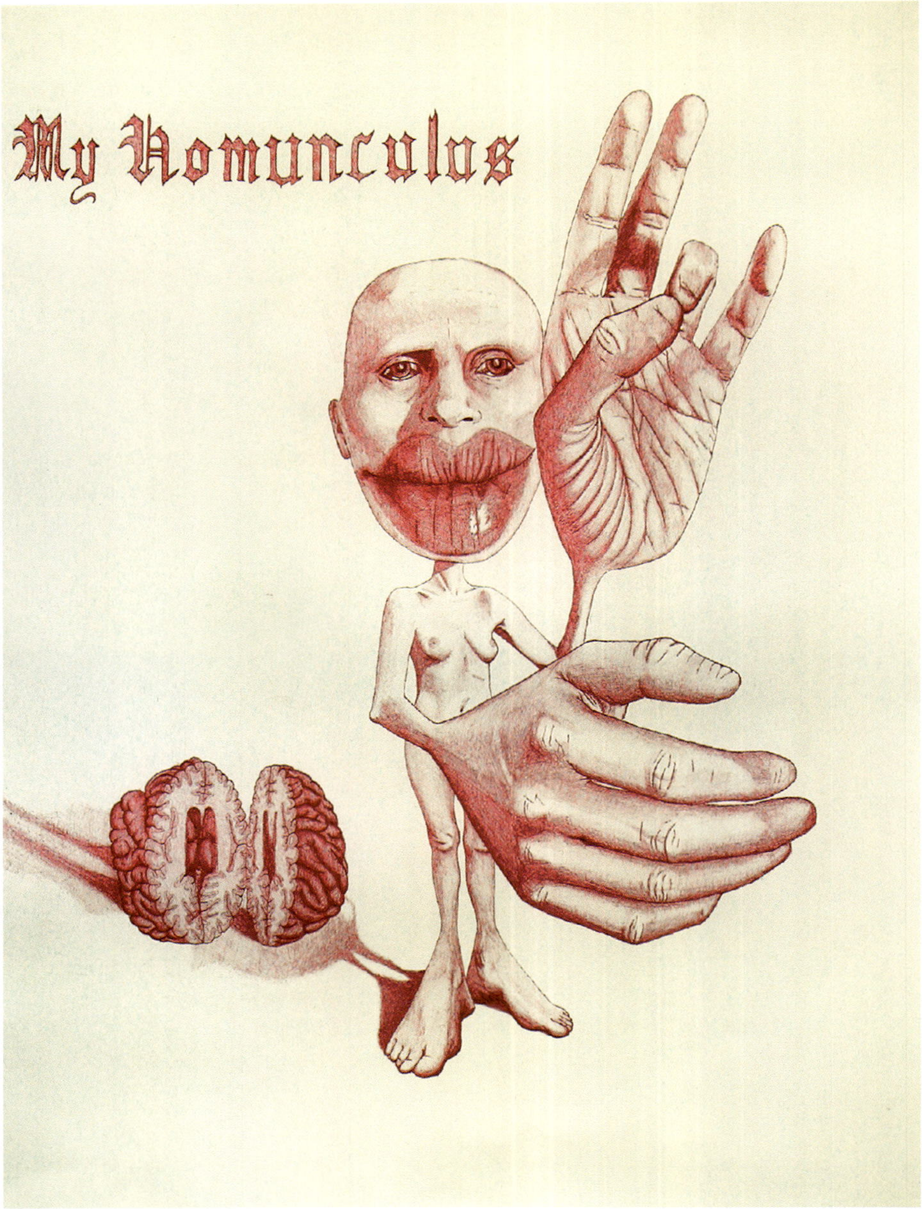

ERIN COSGROVE Born 1969, Saint Paul, Minnesota. Resides Los Angeles, California
My Homunculus, 2002 (detail) Ink on paper, two sheets Drawing: 30 x 22 in. (76.2 x 55.9 cm); letter: 11 x 8 1/2 in. (27.9 x 21.6 cm)
Collection of the artist

Gentle Viewer,

While I have perhaps failed in bringing to you an image of a traditionally imagined, ethereal God,[1] I hope you will accept this humble rendering of my homunculus. A homunculus is that diminutive being inside one's head who perceives the world and thinks, plans, and executes all of our actions. Picture, if you will, the *id creature* who mans the control room in the center of the brain, monitoring gauges, pulling levers, pushing buttons, and thereby commanding the human body in all matters mental and physical.

This rendition of my homunculus is a result of fastidious body-mapping. The distortion of its features is based on the proportional amount of cerebral cortex used to process touch receptors. This method of visualizing the homunculus may not be as effective as the alchemist version of inserting semen and blood of the creator into a horse womb and letting said amalgam incubate for forty days; I nevertheless must succumb to the scientific fashion of the time.

It would be impossibly bad manners to claim that my homunculus is the first mover. It is, however, the first mover in wholly personal terms. As the carrier of my human soul, it stands as reminder of my connection with the immutable cosmic forces and, God willing, executes God's will.

Sincerely,

Erin Cosgrove

1. Upon reflection, I am sure we all recognize that an achievement of this kind is impossible in nature and that any such attempt on my behalf is foredoomed to failure.

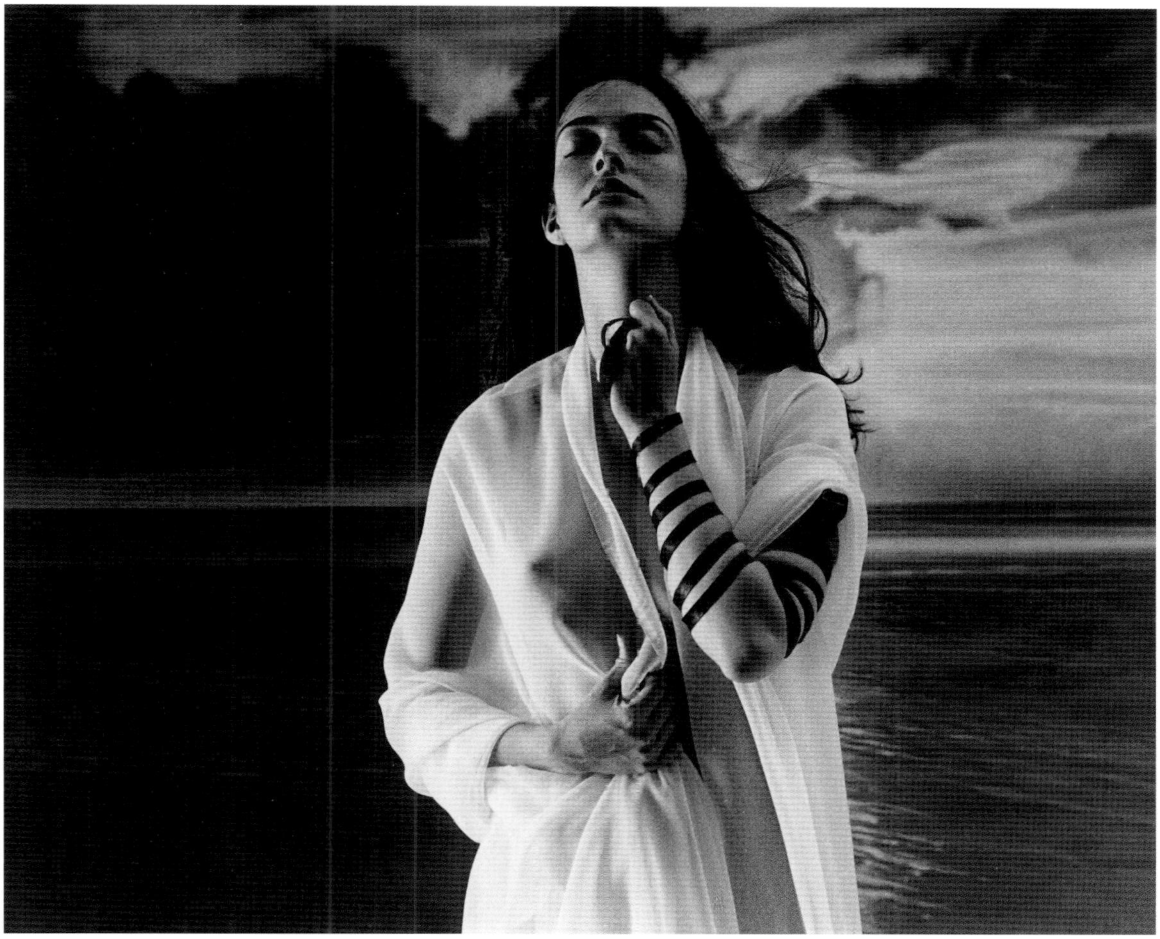

LEONARD NIMOY Born 1931, Boston, Massachusetts. Resides Beverly Hills, California
Shekhina, 2002 Gelatin silver print 20 x 24 in. (50.8 x 61 cm) Collection of the artist

I enjoy the female figure in sculpture, I enjoy it in painting, I enjoy it in the flesh—and then to discover that I was able to find a spirituality in it made me even more comfortable with it. It gave me a broader context as well: I had been working more with line, light, and form, but now I find myself dealing in much more depth with the issues involved. Most of the women who have seen the work, including some female rabbis, have been extremely supportive, but the question has come up of whether I'm limiting the vision of Shekhina, which is understood to be the feminine aspect of the divine. My response is that this is my Shekhina and if others see her differently, so be it.

This is my Shekhina. This is the way I experience her: she is fully female. In one of my images she is pregnant with a spiritual light. In another she has given birth to a spiritual light. In some images she is more sensual than maternal. In some she is very mysterious; in some she is very frank, and faces the camera directly; in others she is veiled. Sometimes I capture her at rest, sometimes in motion, and sometimes in meditation.

My dream concept is that I am trying to photograph what is essentially invisible.

Excerpted from "Trying to Capture the Invisible," an interview with Leonard Nimoy by Anne A. Simpkinson, originally published on the beliefnet.com website.

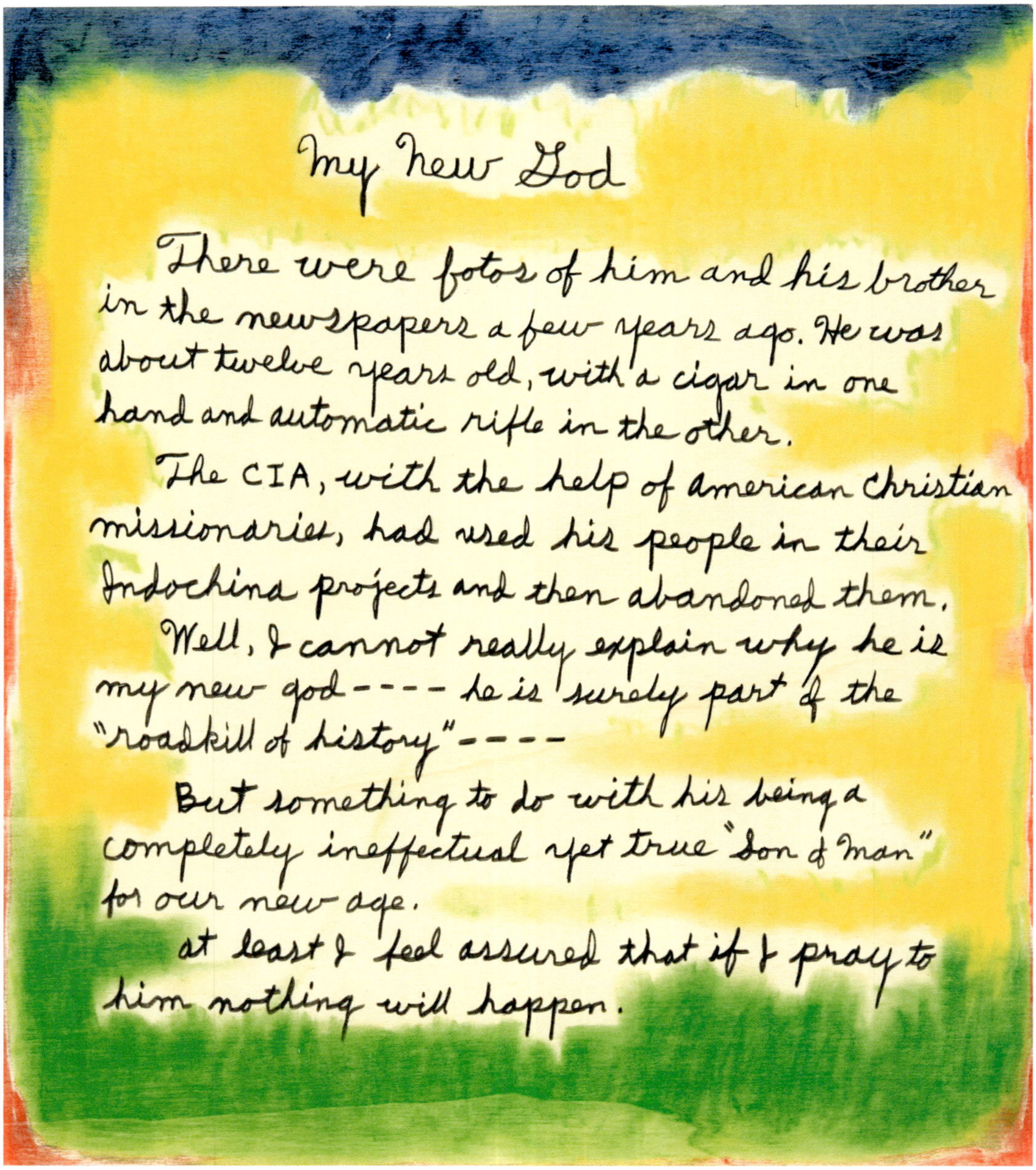

<u>JIMMIE DURHAM</u> Born 1940, Arkansas. Resides Berlin, Germany
My New God, 2002 Graphite and pastel on plywood 14 x 12 1/2 in. (35.6 x 31.8 cm) Collection of the artist

I have tried to be sensibly unheroic and practical in making a piece for the project of seeing god.

I want there to be no god, but just as important, I want there to be no more belief. No belief in anything, because it is anticuriosity, antiintellect, antiscience, antihuman; and for my own practice it would be antiart.

To *pretend* that there is god, though, is no more than a mental exercise. The Dutch artist Henk Visch (quoting someone else) said, "If you want to look god in the eye how close would you need to get? You would have to try to look at what god is looking at." Well, if there was god I would require that he look at this actual world.

I would want him to see the desperate child in the forest, and say, "Oh, you poor, brave, monstrous boy! Come up here and sit at My Right Hand."

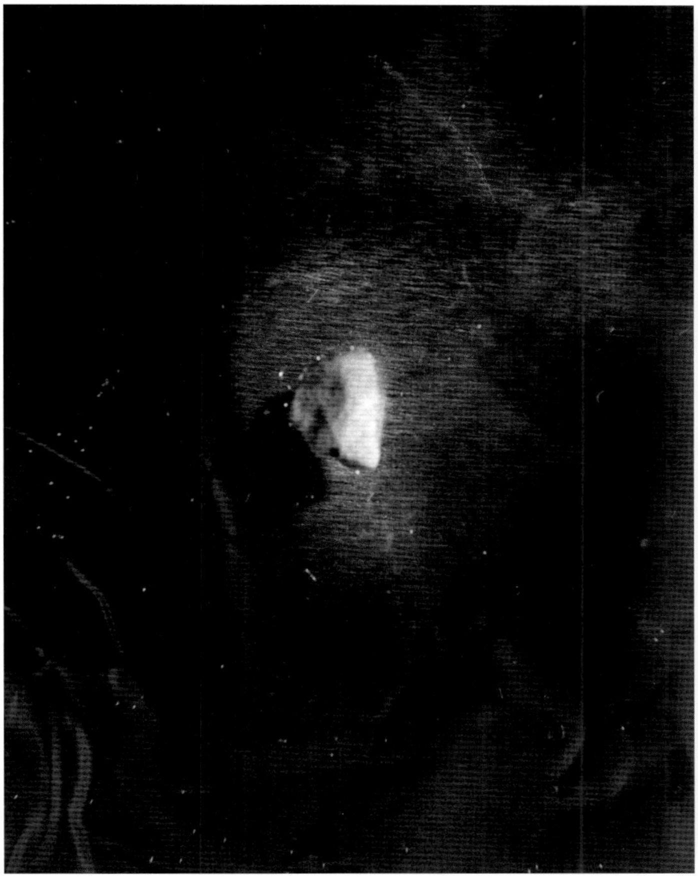 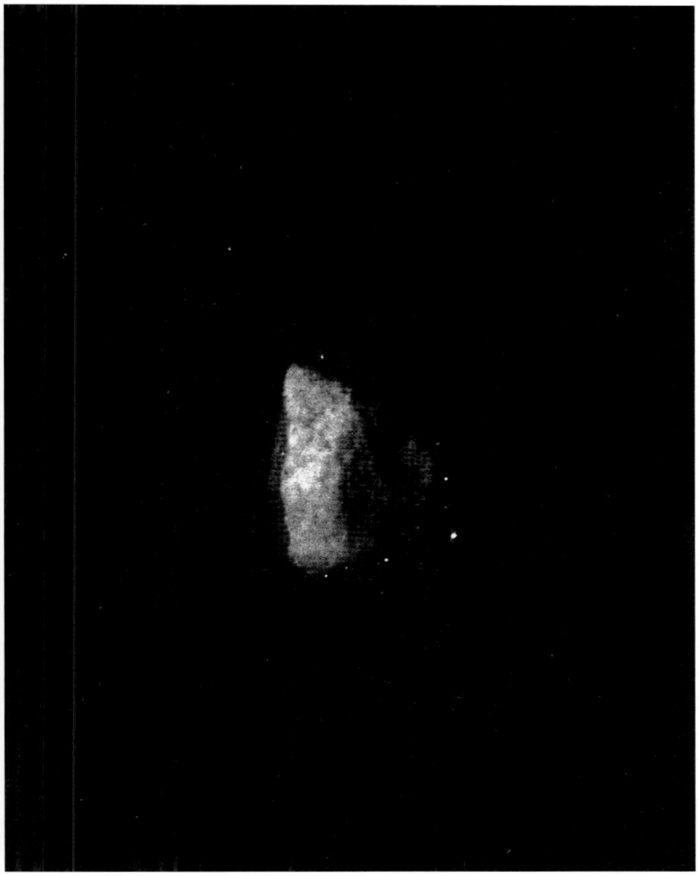

MIKE KELLEY Born 1954, Detroit, Michigan. Resides Los Angeles, California

The Two Faces of God, 2002 Two gelatin silver prints 10 x 8 in. (25.4 x 20.3 cm) each Collection of the artist

My contribution to *100 Artists See God* is a photograph of a god substitute. Although I am now an atheist, I was raised Catholic, and the fear of a vengeful God was instilled in me young. During moments of stress, fear, or depression I sometimes find myself reverting to prayer as a way to calm myself down. Since I no longer believe in a supreme being, this provokes an intellectual dilemma.

In response I have focused my prayer upon a common object: a tiny stone pulled from my boot. This object appeals to me as a god substitute, first, because the smallness of a pebble strikes me as a visual antidote to the pompous and spectacular image of the God of my youth. Second, if I were attracted to any religion, it would have to be nature worship. Third, any pebble can perform the function of god substitute; one is as good as another. The democratic nature of such "holiness" appeals to me.

To present a pebble itself in this context would be like presenting an idol, and thus outside the aesthetic bracket of an art exhibition. Instead I will present an iconic depiction of a pebble, either as a simple framed photograph or as a photograph printed on "holy cards"—those small cards, often found in Catholic churches, that generally show Christ or a saint on one side and a prayer on the other. If I decide to print holy cards, they will be available free to the viewer.

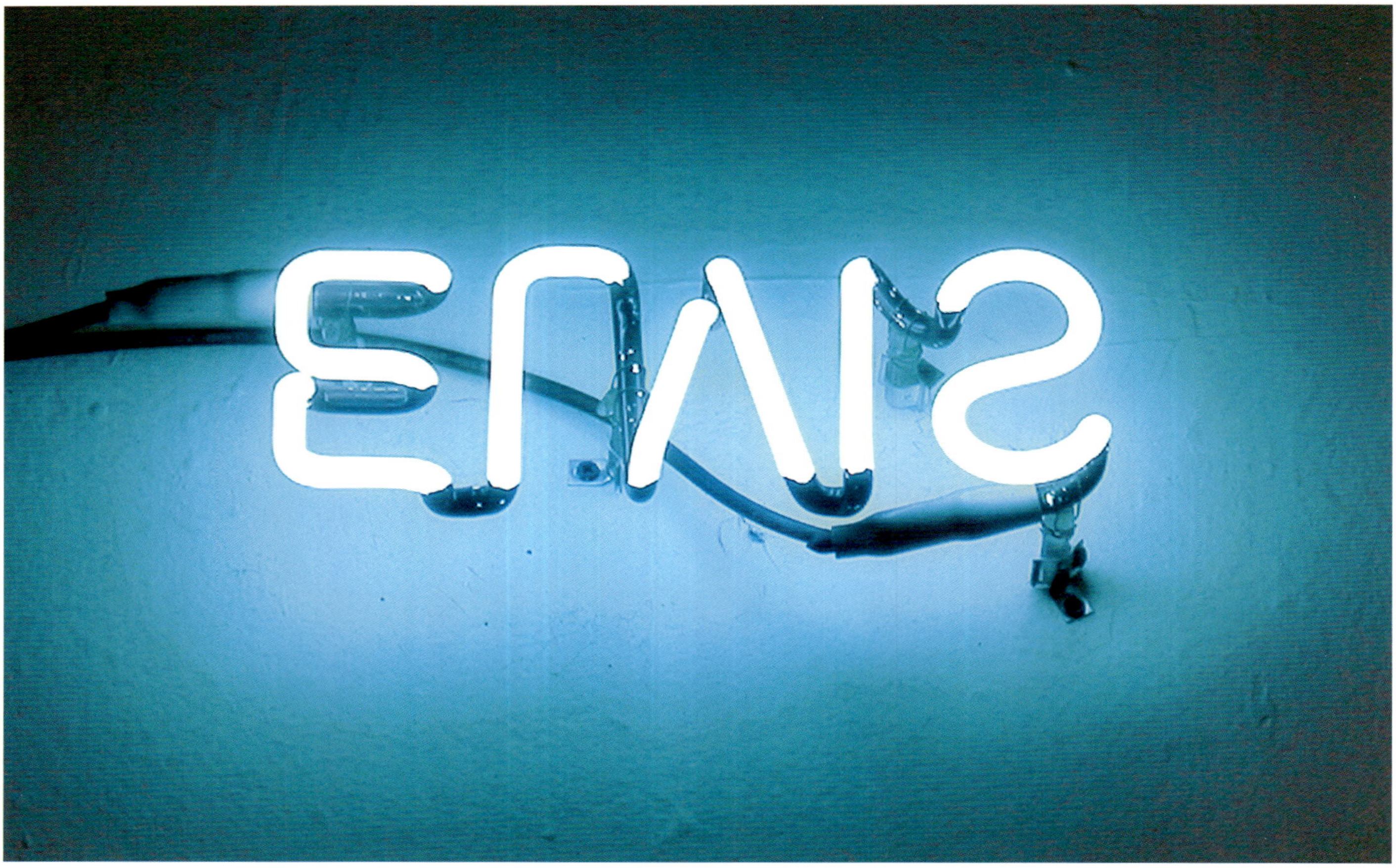

TERRY ALLEN Born 1943, Wichita, Kansas. Resides Santa Fe, New Mexico
Jesus (upside down backwards), 1993 Neon 4 x 12 in. (10.2 x 30.5 cm) Collection of David Byrne and Adelle Lutz

The only difference I can see in how the culture regards ELVIS son of Vernon and JESUS son of God is, to my knowledge, JESUS never recorded anything called "DO THE CLAM." Even Bob Dylan said, after nearly dying from a rare heart virus, "Man, for a while there I thought I was going to see Elvis."

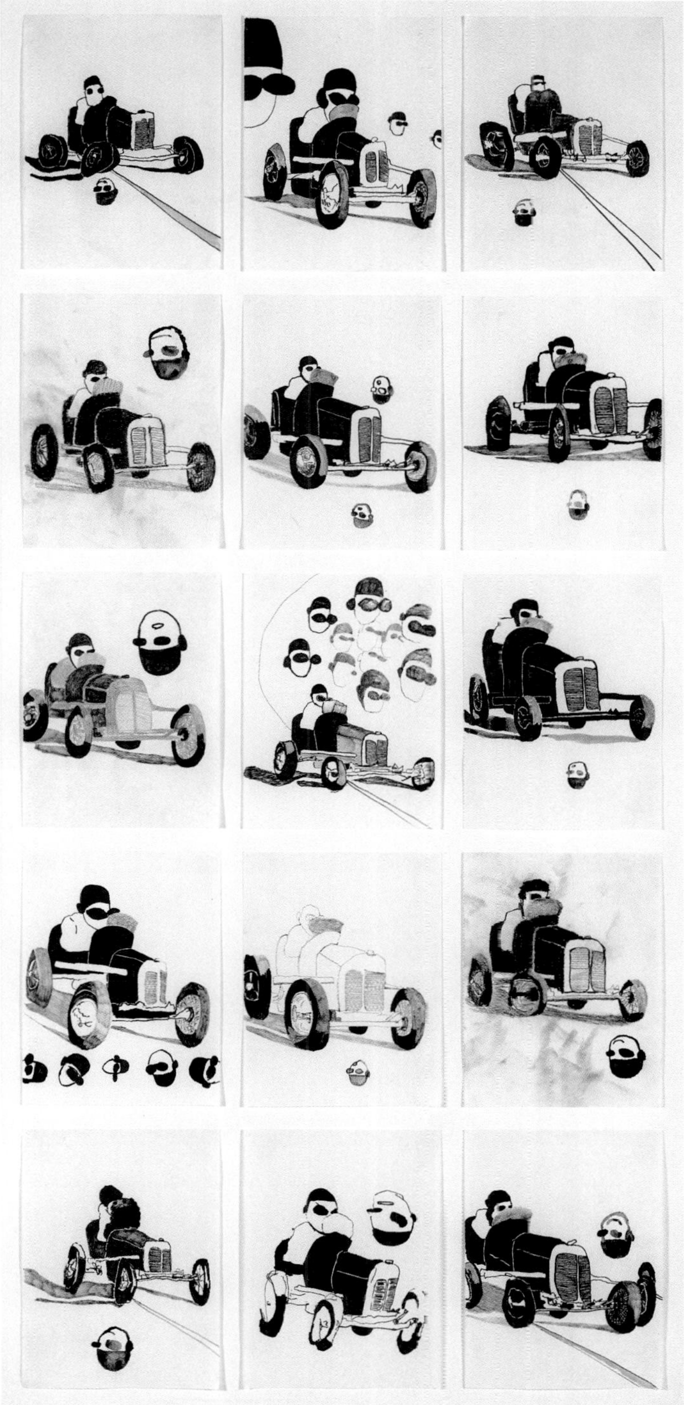

BENJAMIN WEISSMAN Born 1957, Los Angeles, California. Resides Los Angeles, California
Heads & Cars, 1995 Gouache on paper Framed: 64 x 33 in. (162.6 x 83.8 cm) Collection of the artist

SEEING JOHN

I see the god we call John all the time but He doesn't see me. He senses how needy I am and turns His back. I understand. It is better to help someone who is strong and self-sufficient, who will not paw after him, arms waving, pleading for a life-preserver. John is tall and his back is beautiful, a gentle slope. His hair is long and white like a shimmering snowfield. Standing behind Him, never in front, I have an impulse to ski down His steep silky locks. His hair is the only snow that means anything to me.

Then one day while driving the motorcar I experience an epiphany: I see my own head coming off and landing in front of me. My skull multiplies into many heads that grin and taunt me to run over them. In my goggles and helmet my disconnected head appears more cheerful to me than in any bathroom mirror, which makes me less interested in killing myself. This is what John will do. He will take your head off and place it in front of you and ask you to reconsider the violence you are ready to inflict on yourself. When I saw all these heads of mine, removed from their proper trunk, the stem of my neck, I thought to myself, You are a handsome man, you really are, maybe someone will fall in love with me. I glanced in the rearview. I was blushing.

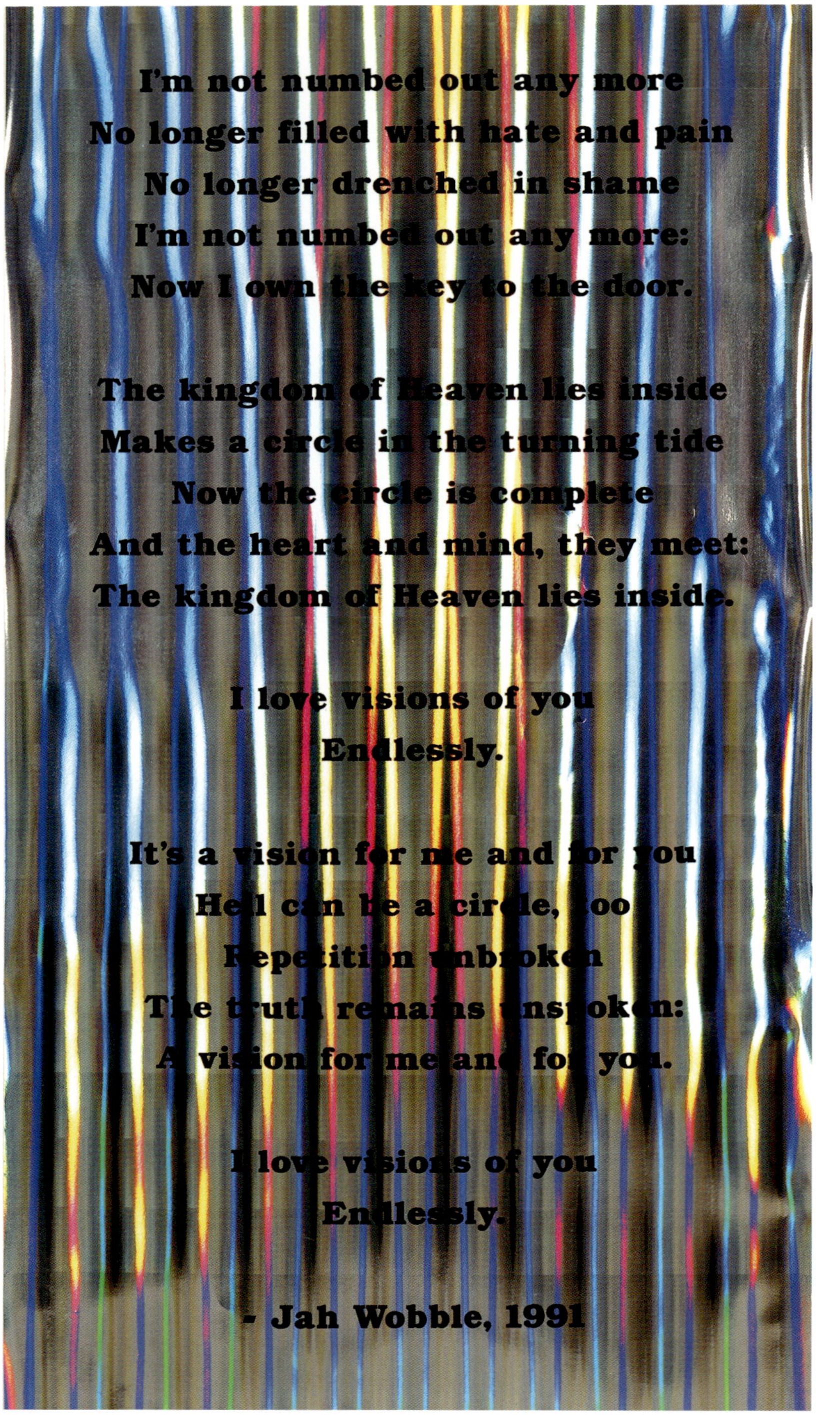

<u>CHRIS WILDER</u> Born 1957, Long Beach, California. Resides Los Angeles, California
Visions of You, 2002 (detail) Silkscreen on holographic-foil wallpaper 72 x 24 1/2 in. (182.9 x 62.2 cm) Collection of the artist

ARTISTS SEE GOD AS THE EXTRAORDINARY FORCE OF NATURE

Every religion sees god in nature, whether or not it formally expresses that idea. Some notion of the relationship between god and nature is fundamental to any culture's world view.

In general, Western art both venerates and fears the natural world, because it understands human beings as separate from nature. Nature is different from human culture, it does not follow the same rules. God works through nature in beautiful and terrible ways. God is wonderment, which is best expressed in nature, spectacular and cruel.

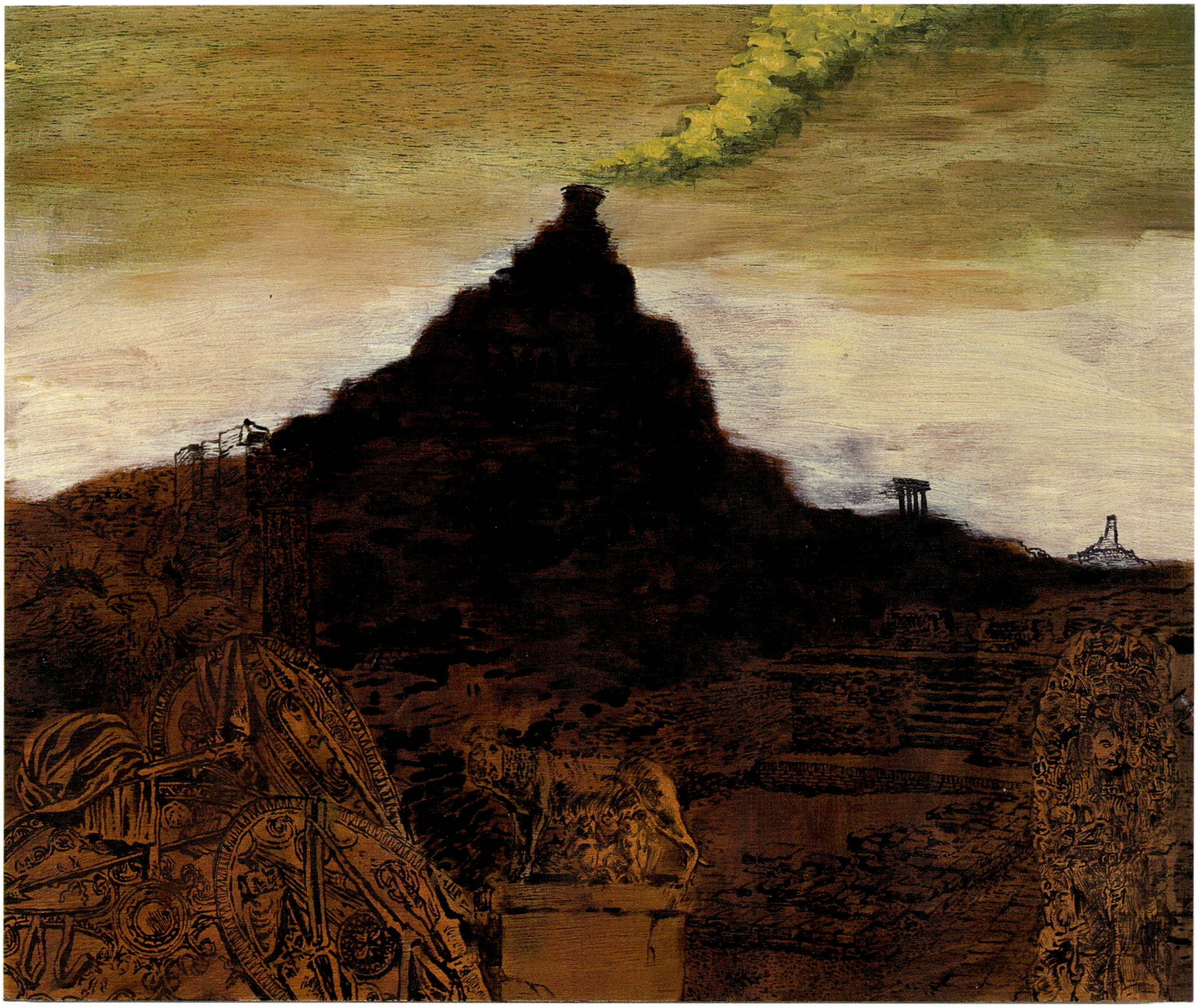

JP MUNRO Born 1975, Inglewood, California. Resides Los Angeles, California
The Mountain of Tears, 2002 Oil on panel 10 x 12 in. (25.4 x 30.5 cm) Collection of the artist. Courtesy China Art Objects Galleries, Los Angeles

Heraclitus says that "in the matter of wisdom, beauty, and every other thing, in contrast with God the wisest of mankind will appear an ape." Similarly, a mortal makes a poor reporter on the doings and appearances of the gods. Let us look instead at the mountain of tears, a physical manifestation of centuries of human desire and pain, a representation of the godlike in history.

The mountain's stones are baked in sweat and bathed in blood. They are the concrete embodiment of the wishes and misunderstandings that are the glue of the psychic firmament. As hope softly slips away, the mountain creeps higher, a volcano belching forth its own mass and girth, bubbling up faster than the icecaps can melt. We have passed the point of worry to the point of jollity:

the Mountain of Tears,
the Mountain of Giggles,
the Mountain of Music.

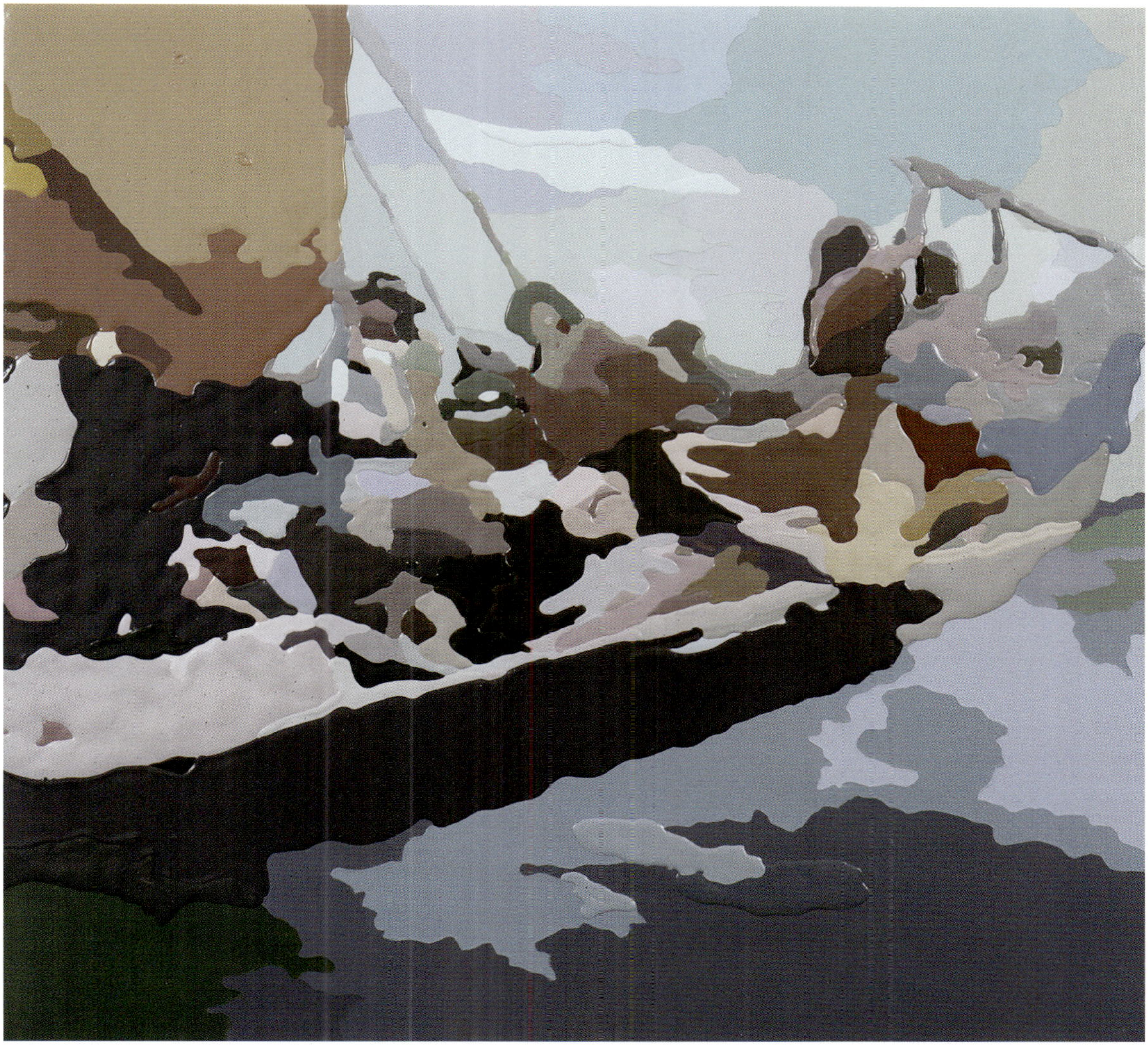

ERIC NIEBUHR Born 1972, La Marque, Texas. Resides Los Angeles, California
How Fast It Could End, 2003 Acrylic on canvas on panel 20 x 22 in. (50.8 x 55.9 cm) Collection of the artist. Courtesy Mary Goldman Gallery, Los Angeles

The painting *How Fast It Could End* comes out of my continued interest in classical religious imagery, science fiction, and computer-aided abstraction. It was inspired by a scene in the religious film *Jesus* where Christ calms the turbulent waters. I took the painting's title from the song "Overhead," by the band Low, from their album *Things We Lost in the Fire*.

"Overhead"

Wanted—bring him back alive
if you can
All said—you can tell your lies to
the dead
Overhead—you don't have
to like
What you're fed
Overhead
Overhead

Wanted—bring him back alive
if you can
Trusted—you don't know how
fast it could end
Overhead—you don't have
to like
What you're fed
Overhead
Overhead
Overhead
Overhead

By Low, from *Things We Lost In the Fire*, vinyl version, 2001

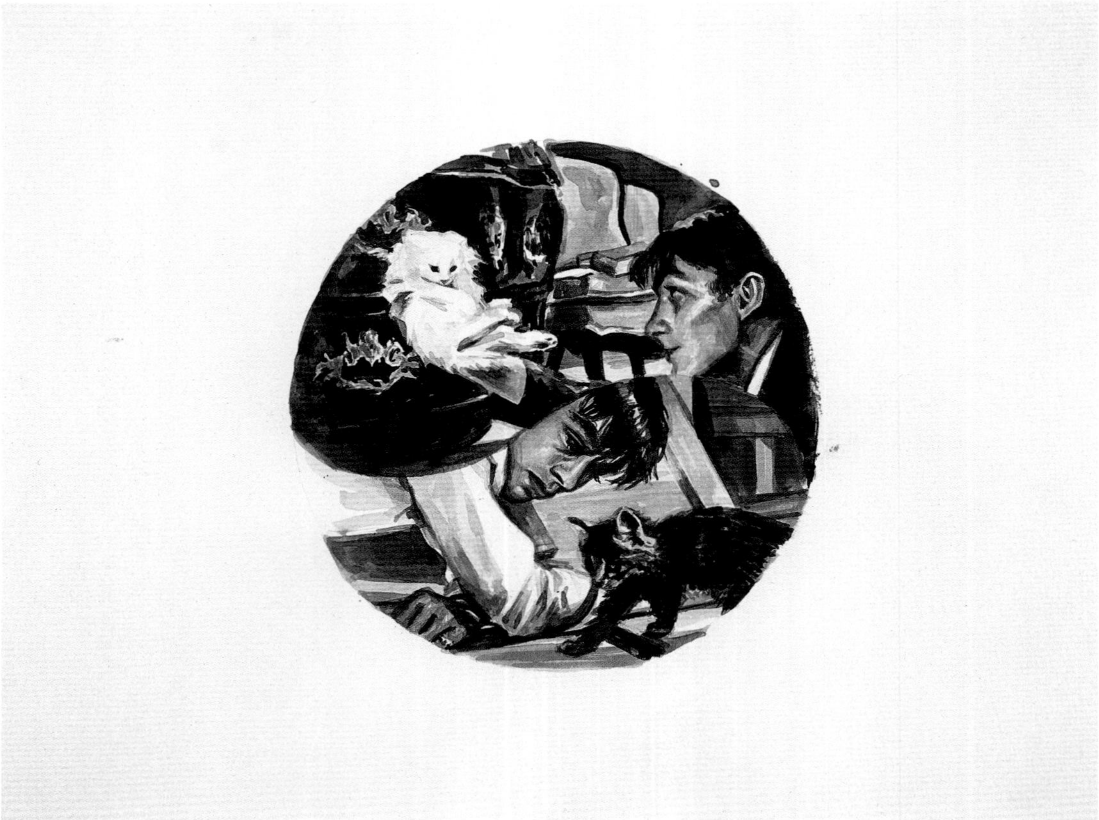

DELIA BROWN Born 1969, Berkeley, California. Resides Los Angeles, California
Yin & Yang (Boccacio '70 and Les Félins) #4, 2002 Ink on paper 9 1/2 x 9 1/2 in. (22.9 x 22.9 cm) Collection of Delia Brown. Courtesy of the artist and D'Amelio Terras, New York

I collected these images while researching films that used kittens as foils for particular aspects of humanness. The top part of *Yin & Yang* is a still from Luchino Visconti's episode of the collectively made movie *Boccacio '70*. The bottom half is from *Les Félins*, a French film of 1964 starring Alain Delon and Jane Fonda. When I acquired these images I recognized that a task had been given to me.

I believe it is beyond coincidence that these two images combine to create a yin-and-yang form. A philosophy that recognizes opposites as complements is a philosophy of peace. The man on his knees observing the tabby kitten is a picture of pathos, of man humbled before innocence, apprehending his own existential sadness in the creature's dark eyes and tiny, awkward body. The man lifting up the fluffy white kitten, as if offering heaven a small slice of its own perfect self, represents chivalry, love, and faith.

Only one mind that unites all things can bring about such a symbolic alignment for us to notice. The omniscient field of intelligence that I perceive as "God" makes meaning available to us at every moment, and we may live with or without it. Art, and the coming together of disparate elements to engender new symbolic meanings, is one of our ways of elucidating and acknowledging that gift.

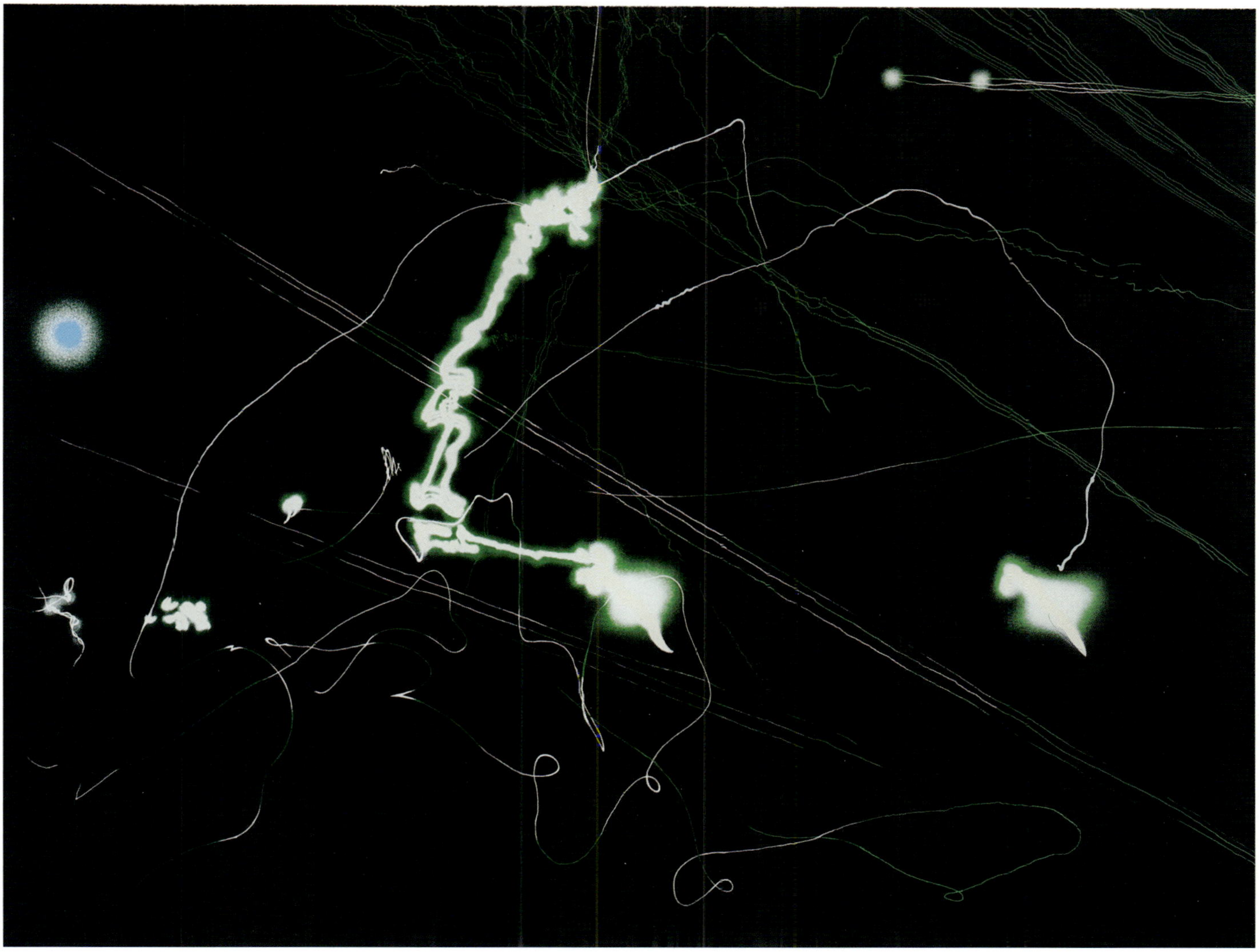

JACK GOLDSTEIN Born 1945, Montreal, Canada. Died 2003, Los Angeles, California
Untitled, 1983 Lithograph and silkscreen on paper Framed: 32 1/2 x 42 1/2 in. (82.6 x 108 cm) Artist's proof from an edition of 55
Collection of Brian Butler. Courtesy 1301PE, Los Angeles

GREAT GOD! BUT
FOR ONE SINGLE
INSTANT SHOW
THYSELF

"no, you are not
someone apart, you are myself,
you and i and
nothing more"

"Lu-nar
paths, of the
de-part-ed,

start here

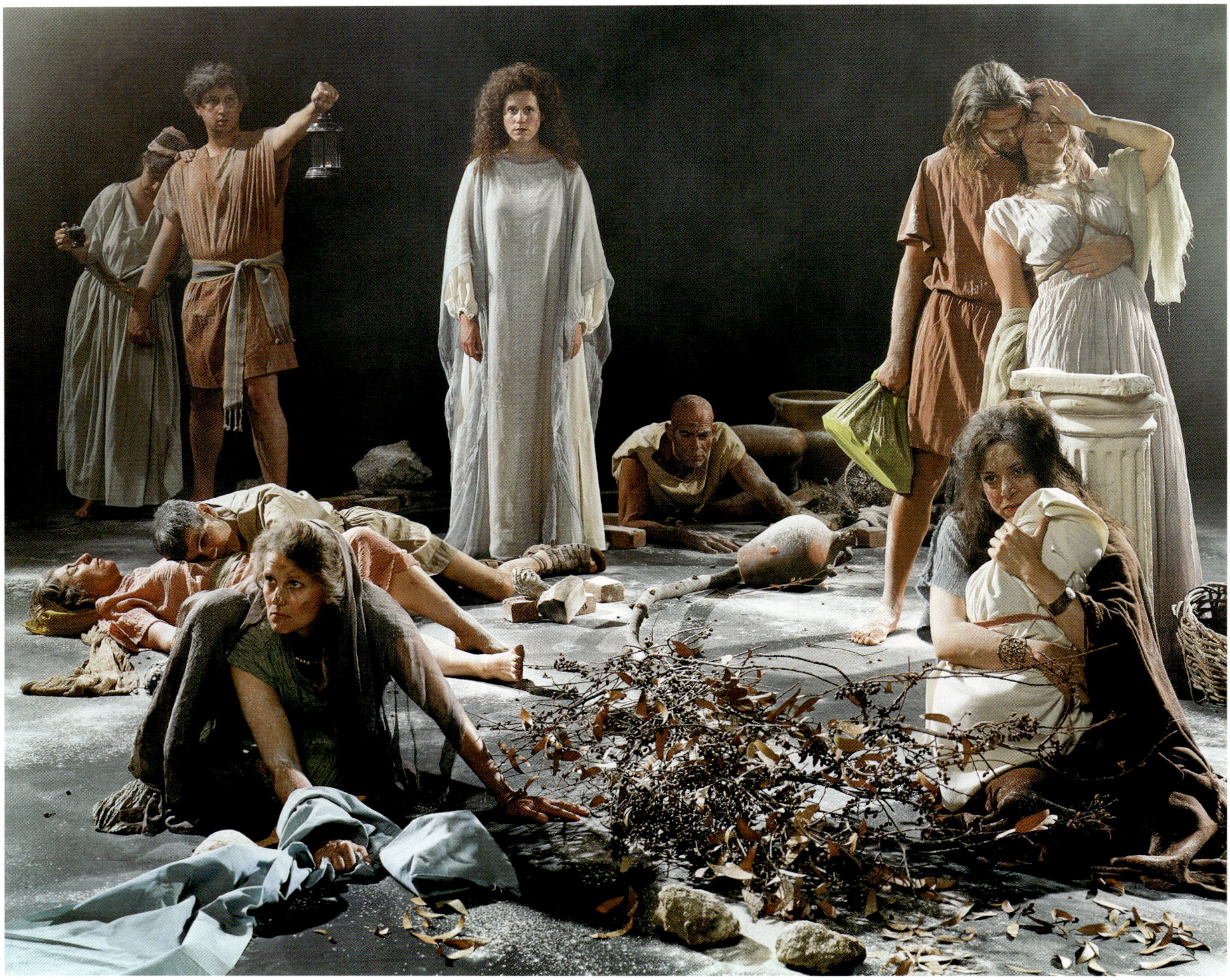

<u>ELEANOR ANTIN</u> Born 1935, New York, New York. Resides Del Mar, California
The Last Day, from "The Last Days of Pompeii," 2002 Chromogenic print 20 x 40 in. (50.8 x 101.6 cm) Courtesy Ronald Feldman Fine Arts, New York

In our chaotic and destructive world, the problem of trying to imagine an omnipotent, omniscient, and benevolent power that can be called God seems an amazing feat of mind that I'm not sure I'm up to. Shall we know Him by His acts? "The Last Days of Pompeii" looks at a typically arbitrary event that one beautiful sunny morning in August slaughtered grandmothers and children, singer and slaves, vandals and villains, pimps and procuresses, and suggests a causal force that is either an absentee landlord, a demonic trickster, a psychotic, or an Alzheimer case.

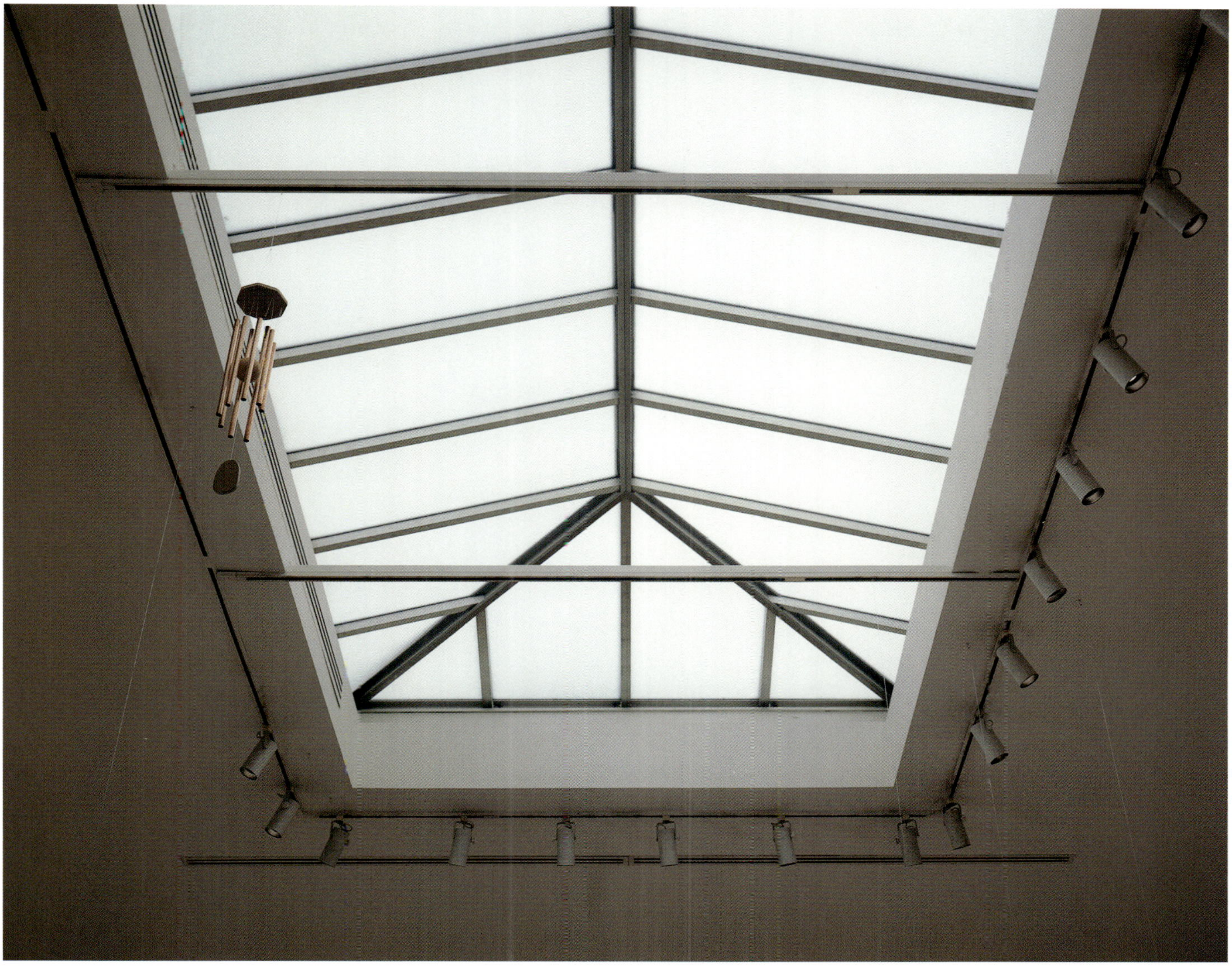

MUNGO THOMSON Born 1969, Davis, California. Resides Los Angeles, California
Wind Chime, 2000 (installation view) Wood, copper, and monofilament 42 1/2 x 6 x 6 in. (108 x 15.2 x 15.2 cm) Collection of the artist. Courtesy Margo Leavin Gallery, Los Angeles

the temple bell stops
but the sound keeps coming
out of the flowers
—Basho Matsuo (1644–94)

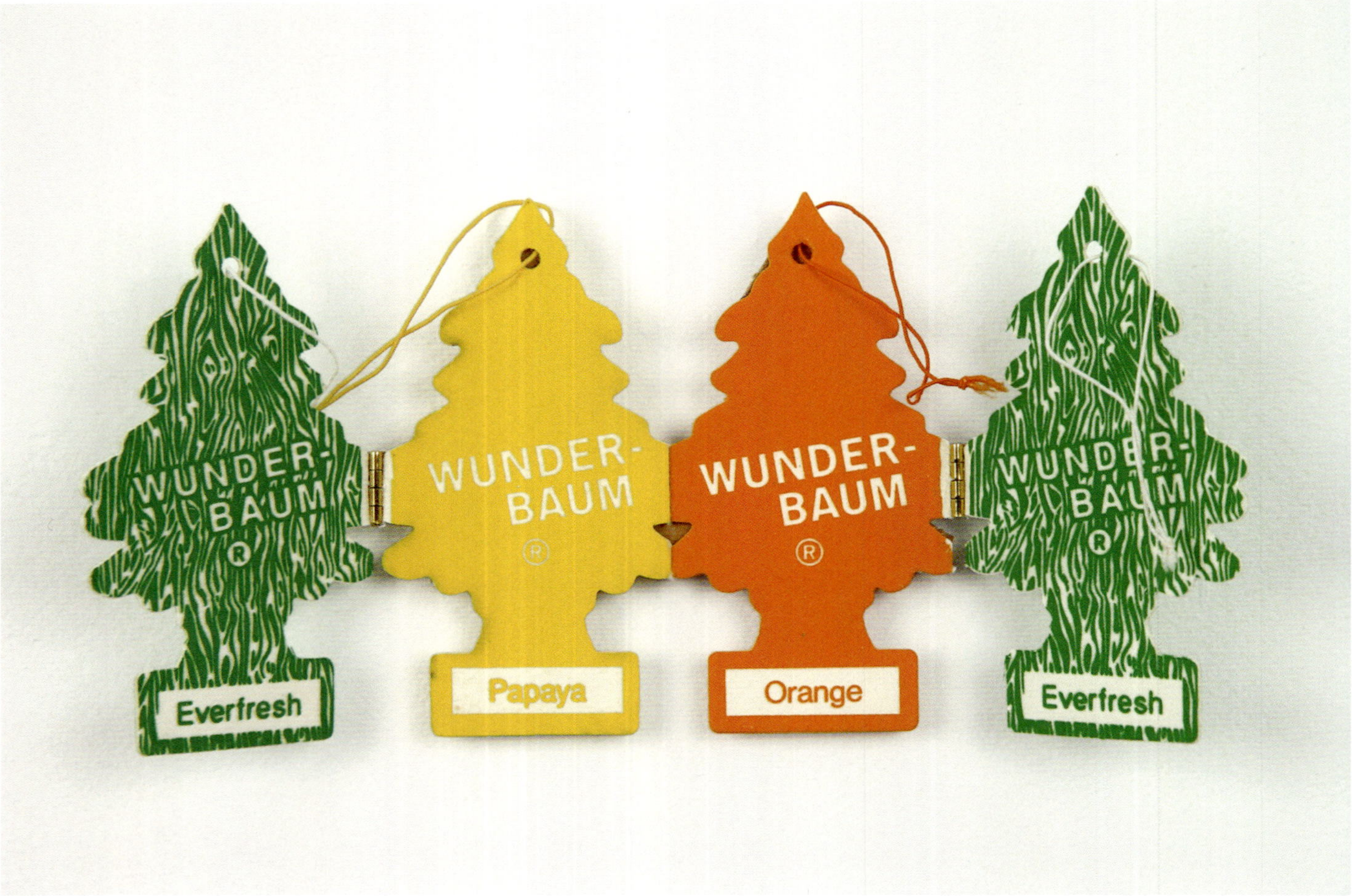

RITA McBRIDE Born 1960, Des Moines, Iowa. Resides New York, New York
Polyptych, 2003 Air fresheners, cardboard, and brass hinges Open: 4 3/4 x 10 1/2 x 1/16 in. (12 x 26.7 x .4 cm); closed: 4 3/4 x 5 1/4 x 1 1/2 in. (12 x 13.3 x 3.8 cm) Collection of the artist. Courtesy Alexander and Bonin, New York

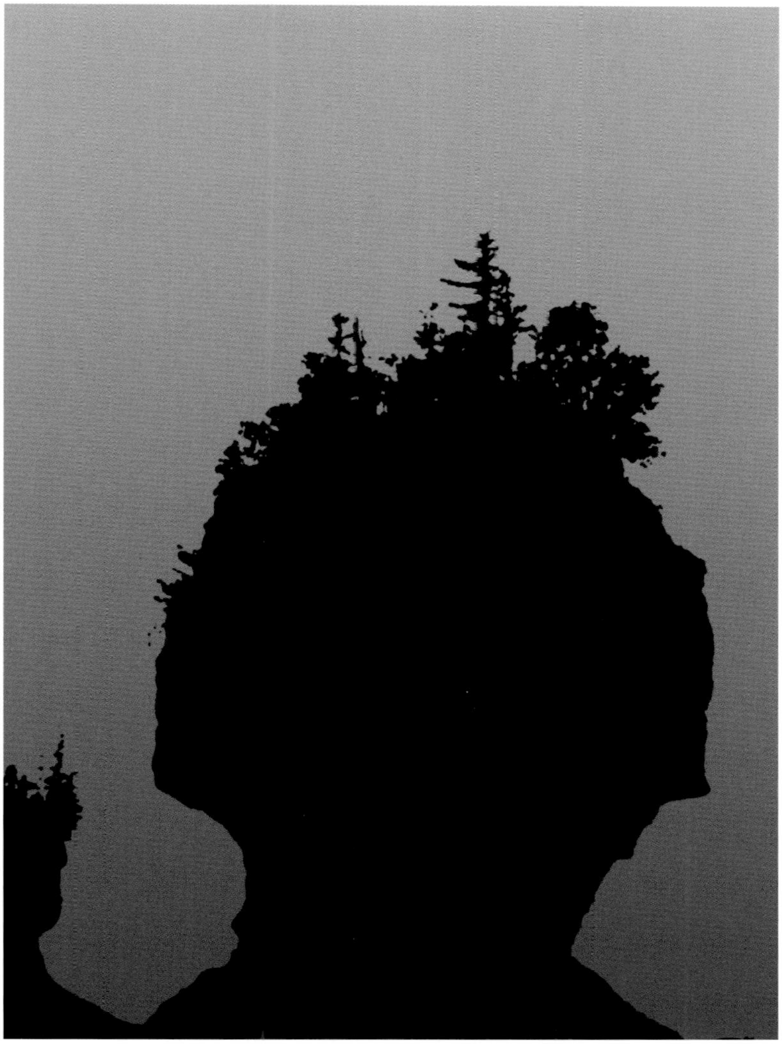

GLEN WALTER RUBSAMEN Born 1957, Los Angeles, California. Resides New York, New York
Hopewell 2, 2003 Oil on linen on panel 23 1/2 x 15 3/4 in. (60 x 40 cm) Collection of the artist

ARTISTS SEE GOD AS THE GREAT ORGANIZER

There is no greater job god can do than organize the world. Most religions provide a cosmology—some basic theory of the organization of the universe. Religions point us to what is important and help to establish cause and effect. Artists are like gods in the basic respect that they organize. An artist says this and not that. An artist says here and not there. There is no greater job an artist can do than organize the world.

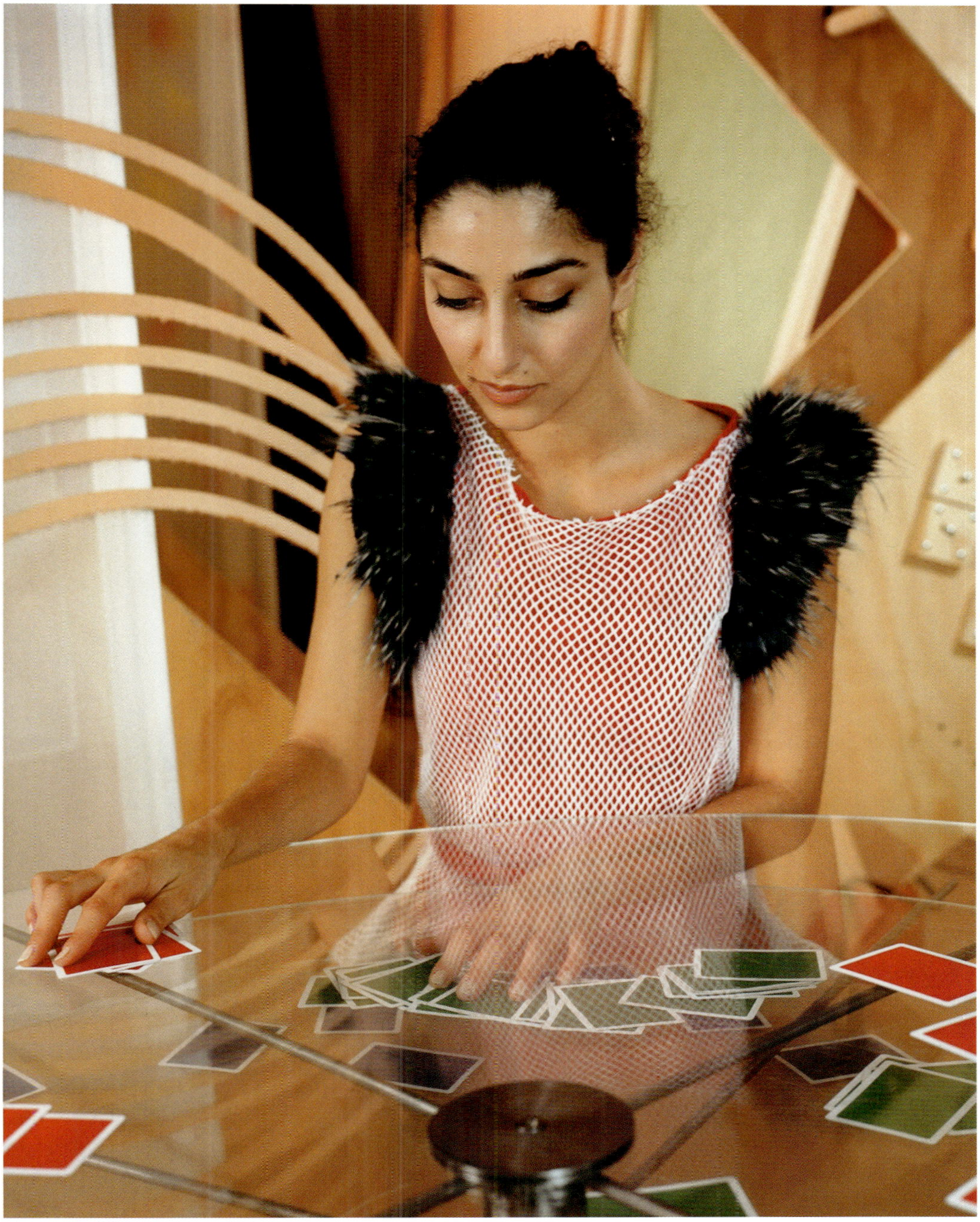

DARIA MARTIN Born 1973, San Francisco, California. Resides London, England
Production still from *Closeup Gallery*, 2003 UltraChrome digital print 24 x 20 in (61 x 50.8 cm) Collection of the artist

My films are utopias made by hand: idealized places created through fragile means. If a form of spirituality is embodied in these worlds, it is, like the medium of film itself, both materially solid and elusive—a belief in fantasy made flesh.

This still is drawn from *Closeup Gallery*, a film focusing intimately on the theater of close-up card magic. A sleight-of-hand artist and an actress play an enigmatic game in which they manipulate colored cards at a multilayered wheellike table. The game is a conduit both between the two actors and between the film and the audience: a method of communicating a secret code, a way to both hide and reveal meaning. Revolving like cards on the rotating table, notions of fate, fortune, chance, deception, and revelation emerge, shuffle, and disappear.

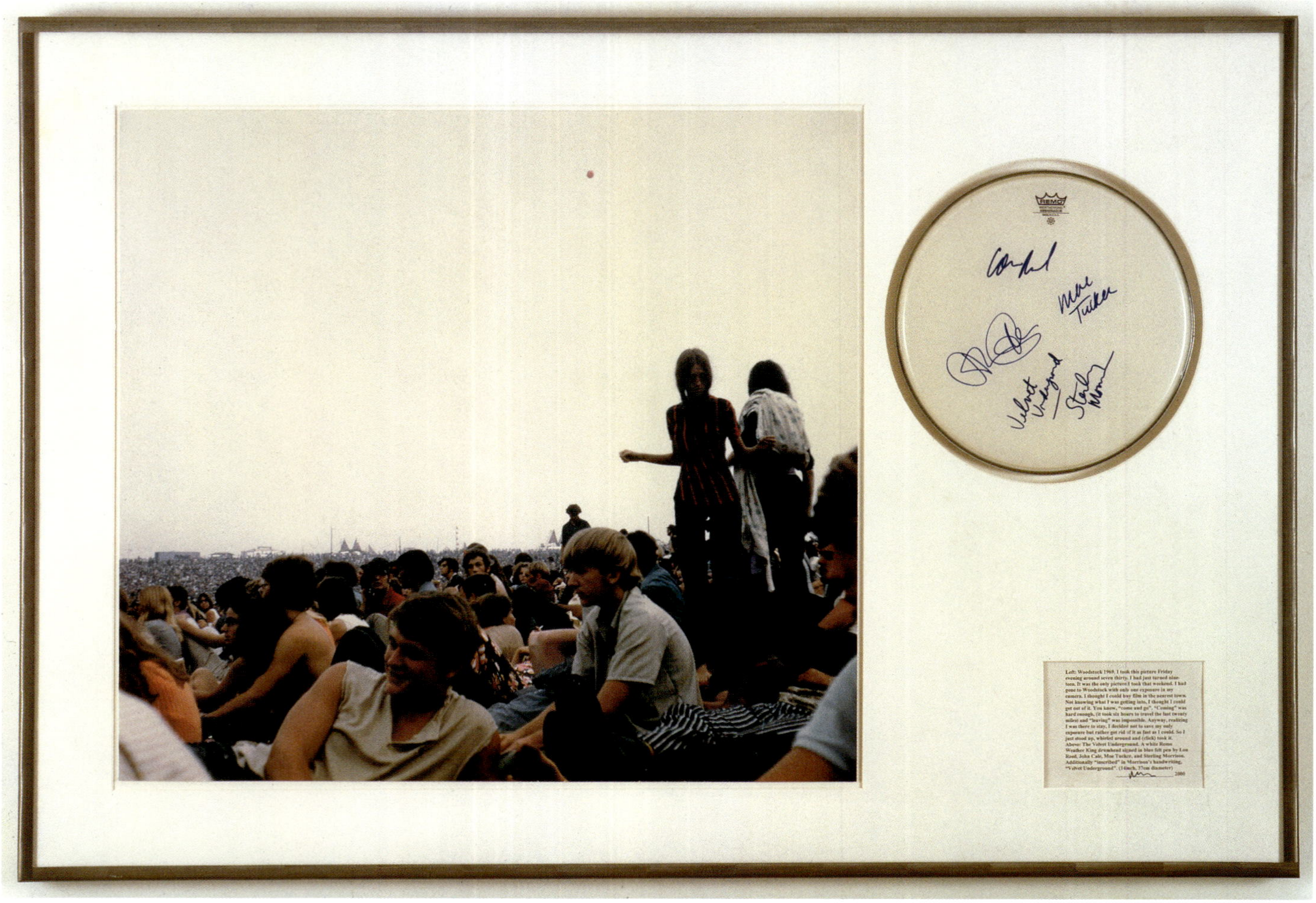

RICHARD PRINCE Born 1949, Panama Canal Zone. Resides New York, New York
Untitled (Publicity), 2000 One Ektacolor photograph by Richard Prince and one drumhead signed by the Velvet Underground
Framed: 41 x 61 in. (104.1 x 154.9 cm) Collection of the artist. Courtesy Barbara Gladstone Gallery, New York

Woodstock 1969. I took this picture Friday evening around seven thirty. I had just turned nineteen. It was the only picture I took that evening. I had gone to Woodstock with only one exposure in my camera. I thought I could buy film in the nearest town. Not knowing what I was getting into, I thought I could get out of it. You know, "come and go." "Coming" was hard enough, (it took six hours to travel the last twenty miles) and "leaving" was impossible. Anyway, realizing I was there to stay, I decided not to save my only exposure but rather to get rid of it as fast as I could. So I just stood up, whirled around and (click) took it.

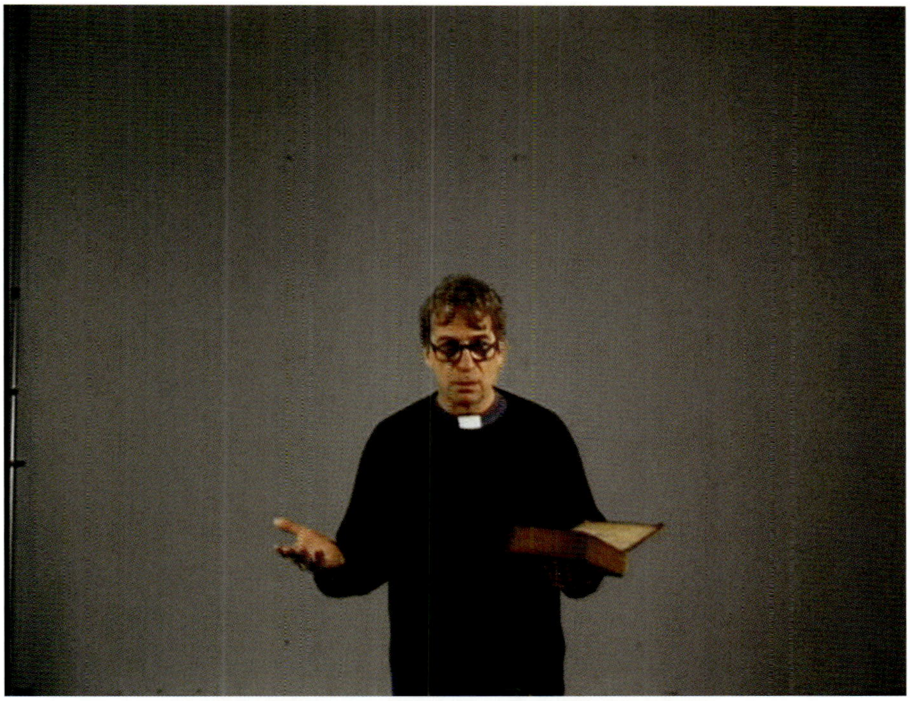

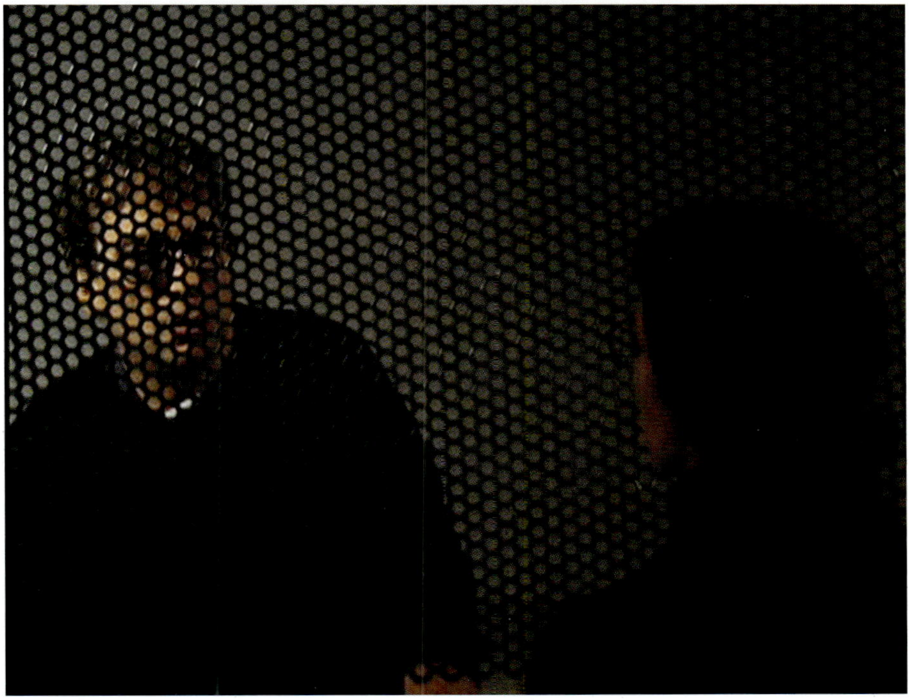

WILLIAM WEGMAN Born 1943, Longmeadow, Massachusetts. Resides New York, New York
"Minister" and "Confession," excerpts from *Reel 9*, 1999 (video stills) DVD 2 minutes 56 seconds and 2 minutes 11 seconds respectively
Collection of the artist

I don't believe in God, but I do believe in religions...that they exist.

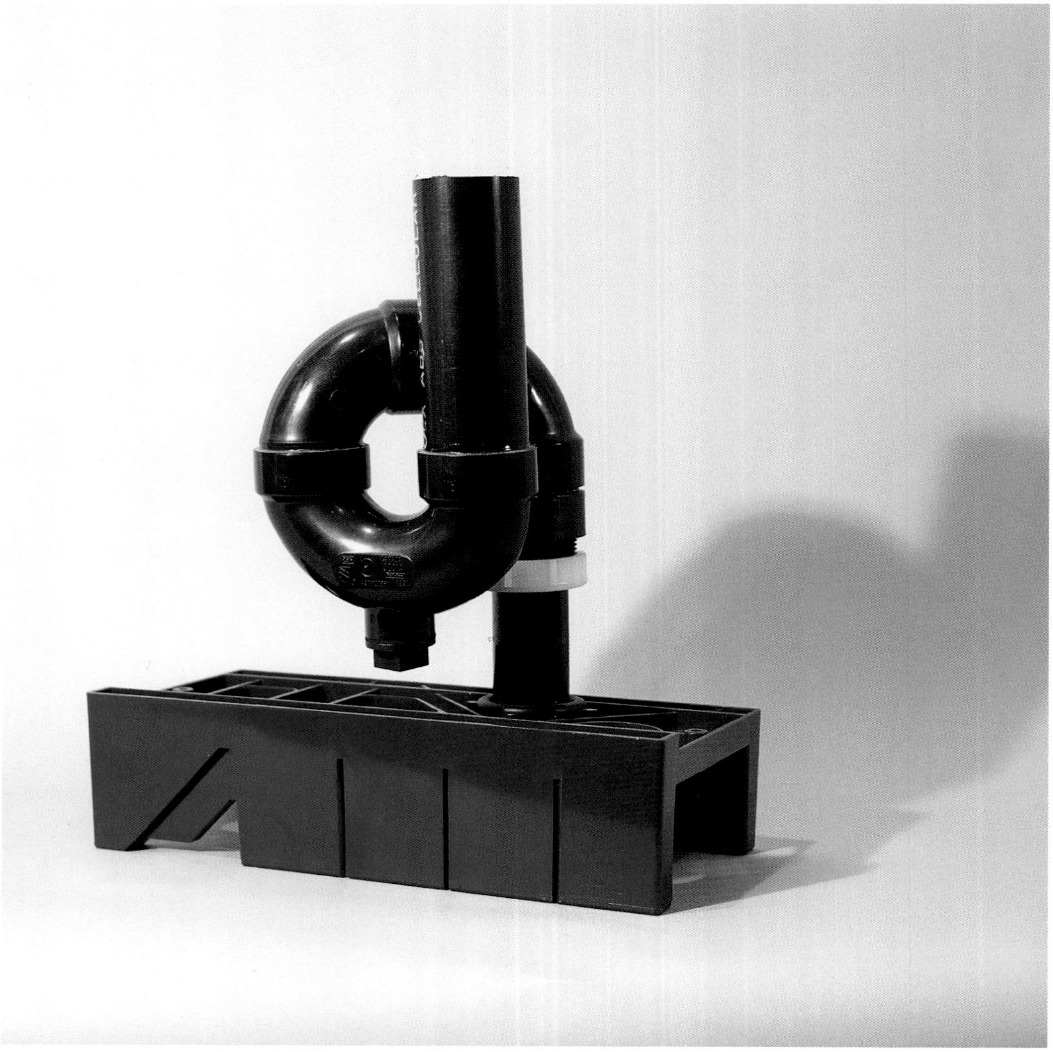

T. KELLY MASON Born 1964, Hollywood, California. Resides Los Angeles, California
Plastic God, 1997 (detail) Plastic, birch plywood, and Plexiglas 20 x 14 x 20 in. (50.8 x 35.6 x 50.8 cm) overall Collection of the artist

I made this piece after a work titled *God* (ca. 1917) in the collection of the Philadelphia Museum of Art. Although the work has long been attributed to Morton Schamberg exclusively, it has recently been discussed as a collaborative work between Schamberg and Baroness Elsa von Freytag-Loringhoven (1874–1927). Schamberg was part of the first generation of American abstract painters—Charles Demuth, Arthur B. Dove, Marsden Hartley, Charles Sheeler, et al. The baroness made her way through the salons of the early-twentieth-century New York avant-garde wearing black lipstick, shaved head stained purple, postage stamps stuck to her cheeks, toy soldiers sewn to her skirt, stalking William Carlos Williams. At the end of the twentieth century she was reinvented as a proto-punk gender-political artist, although eyewitnesses swore she was simply mad. Things change. Coincidences happen. I made the piece a few years back as a gift for someone and for myself. It seemed the obvious choice for the exhibition.

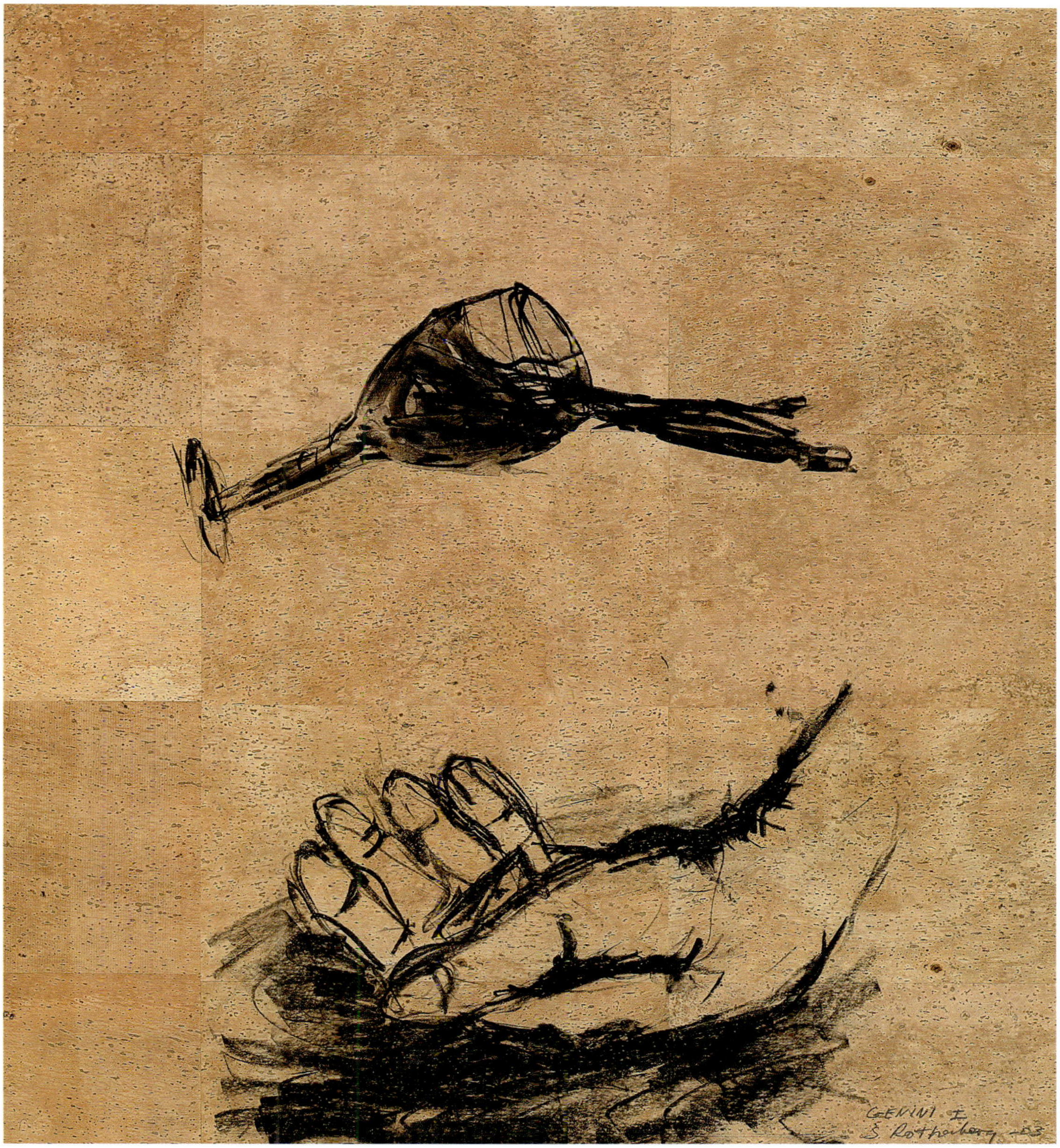

SUSAN ROTHENBERG Born 1945, Buffalo, New York. Resides Galisteo, New Mexico
Uncorked, 2003 Two-color lithograph/screenprint 24 x 22 in. (61 x 55.9 cm) Edition: 20/58 Collection of Gemini G.E.L. LLC

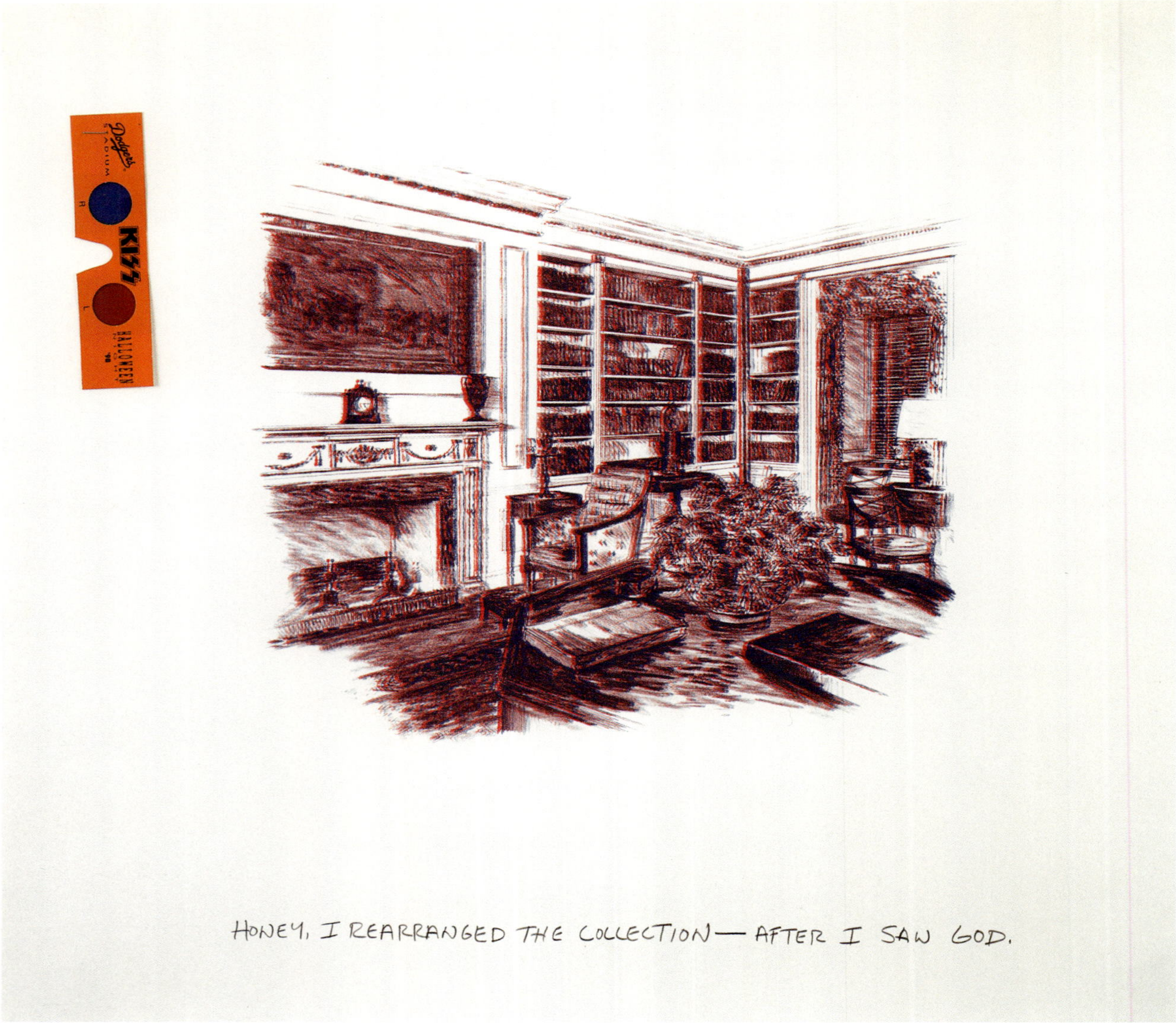

ALLEN RUPPERSBERG Born 1944, Cleveland, Ohio. Resides New York, New York, and Santa Monica, California
Honey, I Rearranged the Collection After I Saw God, 2002 Silkscreen, graphite, and 3-D glasses 22 x 25 in. (55.9 x 63.5 cm)
Collection of the artist. Courtesy Margo Leavin Gallery, Los Angeles

I like God.

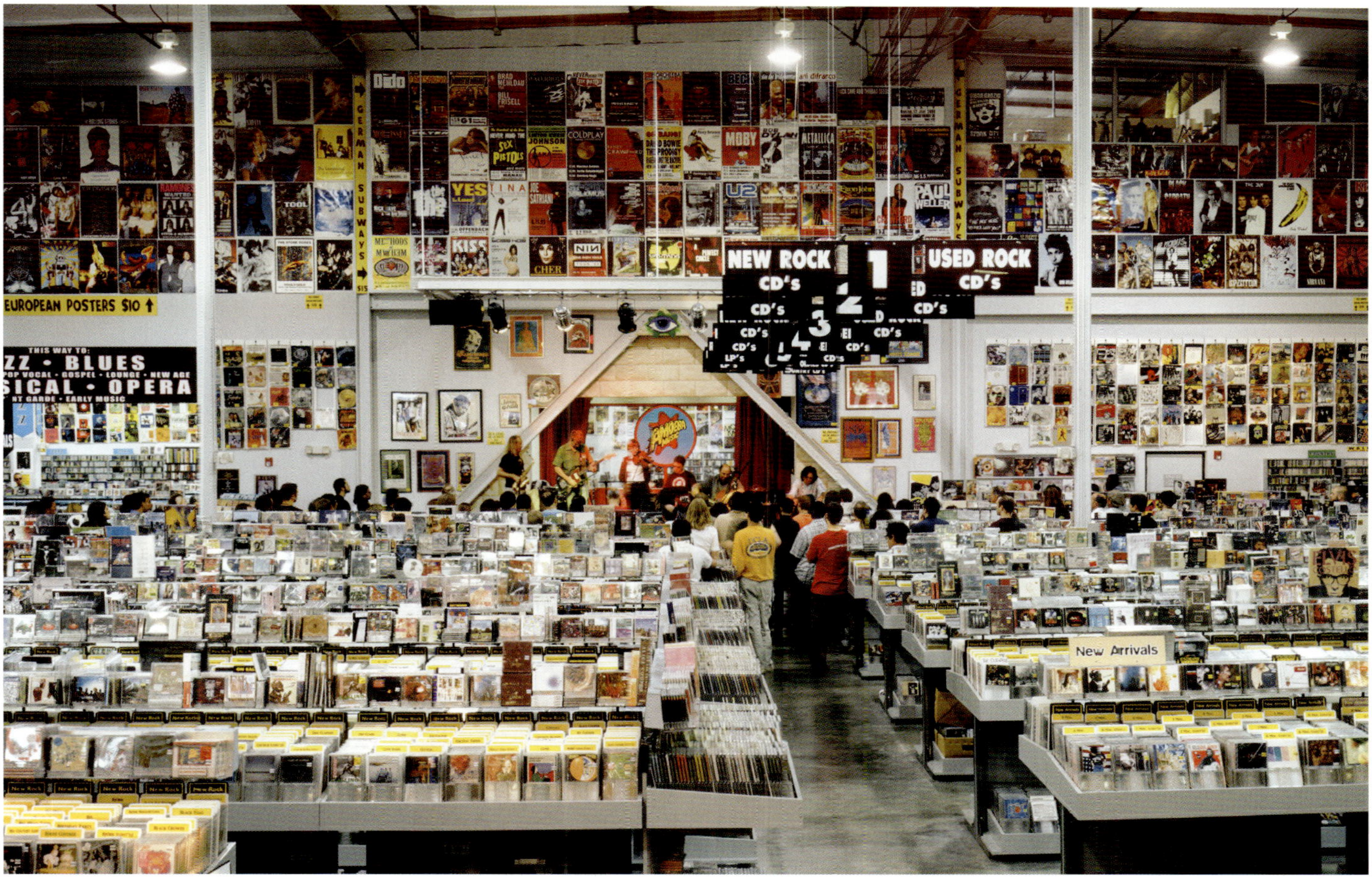

CINDY BERNARD Born 1969, San Pedro, California. Resides Los Angeles, California
July 25, 2002 (no. 1), 2002 Chromogenic print 30 x 46 7/8 in. (76.2 x 119.4 cm) Collection of Jane Hart. Courtesy the artist and lemon sky projects + editions, Miami

In the title *100 Artists See God*, I was struck by the reiteration of the priority so commonly given to sight over sound in our culture. I was interested in including an image that would refer to sound, and whose genesis would lie in sound and listening—since for me, admittedly an agnostic, those moments that are close to transcendence tend to be aural, not visual. My recent photographs of concerts I've organized depict a heightened yet compressed version of the temporal experience of the event—an image more closely resembling my experience and expectations as a producer than an image from a single transparency or negative is capable of representing.

In July 2002, I organized an in-store improvisation at Amoeba Music in Hollywood to celebrate the release of "soundCd no. 1: Live recordings of experimental improvisations organized as a part of sound. 1998–2001." Working with a director of photography, I shot eighteen transparencies that when combined, heighten different aspects of the experience of the performance. In *July 25, 2002 (no. 1)*, I combine six transparencies in order to eliminate anyone not paying attention to the musicians on the stage, emphasizing the exchange between audience and performer.

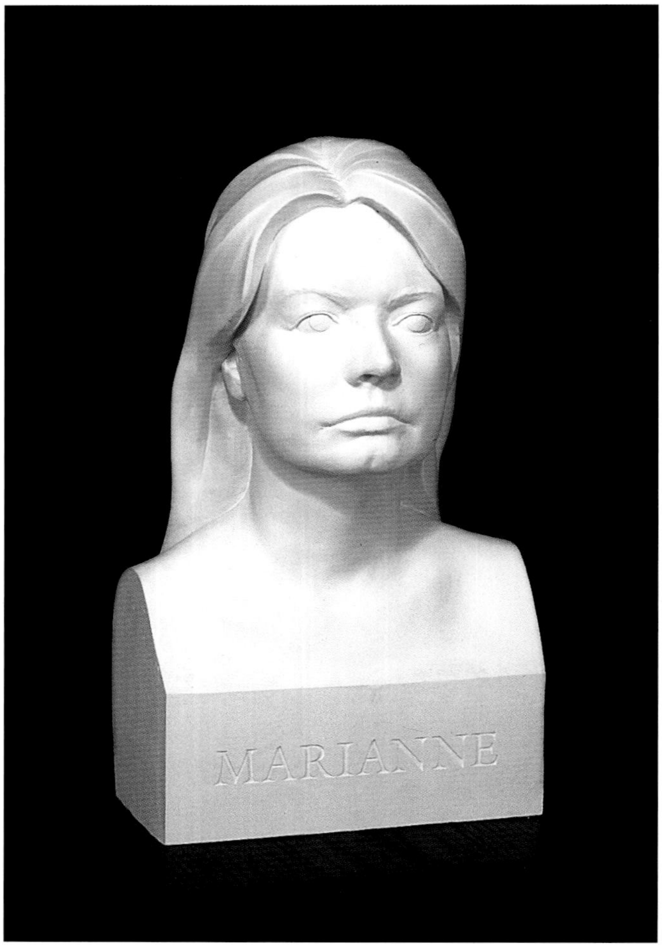

MÅNS WRANGE in collaboration with IGOR ISAKSSON Wrange born 1961, Åhus, Sweden. Resides Stockholm, Sweden
Isaksson born 1963, Strom, Sweden. Resides Stockholm, Sweden.
The Average Citizen, 1999 Plastic bust and inkjet print Bust: 11 x 20 x 7 in. (27.9 x 50.8 x 17.8 cm); framed print: 37 x 28 in. (94 x 71.1 cm)
Collection of the artist. Courtesy Andrehn-Schiptjenko Gallery, Stockholm

"God is dead," said Nietzsche, who, in the late nineteenth century, replaced God with Superman. A few decades later the social engineers of Sweden have replaced God with the statistically average man. In our modern welfare state, statistical studies have replaced the Bible as our guide in law and government, and statisticians are the new prophets who predict the future by interpreting the charts. Statistics have become the new religion, and the average has become the canon by which everything else is measured.

The Average Citizen is a ten-year project aiming to change society in accordance with the opinions of a statistically average citizen. The Swedish Central Bureau of Statistics helped us to create an "average citizen profile," and a media campaign was conducted to find someone fitting it: female, forty, single, childless, living in a two-room-and-kitchen apartment, etc. That person was found, her name is Marianne, and we are disseminating her social views to the Swedish public that she statistically represents. The intention is ultimately to influence public opinion. When, for example, we inserted one of Marianne's opinions into a line of dialogue in a Swedish TV series, 28.6 percent of the country's viewing population heard it. An opinion poll then established that it had convinced 6.2 percent of the public. While Mies van der Rohe declared that "God is in the details," his Swedish contemporaries, the functionalist architects who designed for the average citizen, might well have declared that "God is in the statistics."

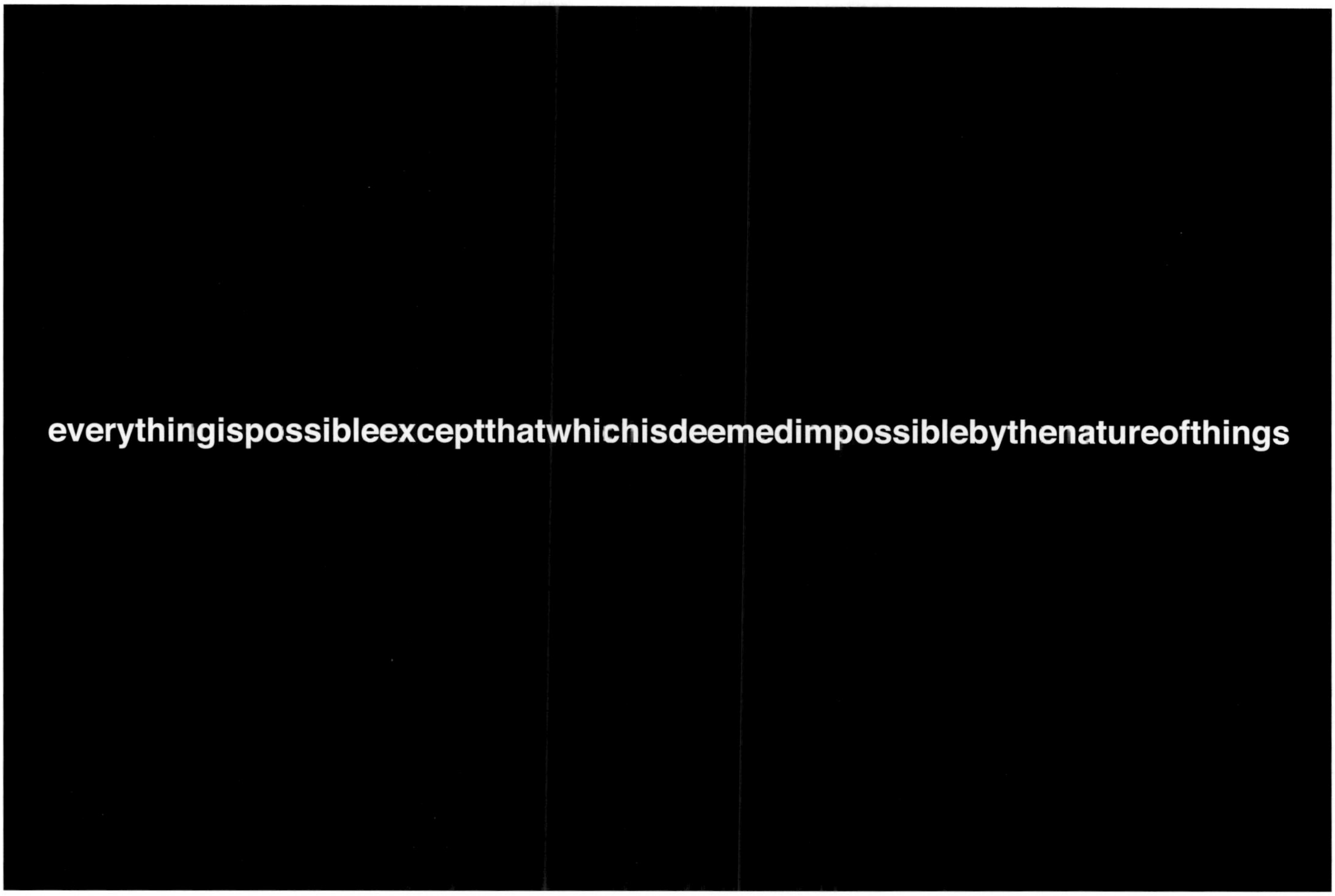

LIAM GILLICK Born 1964, Aylesbury, England. Resides London, England, and New York, New York
Everythingispossibleexceptthatwhichisdeemedimpossiblebythenatureofthings, 2001 White vinyl letters or white sign-painting on black wall
Dimensions variable Collection of the artist

ARTISTS SEE GOD AS SOMEONE WHO SUFFERS

The Gospel of Saint Mark describes John the Baptist in the wilderness as dressed in camel's hair and a skin girdle, eating locusts and wild honey.

Emaciated and near death, Gautama sat cross-legged under the bodhi tree, where he was tormented by demons sent by the evil Lord Mara.

Mohammed would spend the month of Ramadan in the cave of Ghar-i-Hira, or the "cave of research."

Jesus spent forty days in the desert, tormented and starving. At the end the Devil approached him and said, "If you are the Son of God, tell these stones to become bread." And Jesus answered, "Man is not to live on bread alone, but on every word that comes from the mouth of God."

Holy persons suffer for good reasons: suffering is instrumental. It purifies, it strengthens, it moves us forward. In modern times the artist has had the role not only of representing the suffering of holy persons but of imitating it. The many legends of the suffering artist can be connected to those religious myths and stories in which an individual achieves enlightenment after a strenuous period of exile.

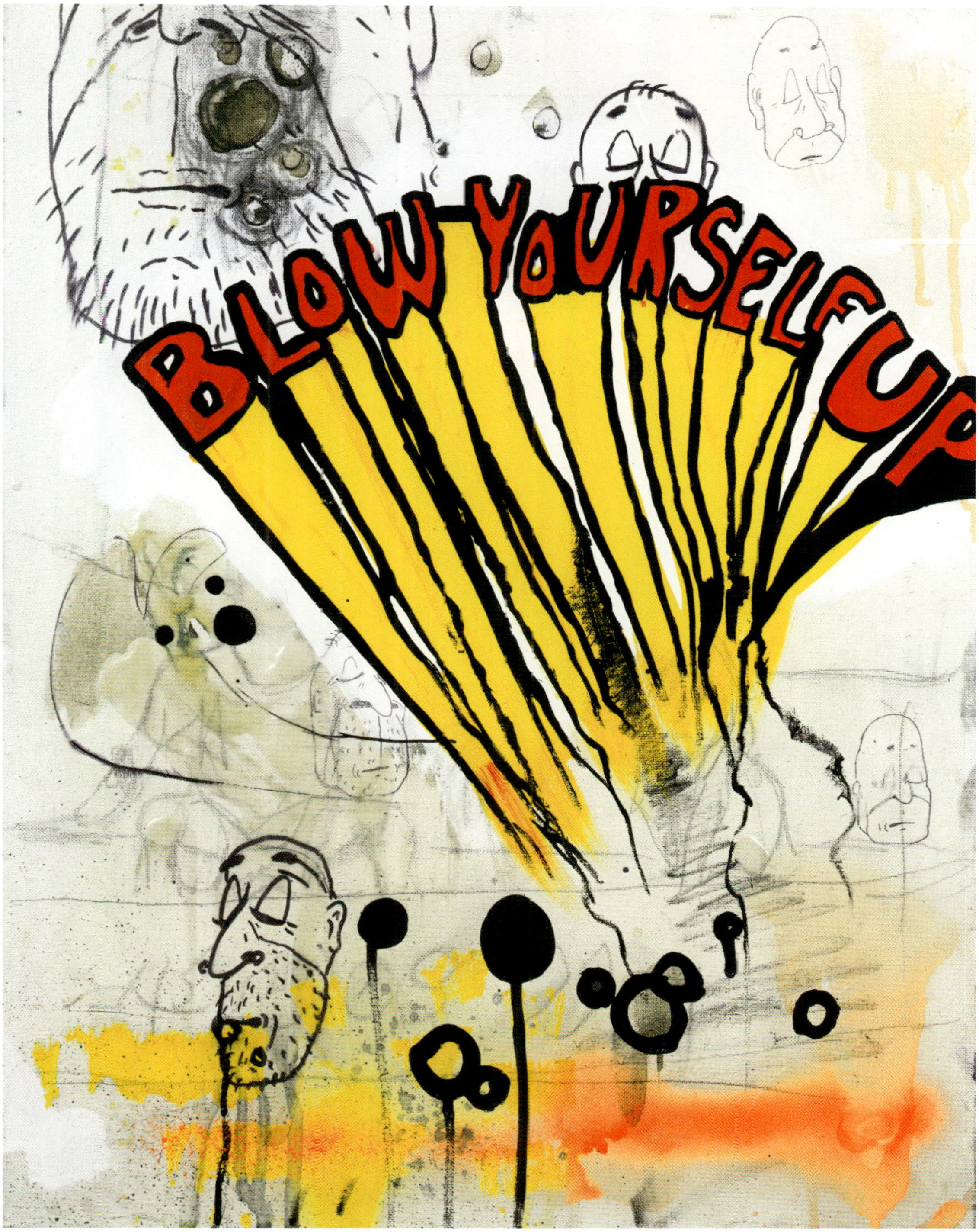

THADDEUS STRODE   Born 1964, Santa Monica, California. Resides Los Angeles, California
Blow Yourself Up: Thus Sayeth the Lord, 2002   Mixed media on canvas   20 x 16 in. (50.8 x 40.6 cm)   Collection of the artist.
Courtesy The Happy Lion Gallery, Los Angeles

In order to reach clarity
and enlightenment, one must
obliterate the conceptual
construct of self.

Blow Yourself Up…

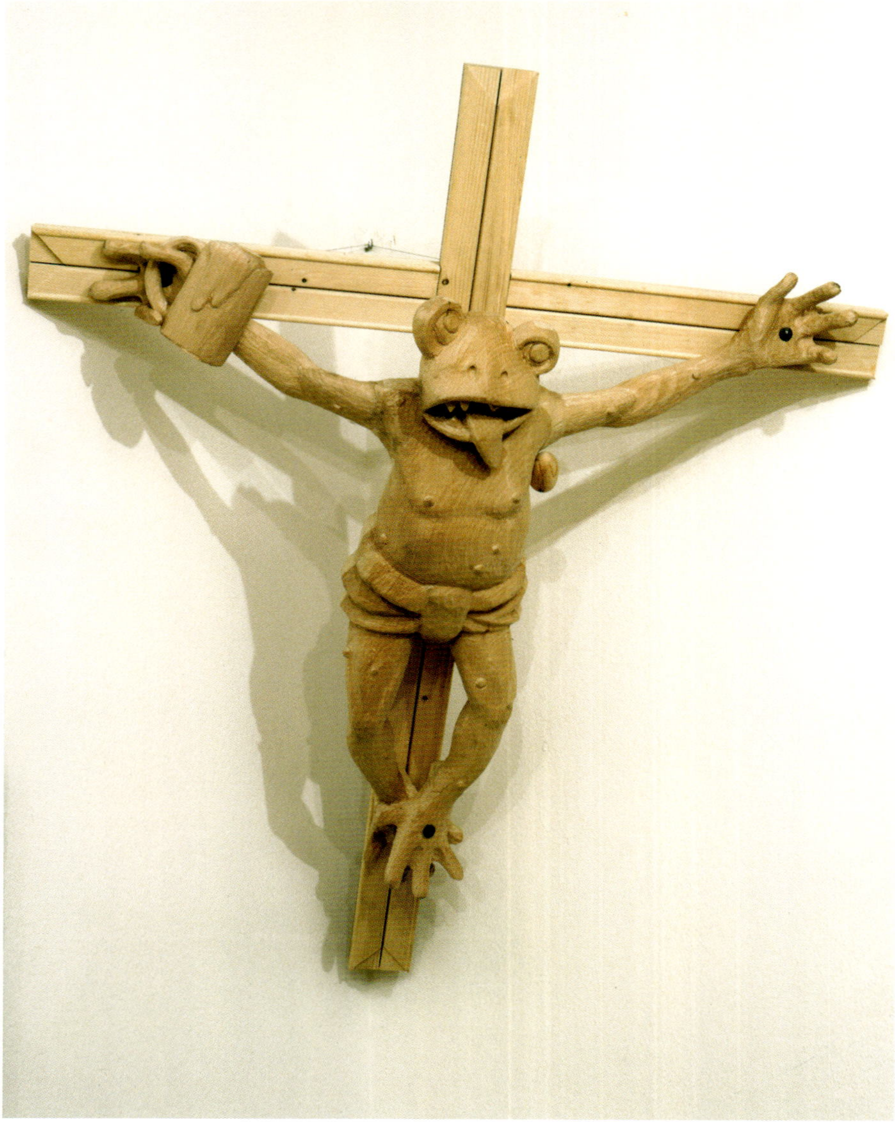

MARTIN KIPPENBERGER Born 1953, Dortmund, Germany. Died 1997, Vienna, Austria
Fred the Frog Rings the Bell, 1990 (a similar work from the same edition is reproduced above) Carved wood and steel nails
51 1/8 x 33 3/8 x 9 3/4 in. (129.5 x 85.1 x 24.8 cm) Artist's proof from an edition of 7 Collection of Norman and Norah Stone, San Francisco. Courtesy Thea Westreich Art Advisory Services

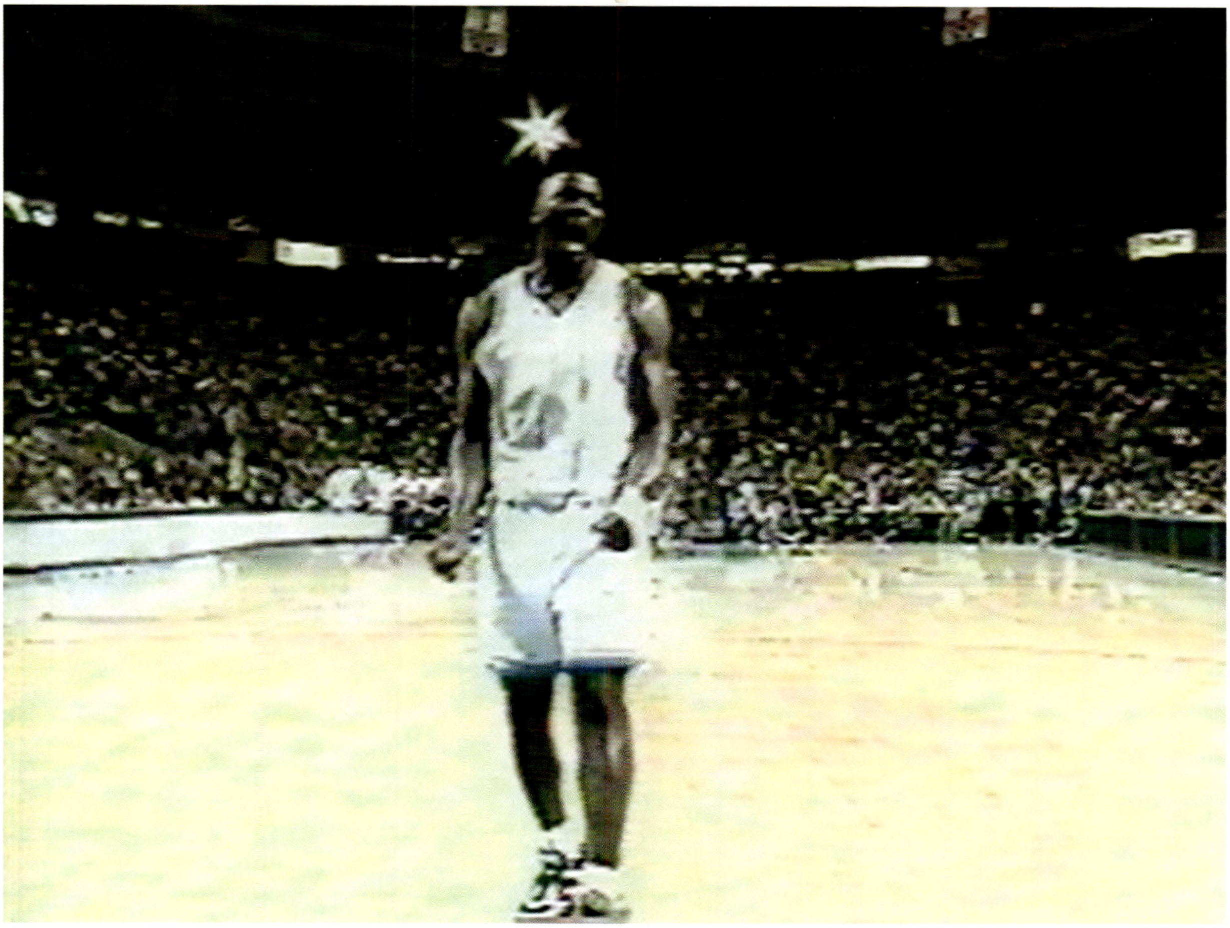

PAUL PFEIFFER Born 1966, Honolulu, Hawaii. Resides New York, New York
Fragment of a Crucifixion (After Francis Bacon), 1999 (video still) DVD and Sony CPJ200 projector Courtesy the artist and The Project, New York

The video sculpture *Fragment of a Crucifixion (After Francis Bacon)* revisits an archetypal theme in art history with specific reference to the 1950 Bacon painting from which it borrows its title. In the video, an athlete stands center court in a crowded arena, flashbulbs popping. The details of the game—team names, sponsors' logos, court markings, even the players themselves (save one)—have been digitally edited out. What remains is a single, screaming black figure in white jersey and shorts, locked immobile at the center of this "crucifixion."

Like Bacon's painting, the video owes much of its formal logic to the long history of art on the Passion of Christ. Yet the genre's compositional devices—heroic frontality, symmetry, the construction of space within an invisible grid extending infinitely back—are here exploited to convey a modern sense of trauma and terror. For Bacon, the quintessential twentieth-century protagonist was represented by the spectacle of the pope paraded before the world's masses, enclosed in a bulletproof-glass case. Bacon shows the pope's gaping, screaming mouth undergoing a transmutation into the sumptuous buildup of the painted surface; the sports star in the video similarly undergoes a transmutation, digitized into a bitmapped pattern of 1's and 0's, encoded as pixels of light, projected as pure information locked in the perpetual replay of a resampled video signal.

The video image in *Fragment* allegorizes the reduction of human subjectivity to that which is wholly consumable. If the hero of the video screams, maybe so should we.

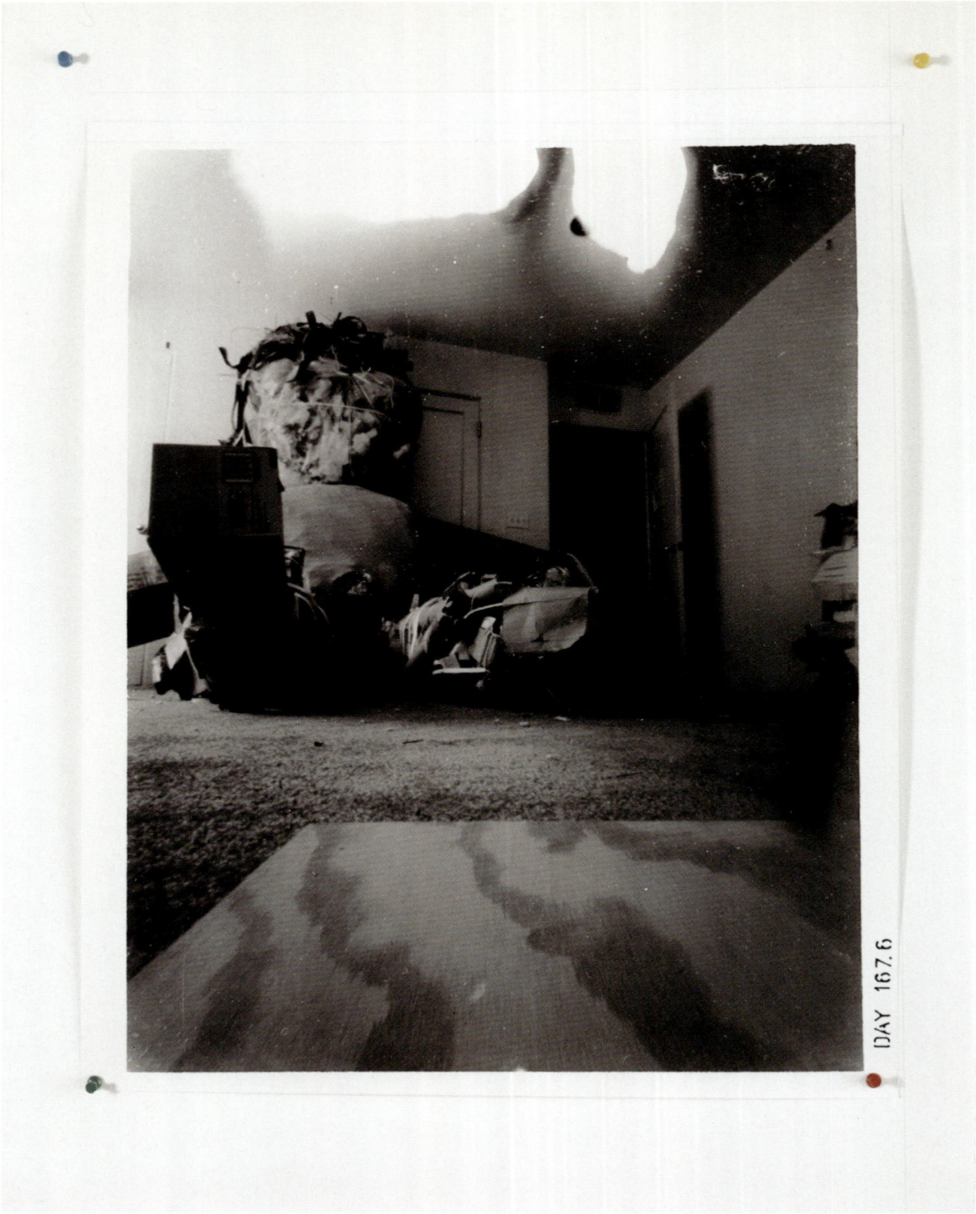

<u>HIRSCH PERLMAN</u> Born 1960, Chicago, Illinois. Resides Los Angeles, California
Day 167.6, 1999–2001 Gelatin silver print on fiber paper, vinyl, and pushpins 30 x 24 in. (76.2 x 61 cm) Collection of the artist. Courtesy Blum & Poe, Los Angeles

DAY 167

Medium-man cannot stand, has no feet, no joints, and no neck. And I have no desire to articulate him further.

It seems we have nothing to say to each other either. Still, I'm reluctant to crush him.

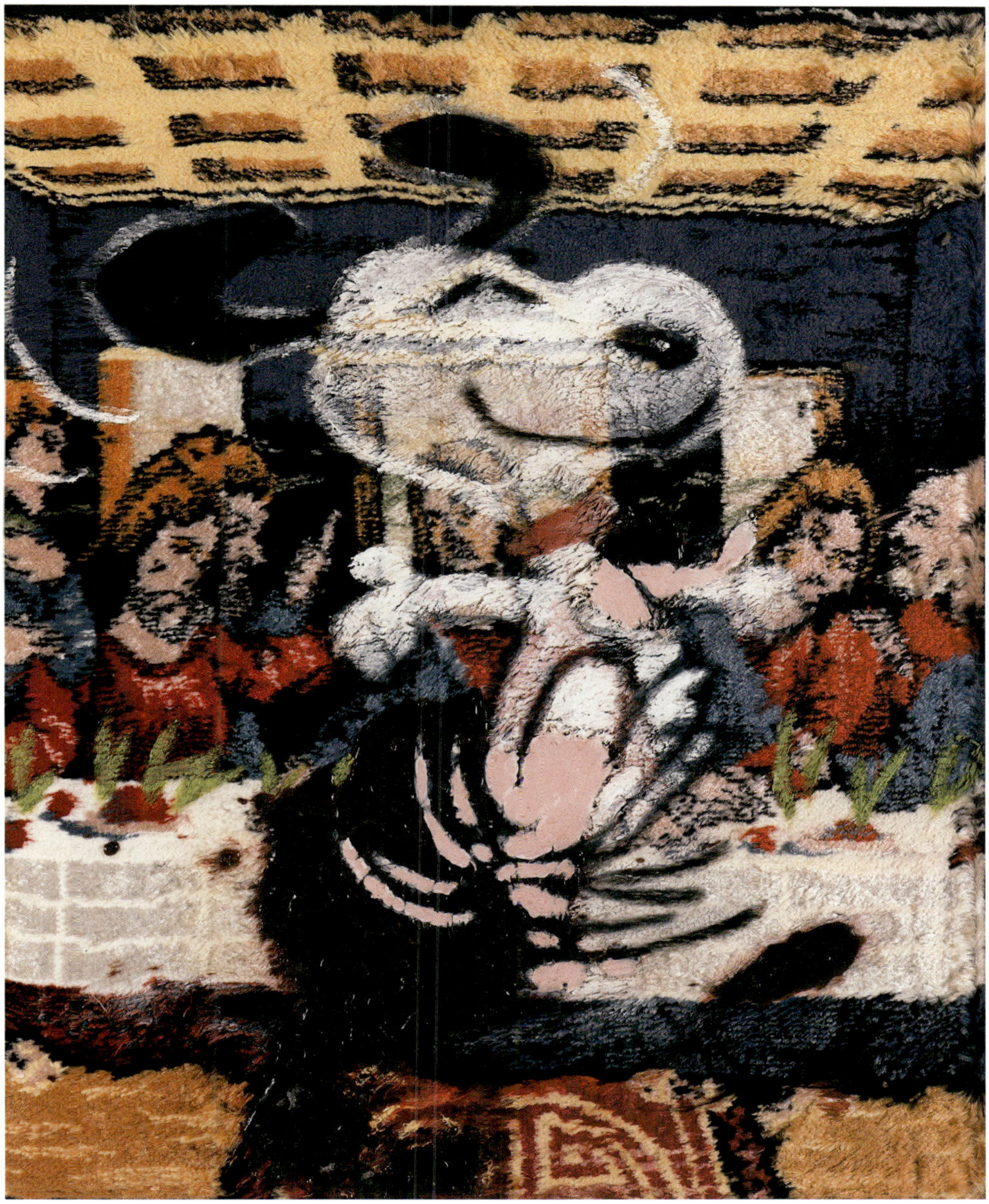

JIM SHAW Born 1952, Midland, Michigan. Resides Los Angeles, California
Oil on Velvet, 1988 Oil on velvet 9 3/8 in. x 6 3/8 in. (23.8 x 17.2 cm) Private collection

This piece, from a narrative series called "My Mirage" (1985-1991), posits a dancing Snoopy atop a torn and bloodied velvet rug illustrating the Last Supper. The rug is a prop from a video in which a dog is sacrificed to Satan in a watered-down version of the Tate-LaBianca ritual murders. In the theology of "Peanuts," Snoopy is supposed to represent the Lord of the Dance, Jesus, although in my cosmology Charlie Brown is a much better candidate. Sometime after the piece was completed and sold, the collector's dog attacked it and ate the dried stage blood, which is made from corn syrup, so I tried to repair it with a new puddle of stage blood. After it lay drying for a month I propped it up for a curator's visit the next day. In the morning I was surprised to find the blood, seemingly solid and dried, had slid down the surface of the painting onto my couch. After more fixing it was returned to its owner, but the incident sparked another piece in the same series, called *Trinity*: a painting in red lines on white of the Red Ghost and two of his simian cohorts blazing destruction, which is then glazed with a thick coat of the same never-drying stage blood, rendering the painting invisible until the stuff slowly slides off the surface.

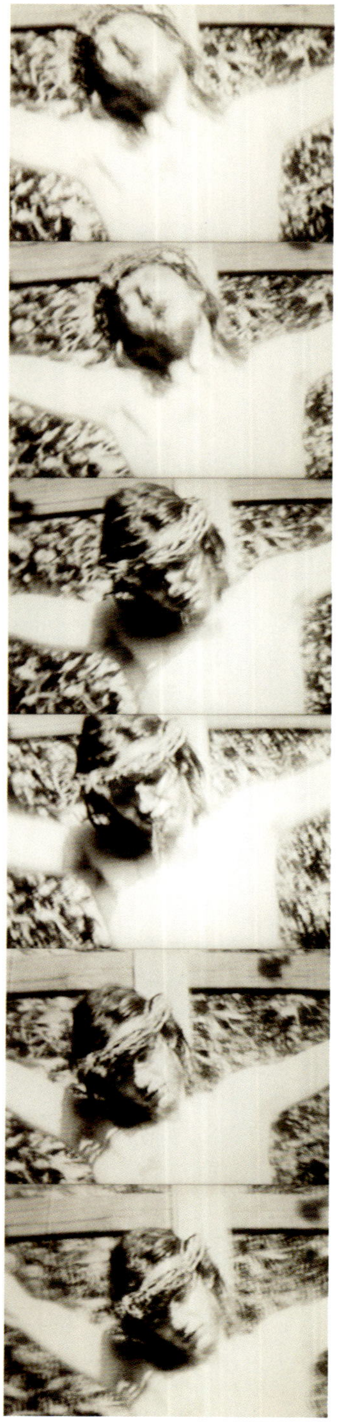

JOHN WATERS Born 1946, Baltimore, Maryland. Resides Baltimore, Maryland
15th Station, 1995 Gelatin silver prints Framed: 37 x 13 3/4 in. (94 x 34.9 cm) Collection of the artist. Courtesy American Fine Arts, Co., New York

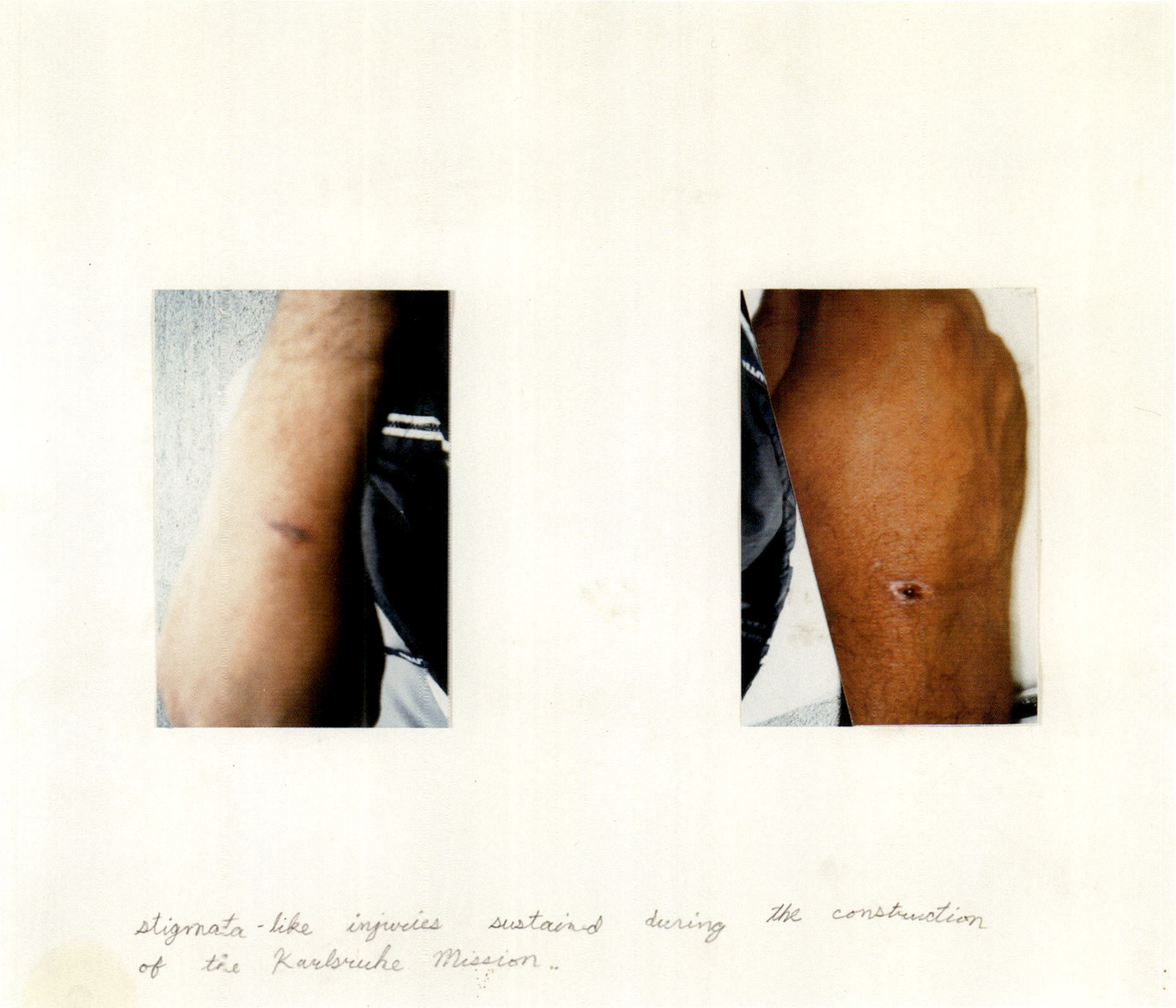

ERIC WESLEY Born 1973, Los Angeles, California. Resides Los Angeles, California
Untitled, 2002 Color photographs on paper 14 x 16 1/4 in. (35.6 x 41.3 cm) Collection of the artist. Courtesy China Art Objects Galleries, Los Angeles

I was working on the installation of a project involving the construction of a kitchen and a mission-style facade. While placing a stainless steel table atop another stainless steel table, I took a nasty fall. The resulting injuries manifested themselves as two cuts on either hand—actually one was more on the arm. I took pictures of these cuts and joked about stigmata and sustaining bodily harm doing God's work.

ARTISTS SEE GOD AS TYRANT

God is a tyrant. His power is absolute. He is a punishing agent, stern and unforgiving, a terrible disembodied force issuing commands. He confuses us with his mysterious behavior. What seems unjust is just on another level: in the eyes of god, who sees everything and never sleeps. He witnesses and remembers our slightest infractions. We exist by his grace. God may sanction democracy but he certainly doesn't participate in it: his desires are the only ones that matter.

Artists are taught to be uncompromising masters who demand their way and are unmoved by the opinions of others. They are mythologized as tyrants, of a kind—concerned only with their own art, their own desires.

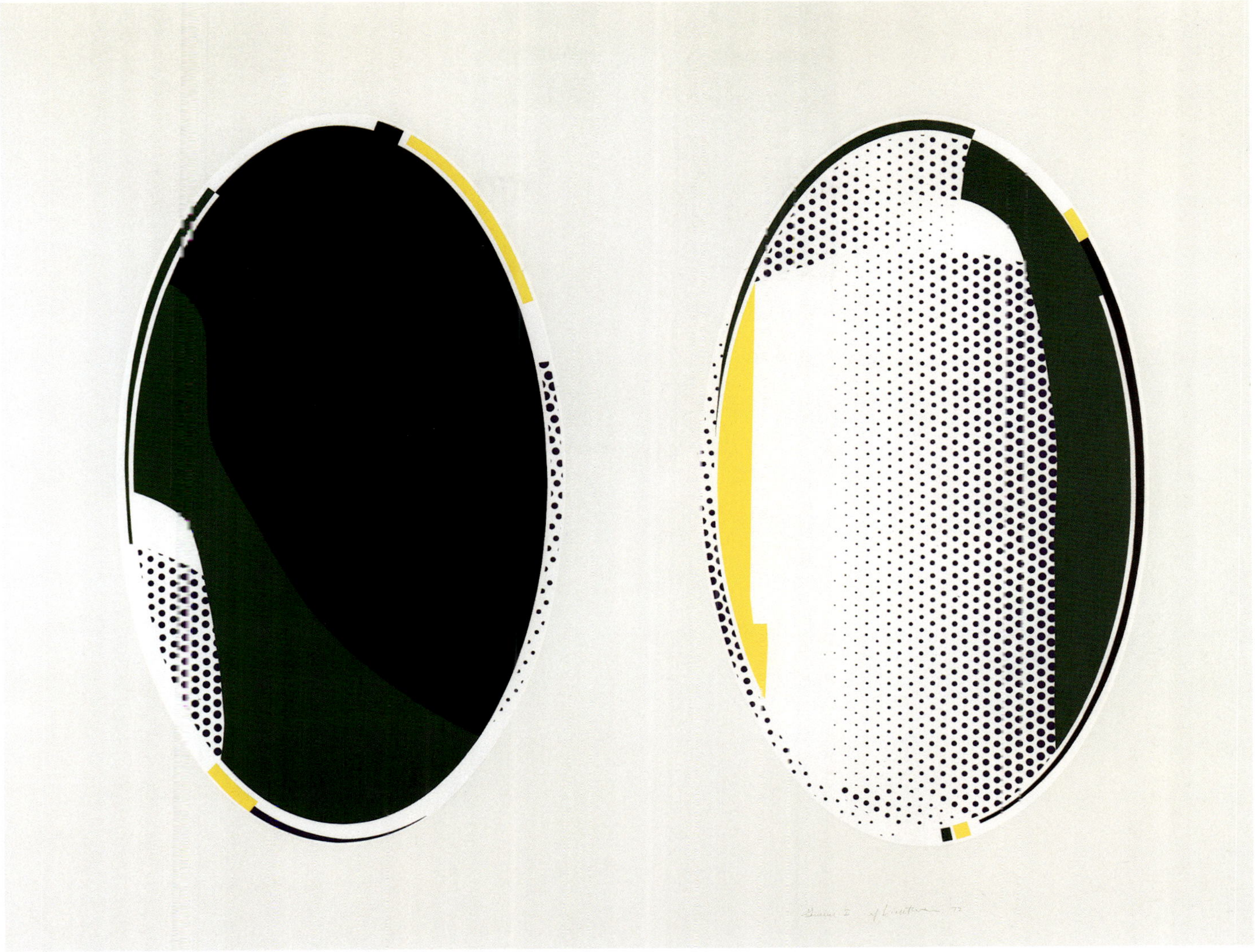

ROY LICHTENSTEIN Born 1923, New York, New York. Died 1997, New York, New York.
Mirror #8, 1972 Five-color lithograph and screenprint 40 3/4 x 53 in. (103.5 x 134.6 cm) Collection of Gemini G.E.L. LLC

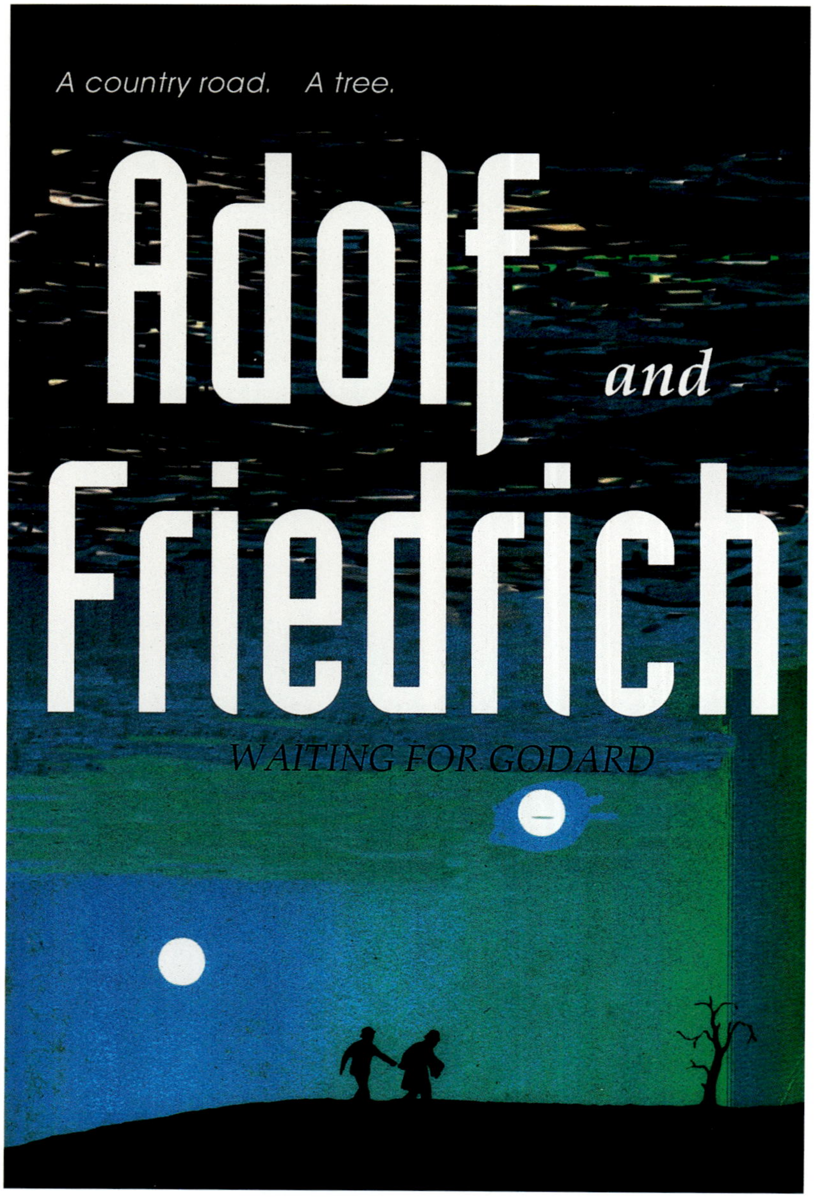

STEVEN WONG Born 1964, Singapore. Resides Singapore

A country road. A tree.[1] *Adolf and Friedrich*[2] *WAITING FOR GODARD*[3], 2002

Four-color offset print 8 1/4 x 5 1/2 in. (21 x 14 cm) Collection of the artist

1 Samuel Beckett, Waiting for Godot, (Grove Press, 1956), Act 1. 2 Barton Byg, "Real History and the Nonexistent Spectator," Landscapes of Resistance (University of California Press, 1995), 233–248. 3 Walter Benjamin, "The Task of the Translator," Illuminations, ed. Hannah Arendt, trans. Harry Zohn (New York: Schocken, 1985), 69–82

In *A Country Road*… I have altered Kenneth Deardoff's jacket design for Samuel Beckett's *Waiting for Godot* to depict Hitler and Nietzsche as the play's characters Vladimir and Estragon. The presence of the filmmaker Jean-Luc Godard is implied but not shown.

Hitler was arrogantly singular, monotheistic, concerned with the worship of a unique, godlike father figure. By contrast, Nietzsche promoted no one goal or stance, and his Dionysian philosophico-political position advanced difference, plurality, the multidirectional, the polytheistic. It was a powerful refusal of fascism, yet Nietzsche has an involuntary reputation as the thinker behind Hitler's philosophy. The idea of Hitler and Nietzsche waiting together in the same frame is wildly incongruous, and if, for Beckett, to wait for a third figure who may never arrive suggests a misplaced faith in the existence of God, it here further suggests the impossibility of correcting the historical record.

Godard, meanwhile, represents the chance not of correcting the historical record but of rendering it more accurately. He stands here as a mode of translation, an understanding aware of its own partisan position. Enabling a critical disruption, Godard reveals the impossibility of an objective historical record. Conventional cinema may be compared to the religion of fascism, in that each constructs a self-enclosed system of value; each generates a world, a space to replace brute reality. Cinema, like fascism, suspends meaning. Godard disrupts such ideological systems, showing that they can only offer selective historical accounts.

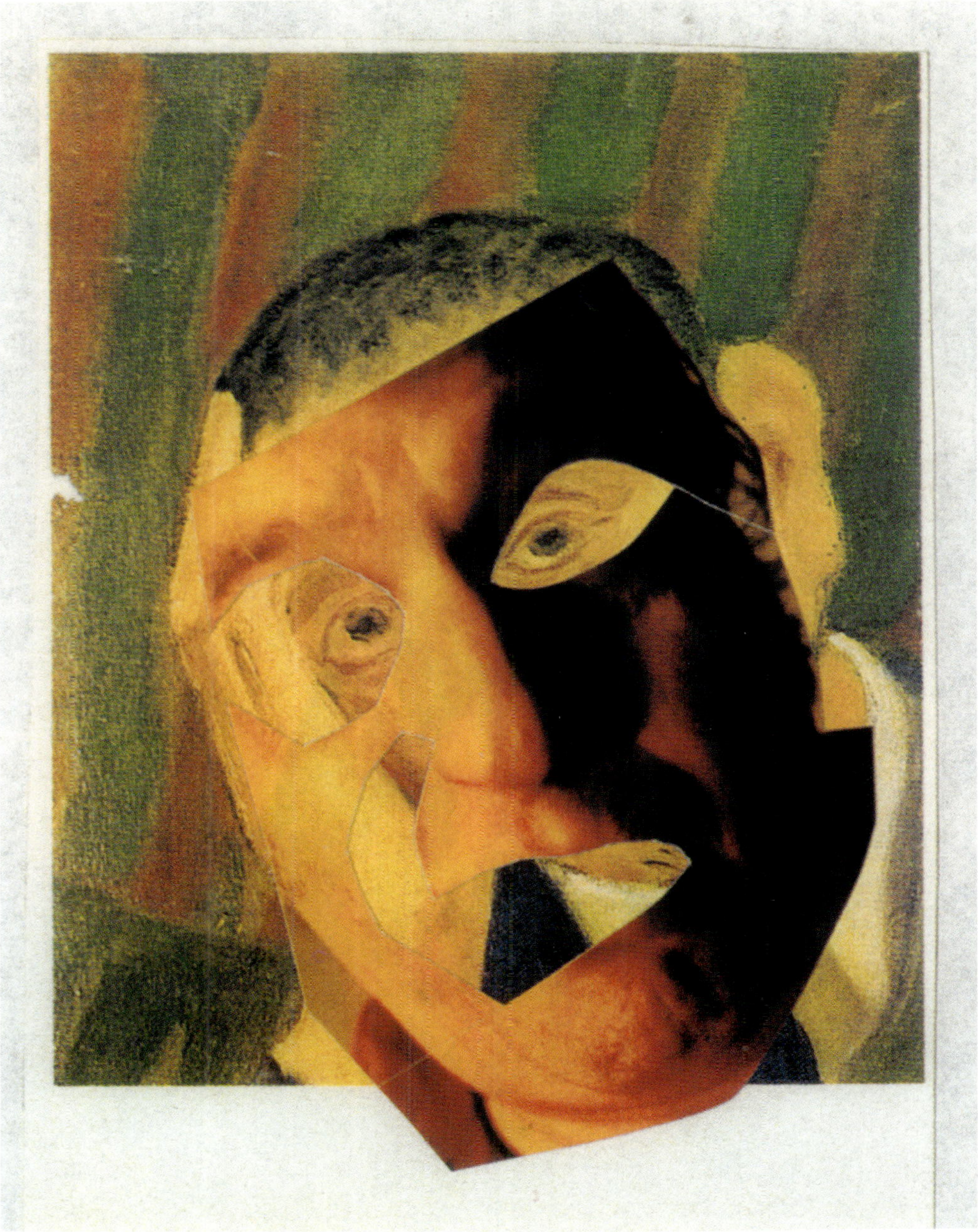

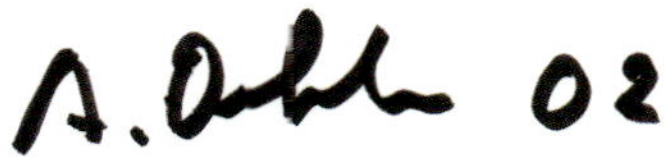

ALBERT OEHLEN Born 1954, Krefeld, Germany. Resides Cologne, Germany
God, 2002 Inkjet print 8 1/4 x 11 3/4 in. (21 x 29.9 cm); framed: 31 1/4 x 26 1/8 in. (79.4 x 66.4 cm) Collection of Mayo J. Thompson, Jr., Los Angeles

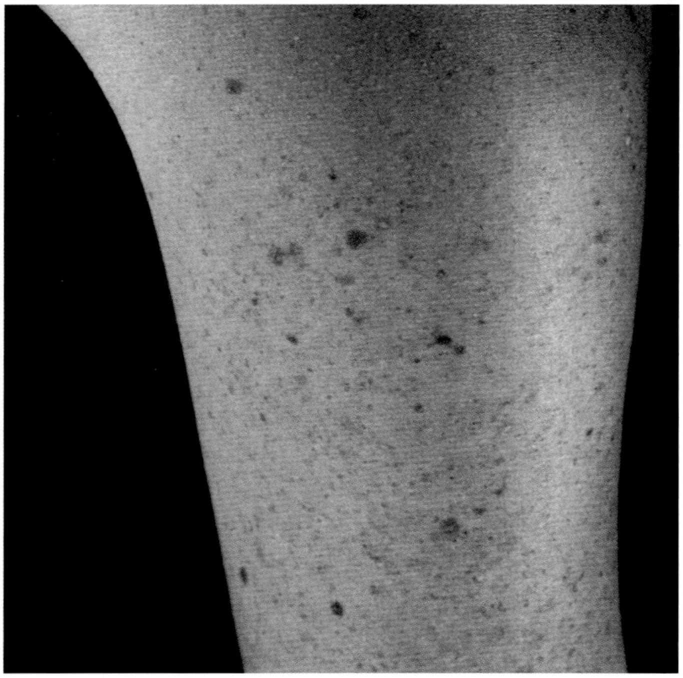

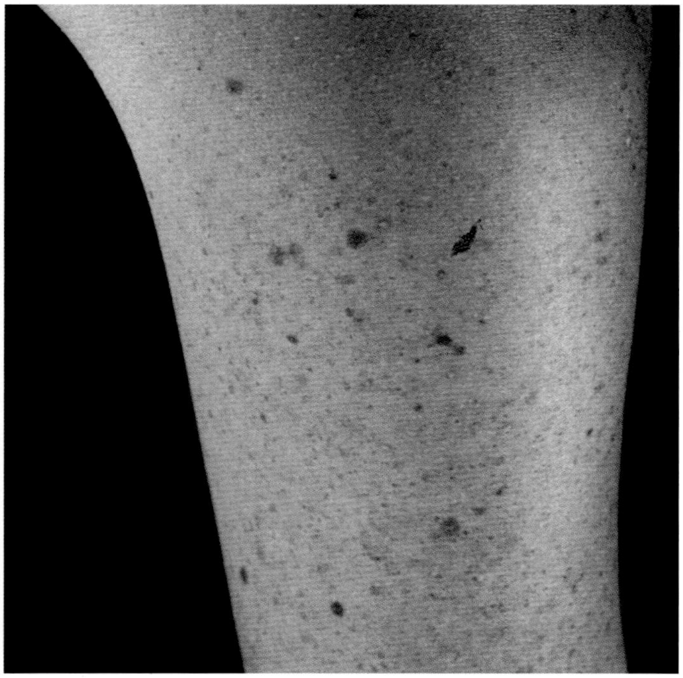

KIM SCHOENSTADT Born 1973, Chicago, Illinois. Resides Venice, California
Freckle Series: Adding Lake Nagawicka, 2002 Two digital prints 10 x 10 in. (25.4 x 25.4 cm) each Collection of the artist. Courtesy lemon sky projects + editions, Miami

I will have a new freckle tattooed onto my body.

The shape of my new freckle will be the shape of Lake Nagawicka, the second of the three bodies of water I have lived on.

We will see if g-d notices. We will see if this addition prevents me from being buried in the Jewish cemetery where the rest of my family are.

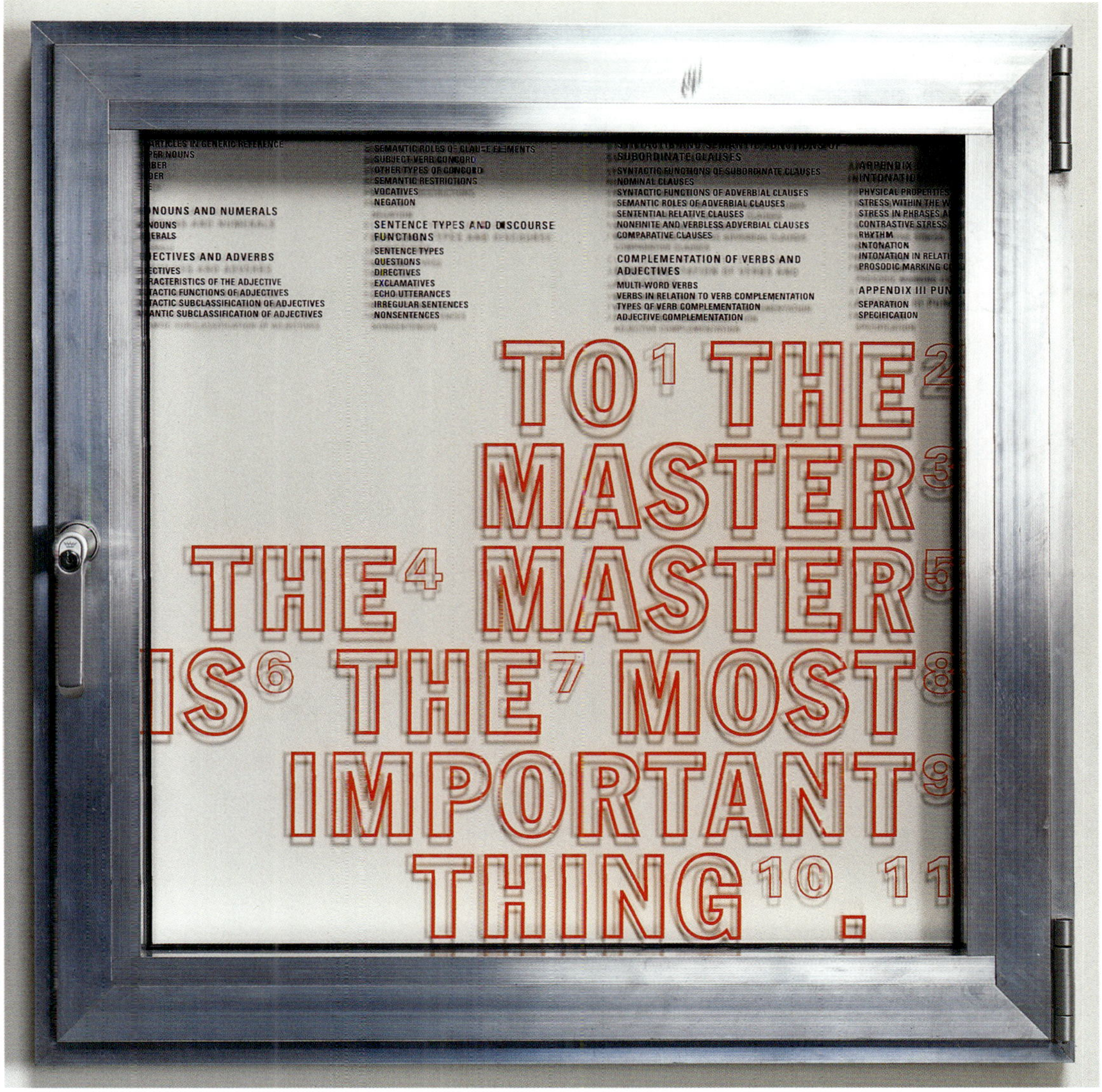

THOMAS LOCHER Born 1956, Munderkingen, Germany. Resides Cologne, Germany
To the Master the Master Is the Most Important Thing, 1999 Silkscreen on glass, aluminum construction 31 1/2 x 31 1/2 x 5 in. (80 x 80 x 12.5 cm) Collection of Cindy Miscikowski and Douglas Ring

That is why the classical Master must legitimize his rule with a reference to some nonsocial, external authority—as soon as the performative mechanism which gives him his charismatic authority is demasked, the Master loses his power.

—Slavoj Žižek, *The Sublime Object of Ideology*, 1989

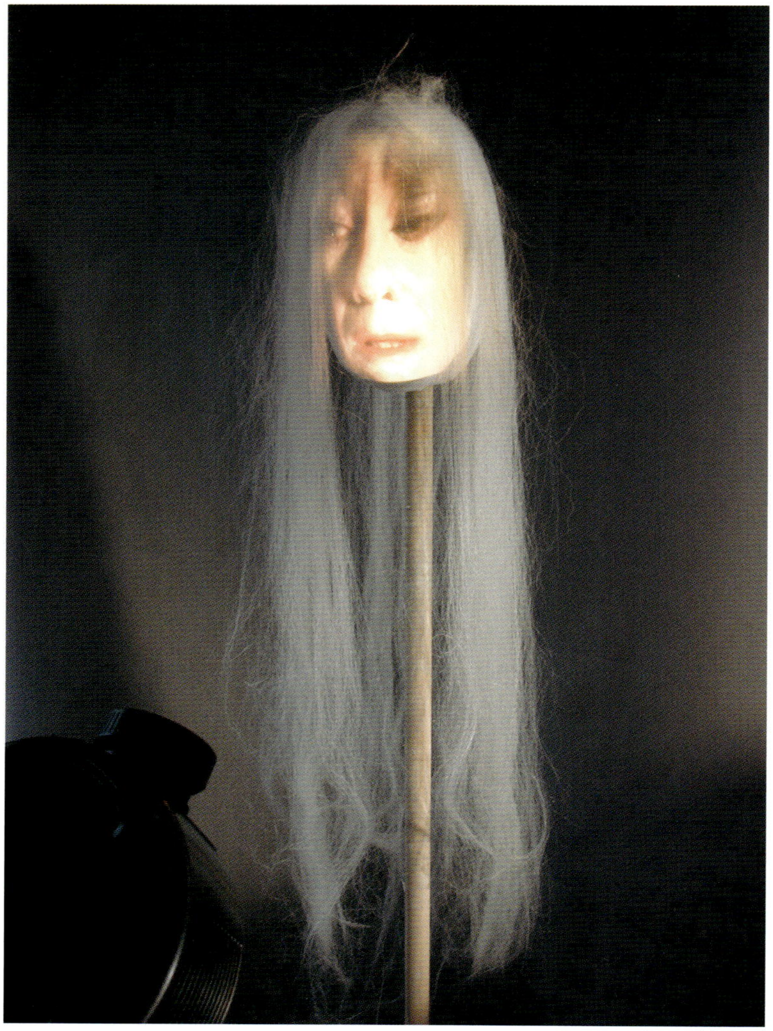

TONY OURSLER Born 1957, New York, New York. Resides New York, New York

DOGOD, 2003 DVD, Sony CPJ200 projector, tripod Dimensions variable Collection of the artist. Courtesy Metro Pictures, New York

DOGOD is an acting out of a very personal deity. This God is an old white man who lives in the sky and has something to do with growing up Catholic. His growth is stunted because I have not developed him in any essential way since I was young. His appearances are unusual, as he rarely addresses his flock openly. Of course he knows everything but won't tell, for reasons that are obscure, yet this is essential to the relationship we have to him. The confusion of life is sorted out behind the scenes in heaven, and we on earth live a hazy morality play, trying to make the correct decisions. DOGOD is in control and out of control at the same time. He is loving, and takes on the guise of authority: long white hair symbolizing wisdom and age, as well as universal sexual appeal symbolized by his makeup. He is also cruel, randomly dispensing disease, violence, and poverty. He is always mysterious, and it is up to the viewer to understand his motivations.

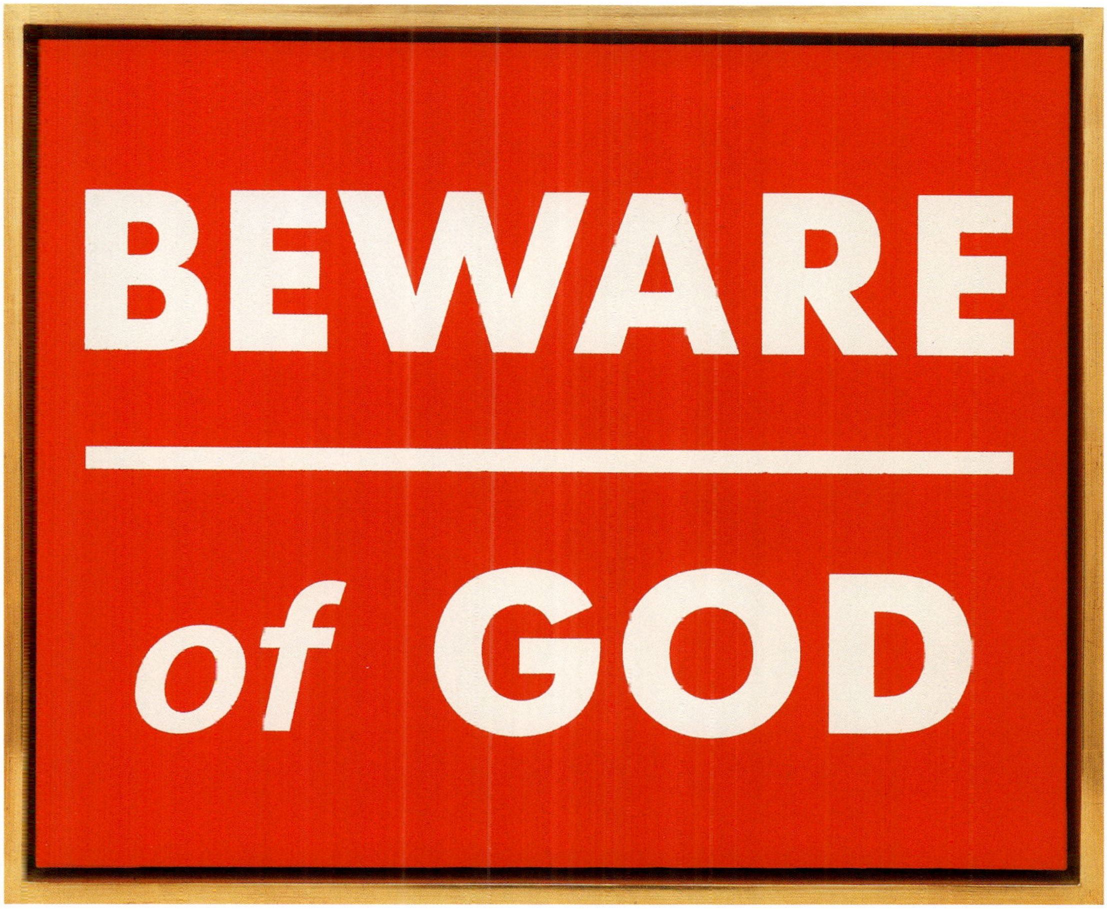

SCOTT GRIEGER Born 1946, Biloxi, Mississippi. Resides Venice, California
Beware of God, 1996 Acrylic on canvas in artist's frame Framed: 17 1/2 x 21 1/2 in. (44.5 x 54.6 cm) Collection of the artist.
Courtesy Patricia Faure Gallery, Santa Monica

I often think there might be
a wrathful God, but we'll bridge
that cross when we come to it.

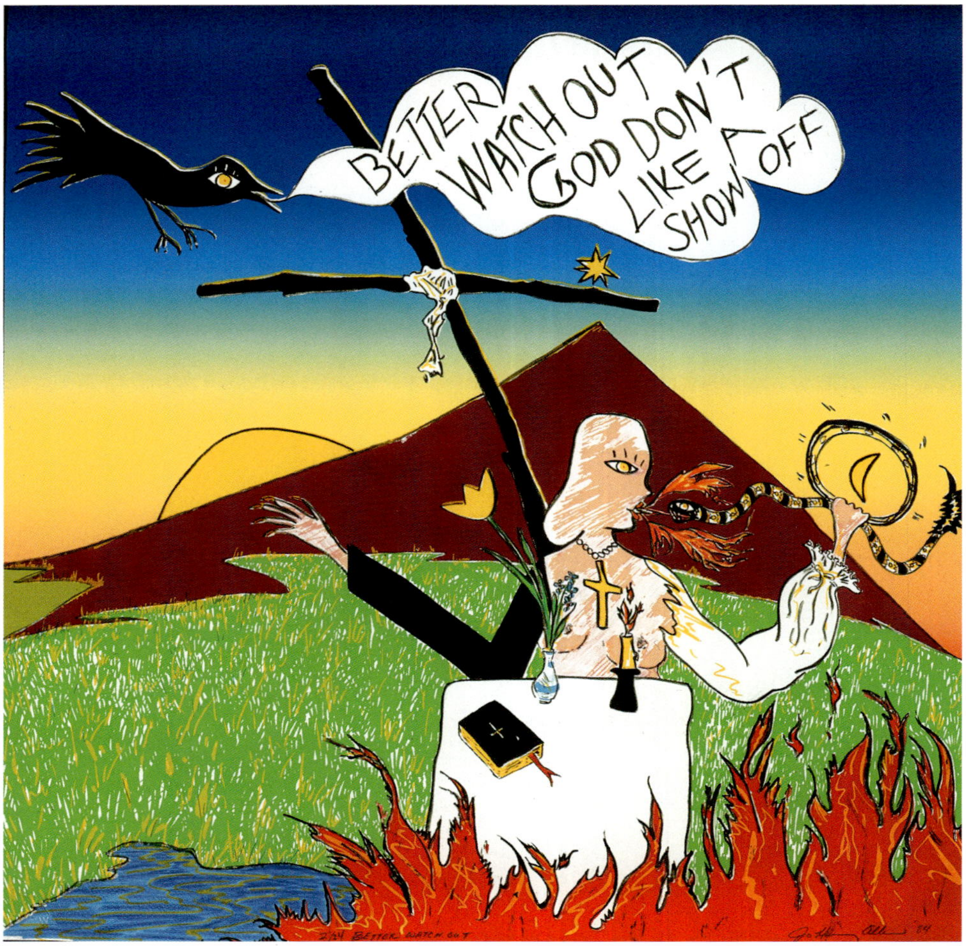

JO HARVEY ALLEN   Born 1942, Lubbock, Texas. Resides Santa Fe, New Mexico
Better Watch Out God Don't Like a Showoff!, 1984   Pencil on lithograph   21 1/2 x 22 in. (54.6 x 55.9 cm)   Collection of Bale Creek Allen

Better Watch Out God Don't Like a Showoff! was made in conjunction with my play *Hally Lou*, about a West Texas tent revivalist. The work-in-progress was produced by the Aspen Art Museum, where I first performed it off the back of a flatbed truck with a thirteen-foot cobra. In 1984 the Museum of Contemporary Art in Los Angeles produced it for the new Japan American Theater, where I added thirty-six live rattlesnakes.

P.S.—I can't help it if God likes me the best.

ARTISTS SEE GOD AS WORD

Several works in the exhibition use language. Seeing image and text as equivalents, or viewing images as language, is a common understanding in modern and contemporary art. The understanding of the primacy of language is supported by mystical and philosophical statements in the Bible. The well-known biblical verse "In the beginning was the Word, .. and the Word was God" (John 1:1) implies that in speaking creation occurs. It is a statement describing the order of things.

UNTIL THE MOON COMES OVER THE MOUNTAIN

LAWRENCE WEINER Born 1942, Bronx, New York. Resides New York, New York
Until the Moon Comes Over the Mountain, 1994 Vinyl on wall Dimensions variable Collection of the artist. Courtesy Marian Goodman Gallery, New York, and Gallery 360°, Tokyo

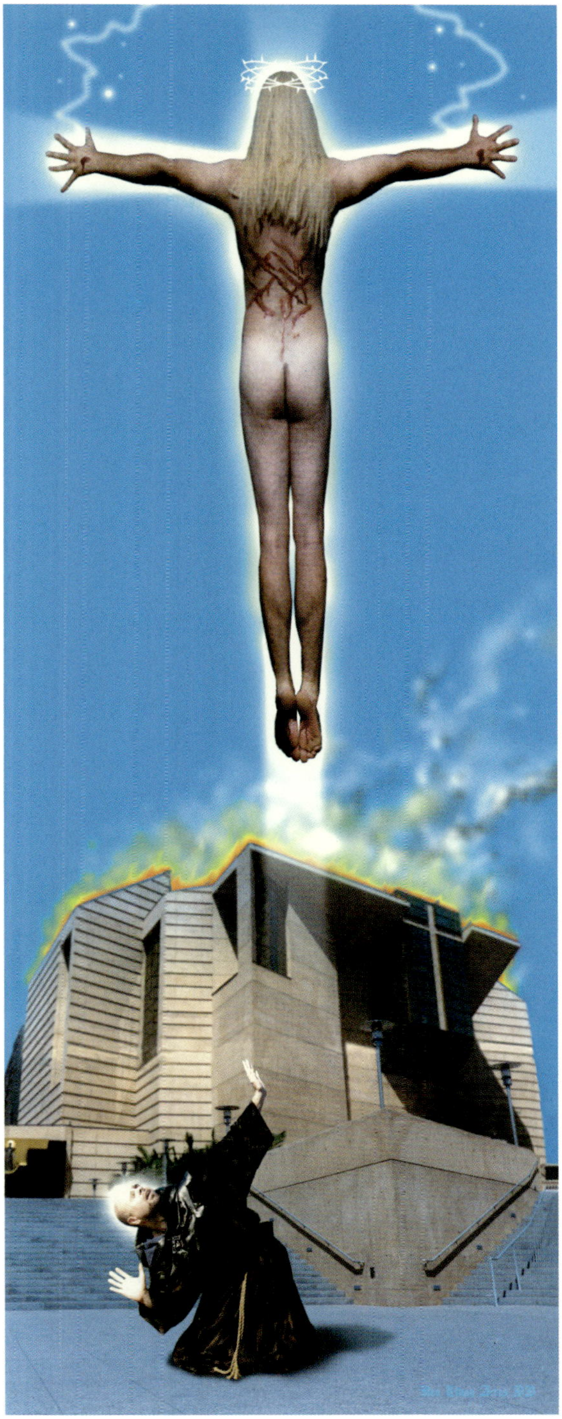

<u>REVEREND ETHAN ACRES</u> Born 1970, Fort Payne, Alabama. Resides San Antonio, Texas
W.W.J.D.?, 2002 Duoprint on Mylar 50 x 20 in. (127 x 50.8 cm) Collection of the artist. Courtesy Patricia Faure Gallery, Santa Monica

My father was the Reverend Albert Satcher, a fire-and-brimstone Southern Baptist minister. When I was ten years old, I would regularly follow Rev. Satcher into some small Alabama or Tennessee church, where voices would cry and lives would be forever marked. Brothers and sisters, I have forever after understood my place: the Gallery is my Church, and in it I am, as Paul wrote in 1 Corinthians 4:10, a "fool for Christ's sake." I wish only to be a spectacle, a Paul of Tarsus a Saint Quentin, a martyr for the pleasure of the public and the high goodness of art, for the glory of my Lord and Savior Jesus Christ. I want to dazzle and seduce… and in the end to pass a little of that Las Vegas Religion into the bloodstreams of all those I clutch in my all-inclusive arms. I believe, Beloved, that you are at a crossroads, and I am giving you a chance to walk a little way with me. Now do not be mistaken, for the journey I am on is not an easy one… it is filled with stones and thorns. But if you take my hand, and trust the childlike faith that still plays in your heart, I will lead you out of the dark valley and into the light of grace and joy. Beat down the devil, my lambs, and help me put the FUN back in FUNDAMENTALISM!

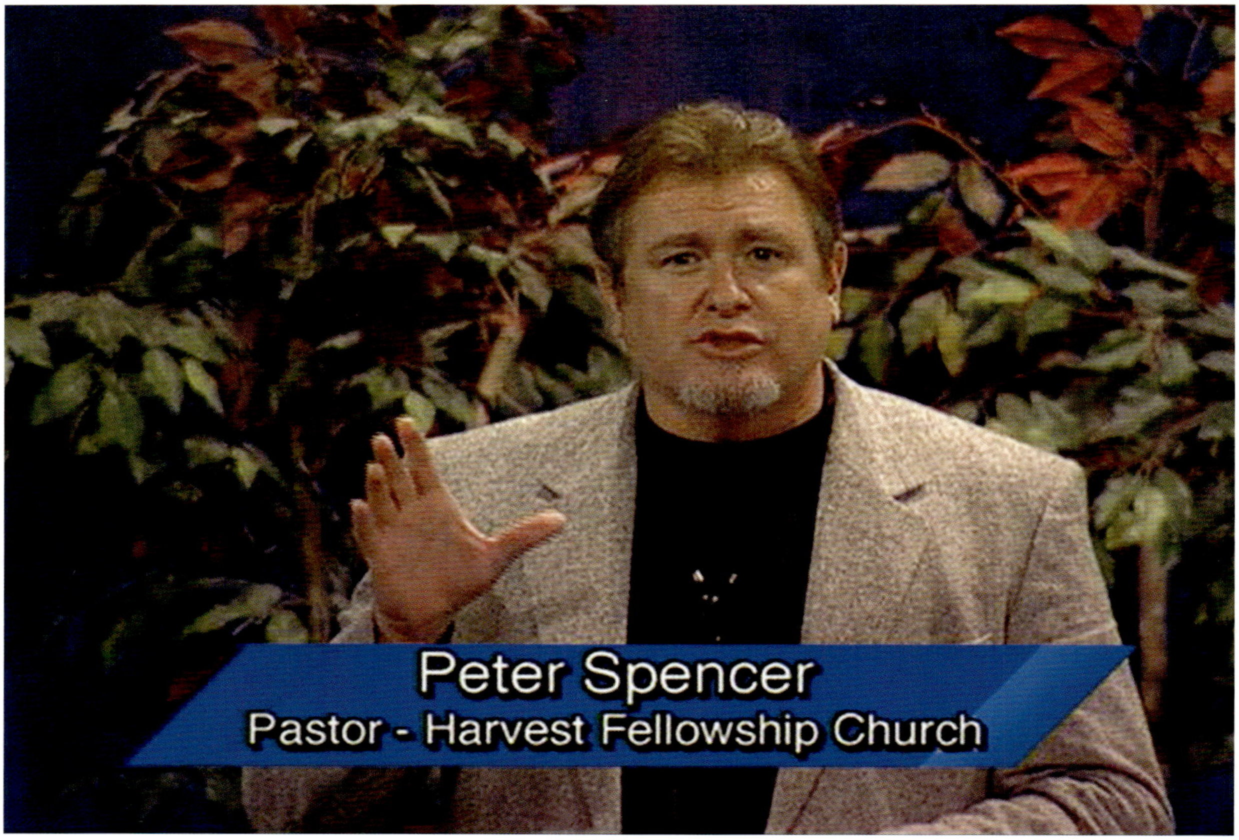

CHRISTIAN JANKOWSKI Born 1968, Göttingen, Germany. Resides Berlin, Germany
The Holy Artwork, 2001 (video still) DVD 15 minutes 47 seconds Collection of the artist. Courtesy Maccarone Inc., New York. Commissioned by ArtPace, San Antonio

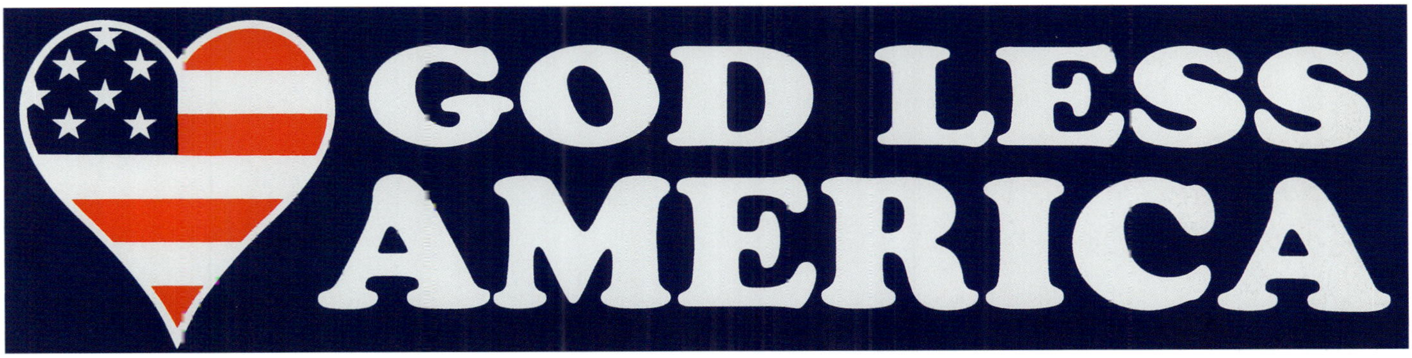

JEREMY DELLER   Born 1966, London, England. Resides London, England
Bumper Sticker, 2003   Vinyl   3 x 11 1/4 in. (7.5 x 28.5 cm)   Collection of the artist

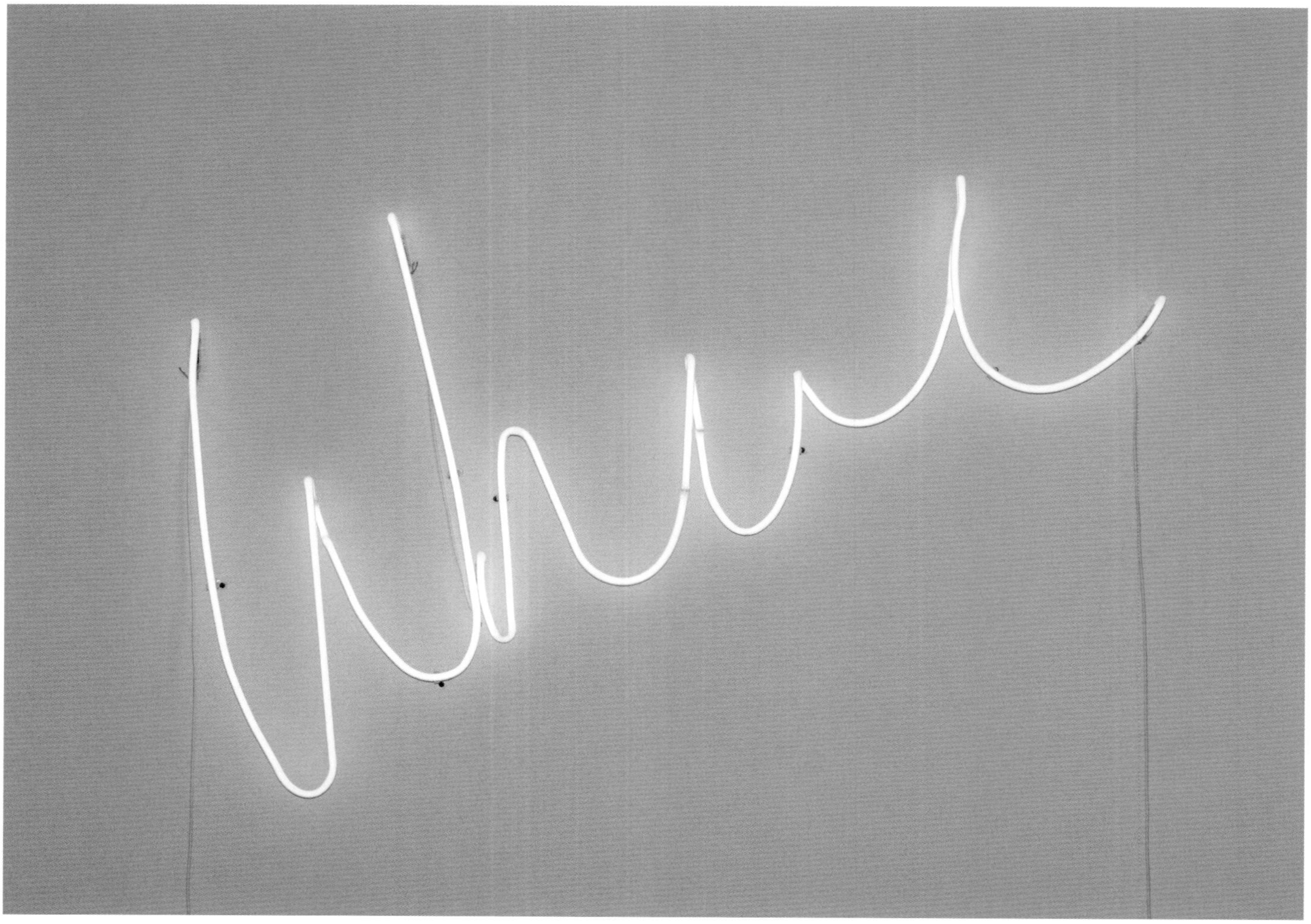

MARY ELLEN CARROLL Born 1961, Danville, Illinois. Resides New York, New York, and Sicily, Italy
Where, What, When, Who, Why, 2002 Neon 39 x 60 x 3 in. (99 x 152.4 x 7.6 cm) Collection of the artist

The idea of expressing the concept of god, which has been presented to us as "one of the most formidable and traditional questions in art," needs to be contextualized within its origin: philosophy. Our dear Wittgenstein, to whom we owe a great deal in the investigations of language and meaning, would certainly agree that it would be too easy and obvious to represent the problem through the tiresome dualism of the sacred and the profane—the question would remain as to what is actually visible. Is the element of faith realizable as a visual response outside language? Presently and historically we know that this has been accomplished, but would placing the onus back on the individual eliminate the problems we are confronted with today in the realm of the social, where all meaning takes place? Is there a near-death experience that we subconsciously desire, wherein we get to see, and that will in turn answer the question, or merely pose it again? Is this the work: the question or the ambitiousness or the ambiguity of the individual meaning in language, rewritten in white neon to be misread as where, what, when, who, and finally why. It is a choice, a sign, like flying from JFK or Newark.

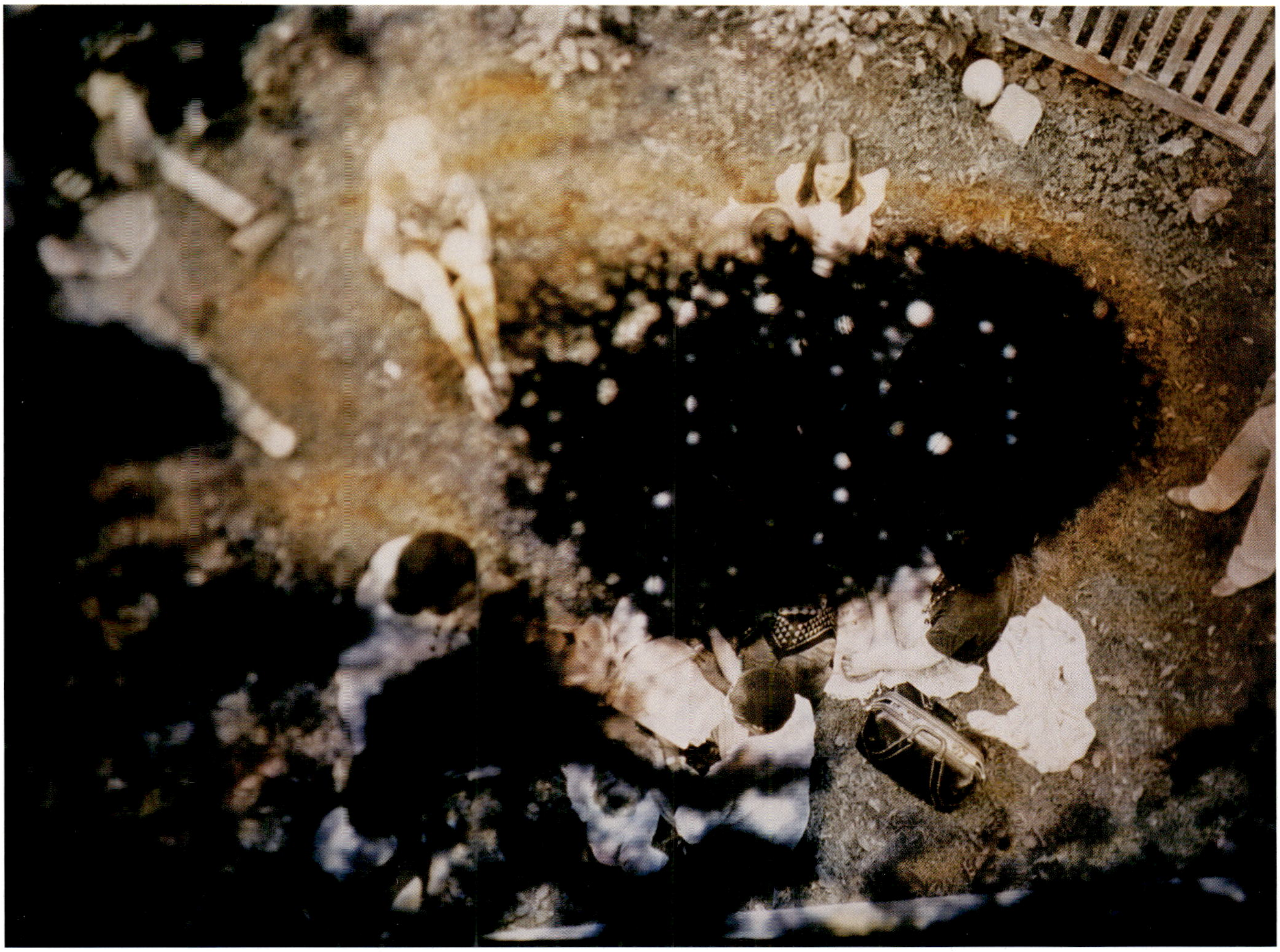

DAVID ASKEVOLD Born 1940, Conrad, Montana. Resides Halifax, Nova Scotia
The Devil's Wishing Well, 1995 Chromogenic print 20 x 24 in. (50.8 x 61 cm) Collection of the artist

I first saw Jesus when I was about three years old, sleeping on a yard-porch-like swinging couch about twenty-five yards in front of our house, under a few trees overlooking the lake. It was around ninety degrees in August and I had fallen asleep, as I sometimes did even before this, on the lap of my sister's best friend, who didn't want to wake me but had the front of her dress stained with the sweat from my head.

The next time Jesus was talking to me. Then someone was calling me from the porch and Jesus just gave me a smile and told me, "Your family needs you now." I woke up in my own pool of pillow sweat. Before someone from my family woke me, he had said he would introduce me to God. I've always resented that interruption.

SIMON PATTERSON

(continued from page 60)

conditions permitted. There were six colours: green, blue, red, purple, yellow and white. The display would last for about five minutes and took place three times a day over a period of one month. The effect was intended to be like a landscape painting with smudges of added colour. The ephemerality of smoke underscored the transience of the supposedly timeless and natural landscape. As the work was time-based, plumes of smoke occurred intermittently, recalling the theatrical device of the 'puff of smoke' (and the trap door) used to cause someone or something to appear or disappear at will. The colours are also linked to coded military markers used both to reveal and conceal. There are no prescribed meanings for the colours other than those that the military might choose to give them on any given day. The hoped-for effect is that of a history painting and a dreamlike evocation of a battlefield: art and the art of war.

The work was partly about drawing attention to the landscape, and to specific vistas, marking out the full extent of the original landscaped estate as laid out by 'Capability' Brown but which is now partly given over to agriculture. The desire was not to intervene permanently in what is already a work of art but to reintegrate, by means of the work, the part of 'Capability' Brown's work that survives with the rest of the new and ever-changing environment.

An unexpected outcome in some of the photographs, particularly those in which the sun's rays break through the cloud of coloured smoke, was the evocation of a clichéd image of divine intervention. All that was missing was the Voice of God, aka John Huston, from the film *The Ten Commandments*.

PHOTO CREDITS

Prudence Cuming Associates Limited, courtesy Gagosian Gallery: p. 29. D'Amelio Terras Gallery, New York: p. 94. Patricia Faure Gallery: p. 129. Ronald Feldman Fine Arts, New York: p. 96. Brian Forrest: pp. 22, 23, 33, 37, 41, 52, 59, 68, 73, 74, 76, 77, 80, 81, 89, 90, 114, 115, 117, 119. Courtesy GBE (Modern): p. 46. © 1982 Gemini G.E.L. and Estate of Roy Lichtenstein: p. 119. © 1995 Gemini G.E.L. and Bruce Nauman: p. 39. © 2003 Gemini G.E.L. and Susan Rothenberg: p. 105. Courtesy Barbara Gladstone Gallery: p. 102. Sean Kelly Gallery: p. 27. Courtesy Margo Leavin Gallery: p. 97. Herbert Lotz: p. 126. Courtesy Matthew Marks Gallery, New York: pp. 69, 71. Fredrik Nilsen: pp. 61, 95. Bill Orcutt, courtesy Alexander & Bonin, New York: p. 98. Douglas M. Parker Studio: pp. 19, 22, 47. Mike Parsons: p. 72. Alan Schaffer: p. 125. Jeffrey Sturges: pp. 32, 65, 88, 116, 131. Pieter Vandermeer: p. 66. Joshua White: p. 21.

<u>INDEX OF ARTISTS</u>

LENDERS TO THE EXHIBITION

Reverend Ethan Acres
Bale Creek Allen
Eleanor Antin
Brienne Arrington
David Askevold
Lillian Ball
Cindy Bernard
Andrea Bowers
Delia Brown
Edgar Bryan
Angela Bulloch
Chris Burden
Brian Butler
David Byrne and Adelle Lutz
Mary Ellen Carroll
Erin Cosgrove
Michael Craig-Martin
Jeremy Deller
Sam Durant
Jimmie Durham
Kenneth L. Freed
Katharina Fritsch
Jonathan Furmanski
Gemini G.E.L., Los Angeles
Jeremy Gilbert-Rolfe
Liam Gillick
Scott Grieger
Andreas Gursky
James Hayward
Micol Hebron
Damien Hirst
Rebecca Horn
Jonathan Horowitz
Darcy Huebler
Christian Jankowski
Larry Johnson
Mike Kelley
Mary Kelly
Martin Kersels
Nicholas Kersulis
Rachel Lachowicz
Norm Laich
Liz Larner
Louise Lawler
Barry Le Va
William Leavitt
Jen Liu
Daria Martin
T. Kelly Mason
Rita McBride
Paul McCarthy
Cindy Miscikowski and Douglas Ring
Carlos Mollura
JP Munro
The Museum of Contemporary Art, Los Angeles
Jennifer Nelson
Eric Niebuhr
Leonard Nimoy
Catherine Opie
Tony Oursler
Jorge Pardo
Simon Patterson
Hirsch Perlman
Luciano Perna
Renée Petropoulos
Raymond Pettibon
Paul Pfeiffer
Nicolette Pot
Richard Prince
Rob Pruitt
David Reed
Victoria Reynolds
Gerhard Richter
Nancy Rubins
Glen Walter Rubsamen
Allen Ruppersberg
Ed Ruscha
Pauline Stella Sanchez
Kim Schoenstadt
Gary Simmons
Barry Sloane
Alexis Smith
Norman and Norah Stone, San Francisco
Thaddeus Strode
Diana Thater
Mayo J. Thompson, Jr., Los Angeles
Mungo Thomson
Thorvaldur Thorsteinsson
Van Valen
John Waters
Marnie Weber
William Wegman
Benjamin Weissman
James Welling
Eric Wesley
John Wesley
Franz West
Chris Wilder
Steven Wong
Måns Wrange
Mario Ybarra, Jr.